SEAF N'T
FL T

A True Story

By Jeff and Clare Curtis

With Steve Eggleston

To my wife, Clare, I will love you always and no matter what happens, we will always be Team Curtis!!

Mr C…

Foreword

This is a story that illustrates a fight for survival, highlights the value of teamwork and pays tribute to the kindness of strangers, who tried to help us even though they had nothing to gain. In fact, you may not call it a story at all, but a true, unadulterated and unelaborated account of one of the most dramatic events that we have ever experienced, written as we remember it.

We decided to write this book, in part, to thank all those involved; from the people who, without ever knowing it, played even the smallest part in this crisis, to those who temporarily stopped their own lives to try and help save the life of our premature child. In part cathartic, written as therapy for what we experienced in May 2016.

The words and opinions in this book are ours; the story is ours to share. The whole debacle felt as if we were living in our own storybook, with no real comprehension of how or when it would end. In it, we have catalogued the vast array of possible outcomes and scenarios we faced, together with the decisions we were forced to make as unprepared parents, in order to try and save the life of our premature baby. Looking back, it all feels unfathomable.

So, Team Curtis invites you to partake of your favourite tipple, find a nice quiet corner somewhere and join us as we relive the rollercoaster of emotions that stretched our British resolve to breaking point.

Acknowledgements

Thanks to Steve Eggleston, who helped to formulate and structure this story; our editor, Sue Kelso Ryan, for her help with my poor grammar and preserving the family emotion we have tried to convey from within, and Alban Low for his cover illustration.

Contents: Part 1

Contents: Part 2

‘Some people want it to happen,
Some people wish it to happen,
Others just make it happen.’

– Team Curtis, May 2016

PART 1

Chapter 1

Survival

{Clare}

I was lying in bed in my bloodstained nightie. I didn't feel as if I was being particularly helpful, but everyone was telling me in no uncertain terms that I needed to relax. *Are they serious?* I remember thinking. Relax was not justifiable in my mind. I was trying to process what the doctor had just said to me, to us. *Labour?* I thought dismissively. *What is this woman talking about?* I had seen the films, the documentaries of birthing and what was required, and even though I hadn't at that point completed the pre-natal course, I was certain that labour pains felt different to constipation. *When was the last time I had gone to the toilet?* I thought logically to myself. *Surely, I'm just constipated?*

Really, this must be a big misunderstanding that was turning into a three-ring circus, a charade of embarrassment at my expense that would eventually amount to nothing. Plus, when I checked again, I could see the bleeding had begun to subside. I was sure that it was just a false alarm.

'It's okay,' Jeff said levelly. 'You just need to rest and make sure the baby is safe.'

I didn't have a choice, so I did as I was being told, knowing that for that moment it was most certainly the best thing for me, and for that matter the baby. I would do whatever it took to ensure a positive outcome. As numb as I was, I would have to muster all of my natural resolve and do exactly what was necessary for the survival of my child. It was terribly hard, and somewhere in the back of my mind I knew tragic things happened when you least expected them.

I also knew worrying would not help or change that. At that point, there simply was no knowing what would happen; either the baby had already miscarried, or it was going to be delivered whenever and wherever it decided to enter the world.

I could see phone calls being made and a plan was put into motion to expedite my move to the best possible place to deliver or remove the miscarried baby. I wouldn't class myself as a particularly religious person, but I lay there hoping, even praying, that my baby was still alive inside me. The not knowing was terrifying. I felt nauseous.

{Jeff}

Poised but concerned, out of Clare's earshot, I spoke to the doctor. 'How are we going to move her?' The weather is horrendous. 'Surely we'll have to wait until it clears?' I reasoned with the doctor, as much as to try to convince myself as her, but to no avail with either.

'Sir, we have no facilities to deliver a premature baby here on this tiny island. Especially a baby that is in a breech position; it's just too dangerous.'

I came to my senses, but I just stared at her, my mind churning like the monstrous waves on the storm-ridden sea outside, searching for any alternative solution.

'Dangerous enough,' the doctor continued, 'that we are going to attempt to get her to some form of medical facilities no matter how basic. We are not going to leave you on your own. Some of my team have volunteered to go with you even though they too will be risking their lives.'

They say you never know how you will react in a crisis until you experience one, and my method – as I was to learn myself – was to latch onto my business persona. No emotion, no second guessing, I made the best decision I felt benefited the situation at that time and ran with it no matter what.

I knew there was no rebuttal to the doctor's last statement; I desperately needed to get help for my blood-soaked wife and even more so, I needed to know if our baby was still alive, although I was very aware that we would be allowing four others to risk their lives in order to save two of ours. To this day I often reflect on this, it could possibly have been one of the most selfish moments of my life, putting others at risk to save my family, but what choice did I have? At that point we were at the mercy of good Samaritans. So, like every emotion that night, I simply eradicated it from my mind; my life had no purpose without my family, so it felt the right decision to make.

What was also very much on my mind at the time was the fact that at the end of a normal gestation period, a baby will naturally turn into the most comfortable position for delivery; head down, bottom up. Our baby had not moved, he was in a breech position. I had read that twenty-five percent of pregnancies were breech at the same stage as Clare was, but they would often turn, unaided, to the correct position. However, only five percent of breech babies were delivered naturally in these modern days. Most doctors preferred the odds of a caesarean delivery promoting a happy outcome, rather than the bravado of delivering a high-risk breech, which might involve a trapped head or a prolapsed umbilical cord with resultant brain damage. Even if the baby survived, it was also possible that the mother would not survive in certain scenarios.

To make things more hazardous for Clare, there was also great concern about the fibroids, as noted by Doctor Amir in our recent visit and in the medical notes. Any detachment of one or more of them could cause Clare to bleed out. A detached fibroid had crossed my mind as being one potential source for the blood. With only basic medical facilities, the likelihood of any spare blood donations would be slim, a thought that chilled me to the bone. *She could be dying right now, bleeding internally.*

All of these things spun circles in my head and I desperately wanted to discuss them with Clare, but she had enough to worry about without me making the situation worse by surmising another potential ailment that could lead to her demise. I wasn't sure what to say to her anyway. I was supposed to be keeping her calm; however I was finding it hard to keep myself calm by then. As much as I hated to admit it at that moment I felt alone, scared, and ill equipped for what was happening inside my wife's body only feet away.

Suddenly there was a knock at the door and the male nurse, who had been frantically making phone calls, rushed to open it.

'It's the buggy!' the doctor exclaimed. 'Clare, Mauroof and Arjun will help you up. Mr Curtis, could you ensure you have everything you need and follow us out?'

'Can you get my bathrobe?' Clare asked me as the two Maldivian men gently started helping her out of the room. 'Not that one!' she shouted crossly as I picked up a heavy towelling robe. 'The light one.'

I was in no mood for a fashion discussion. Not sensing her actual reason for requesting the lighter robe, the one I had picked up was made from towelling, and heavy, far too much for the current humid weather. All I could do was focus on the essentials of our travel.

'Passport, phone and wallet,' I remember repeating to myself. 'Where's my phone charger?' I mumbled as I foraged around the room.

We left the room with the barest of essentials. It never occurred to me that we might never return to that place again.

Outside, there was a torrential downpour amid rolling thunder and cracks of lightning that seemed to shake the heavens; it invoked an eerie sense of the surreal. The buggy turned out to be the type used to whisk the hotels guests about in pampered luxury. Clare and I would normally walk everywhere, but this was not the time nor the place. And thank God for it, the buggy proved invaluable.

{Clare}

Neither Jeff nor I could fathom how we would ever board a small boat, let alone survive a trip across those storm ripped seas. As the buggy worked its way through the sodden vegetation that lined the buggy paths, we heard waves crashing on the nearby shore. It was truly deafening.

'We'll be at the boat soon enough,' Jeff said assuredly to me. 'From there it shouldn't take long to get to the other island, and we can get you the medical help we need,' I did wonder though if he hoped, more than believed, what he had just said.

We were all sitting together in a six-seater buggy, Jeff's arm was wrapped lightly around my shoulders hoping to comfort me and keep me steady as we drove out to the dock. All the seats were full, with driver and navigator up front, we occupied the middle row, as Mauroof and Arjun sat in the rear.

It was pitch black apart from those enormous bolts of lightning that continued to light the night sky. Only as each one ignited could I see the look of concentration on Jeff's face; I wondered if he could see the look of anguish on mine. I knew my baby was dying, or maybe even dead, and without immediate medical care there was no hope of his survival and possibly not even mine.

I tried to smile back at him. But I am sure he could tell from my face as each atmospheric flare erupted skyward that I knew he was making such assurances for my benefit and sanity. By this point, with the world going mad around us, I am not entirely sure either of us believed that the outcome, whatever that was to be, could be a good one.

The driver was moving cautiously. Jeff looked as though he thought we needed to be going much faster. I, on the other hand, couldn't have thanked the driver enough, as my discomfort spiked painfully with every bump. With the rain pouring down translucent plastic flaps like windows had been rolled down, which covered the sides of the buggy and miraculously kept the driving rain out and its occupants dry.

As we left the protective cover formed by the dense overhanging branches, as a multitude of indigenous plants entwined themselves around a wooden-framed walkway to protect the buggy path from the frequent rain, we both saw it. 'Oh, my God!' we mouthed in unison.

What we saw before us was almost unthinkable. The rain was driving into the storm-lashed sea like a thousand arrowheads smashing down and piercing the water. The trees and plants around us were bent sideways, flattened by the sheer power of the howling winds. Exposed fully to the elements for the first time, the once-luxury buggy was being blown precariously to the left side, which meant the wheels on its right side left the ground momentarily. Inside the vehicle we were only protected by the flimsy plastic windows rolled down each side of the buggy and at the back.

And then there were the waves. Where had they come from? The fury they possessed made it clear Poseidon himself could not be any angrier.

Finally, the reason for the driver going slowly became apparent; he was unsure where to go. Earlier that evening the boats had been moored far from the jetty to distance them from being blown dangerously up onto the shore. It hadn't entered anyone's mind that they might be needed in the middle of the night for an emergency evacuation. You could hardly imagine what we saw next; in the roiling cauldron of the storm there were two lone figures in the distance rowing a small boat in the direction of the speedboat moored furthest from the shore. Why the furthest boat, no one could say, but that was clearly their aim. And for every metre of headway, they were pushed back half.

'It will take them all night,' Jeff muttered irritably, but only to me. I knew his impatience came from his concern for me; he knew that they were doing a sterling job in such conditions but as every second ticked away the more dangerous my situation became and getting me to safety rested very much on Jeff's shoulders. 'You have to let them do their thing,' I appealed as I turned to look at my husband. I could clearly see his face; illuminated now by the lights on the jetty, it exhibited a mix of appreciation and frustration toward the men in their precarious vessel and concern for our internal time bomb that ticked away.

I seemed to have become a passive observer, not communicating with those around me and in all of the chaos that surrounded me I had started to find some form of inner calm, almost as if I had accepted my fate, whatever that would be. I knew everyone was doing everything they could, including risking their lives. There literally was no more I could ask of any of them.

After what seemed like an eternity, the men reached and secured the speedboat, somehow managing to get it started. But, as they made their way to the jetty, a new conundrum surfaced; how to get pregnant me onto a boat that was rocking so wildly in these rough seas?

The entourage that surrounded me was assembled from various members of staff who were awoken to help the evacuation. Just living on the islands meant they were seasoned in dealing with life on and around the water and each member of staff took over like pros. Men stepped forward and positioned themselves around me; they held on to my arms, legs and torso firmly but not tightly. They then lifted me expertly down into the boat in one concerted movement without so much as a stumble. Jeff on the other hand, normally so stable, fell into the boat with a huge thump, with about as much grace as a fairy elephant. I saw him cringe as he tried to ignore his mere flesh wounds, which actually consisted of a couple of nasty grazes, but he knew he had larger issues to attend to. I was just thankful he hadn't completely incapacitated himself in the fall.

The boat was a typical, open-sided, Maldivian transport vessel with a fixed roof which helped abate the rain, but the lack of permanent windows meant once again we were only protected by plastic flaps rolled down the sides. Normally used to ferry guests to get around the island and to dive sites nearby, it was not designed for comfort or speed. They positioned me in the middle and toward the rear, trying to provide the most comfortable ride possible in the circumstances. And then we accelerated away.

Of course, in that weather, it still bobbed and bounced up and down like a cork on white-water rapids. I soon became somewhat catatonic as they accelerated to a suitable speed to navigate the waves without breaking the boat. As always, Jeff analysed the situation around him, trying to better assess our predicament, while my body once again shut down, forcing me to rest. All I was capable of doing was just lying there.

Mauroof, the courteous butler, and Arjun, the island's resident nurse, accompanied the two men driving boat and both of us, as we headed out into the black abyss. Both had been brilliant, and it was reassuring to have familiar and friendly faces with us. The doctor had to stay behind since, with Arjun gone, she would be the only medical practitioner left at the hotel island and, with a storm like this, further injuries were a distinct possibility.

I looked around at people faces, which were now lit only by the lights of the boats instrument panel. Despite their obvious competence in this emergency, I couldn't help but notice the bewildered looks on the pilots' faces as one steered and the other navigated us around blindly. I was in no doubt they were asking themselves, *What in hell am I doing out here, in this weather, at this time of night?* I knew that everybody on board was putting their lives at risk to save me and hopefully my baby, and for that I would forever be deeply appreciative, though I would have to wait to tell them that later.

The usual ten-minute ride to what we presumed would be a bigger island took an age. Only after twenty-five minutes did the lights of our hotel island disappear behind us, with no new island visible ahead. At that point we were being hurled around by the enormous swell in an ink-black void. Jeff was beside me, and I was holding on to him for my life, both figuratively and quite literally so, although I was being quiet and reserved, I realised subconsciously I was using every ounce of resolve to rest and conserve energy for what horrors would be thrown at me next.

{Jeff}

I felt a pang of loneliness with my new burden of responsibility for Clare and our baby, mixed with a hint of fear as we pounded into a large wave. The boat bounced clean into the air, chattering my teeth together, it was difficult to find anything to hang on to. The base of the chair sufficed as a makeshift handrail. I realised we were riding in a craft clearly not made for those sea conditions, it was a very dangerous expedition between the islands, but Clare and I had no option; it was the only way to reach any help we so desperately needed.

The others of course did have a choice, although they had not hesitated to come with us in such an emergency. Both Arjun and Mauroof sat at the back of the boat staring into the midnight sky. Their expressions were unreadable but at that point they were in control of the situation and the pilots in control of the boat.

'How are you feeling?' I asked Clare, trying to mask my concern.

She looked up at me helplessly and smiled. By the odd look on her face, it was obvious she wanted to be comforted, but at the same time she needed to concentrate on the horizon. Seasickness was imminent and it was all she could do to hold herself together. I slid my body closer to hers to try to absorb the thunderous reverberations from the hull of the boat when the bow slammed down as it launched off the top of another monstrous wave again and again.

I was wondering if there was a limit to what the boat, and its passengers for that matter, could absorb when Clare's face twisted in pain. She was now having cramps. This was something new.

'Shall we time in between each one?' I suggested as I urgently tried to take her mind off them; we both now realised that these were more than likely contractions.

'Two and a half minutes,' Clare read off my watch, as we both strained to see its face. I wasn't sure at the time but, from what I could recall of what I had read, she must have been getting very close to delivery right then and there in the boat. I briefly considered how much longer we should continue before asking them to stop in the middle of the ocean for Clare to give birth. But with only Arjun the male nurse for help with such a potentially complicated labour, the result almost certainly would have been catastrophic. I knew without any doubt that in that situation not only would we lose the baby, but I'd probably lose Clare too. We somehow had to keep going.

Then, suddenly, out of nowhere, a sight of celestial proportions appeared on the horizon before us; the lights belonging to our destination, Manadhoo Island, terra firma, and a gracious sight at last. As the boat slowed, I began to make out the shape of the port. At that same moment the rains began to subside slightly, almost as if the weather had been mercilessly waiting for us to dock before it got slightly better. However, when we drew near enough to see the dim light cast by the streetlamps, I was filled with a horror. There was nothing there. The island was as small as the one we had left. In the distance, the beam from an old lighthouse circled the island. From the little I could see, most of it consisted of dense undergrowth. Worse, it appeared almost uninhabited.

Where on God's earth are we? I asked myself.

Our vessel struggled to dock at the only jetty, as one wave after another forced our vessel with sheer might far too fast in toward the harbour. We thought we would get smashed into pieces and were so glad when the boat driver managed to dock and tie up the boat with relative ease in the end. Miraculous under such dire conditions.

Now the boat was stable enough, everyone assisted Clare to disembark, helping her to climb out as carefully as they had loaded her in. Then they collectively aided her as she walked over the uneven sand that was littered with old fishing tackle washed up by the storm.

A beaten-up white van appeared, speeding toward us along the port road. I wondered who would be in it at half-past midnight. It stopped a few hundred feet away, just close enough for me to make out the faded lettering on the side: Ambulance. Not the most modern of vehicles, but at least it had an engine and wheels. But it obviously couldn't be driven over the beach, which meant we would have to clamber over to it.

'Jump in here,' I gestured to Clare as we arrived at the battered van. There was a hint of irony in my voice, but it fell on deaf ears, for Clare's mind was obviously somewhere else.

'It's so old and doesn't look that safe,' Clare said looking up at me with concern. She was scared and it was beginning to show. But we had made it this far, we continued to trust our helpers, who were standing waiting to help Clare climb on board.

Despite its label, we were riding in something that once might have been an ambulance. All of those that still rode with us sat on the floor where a stretcher used to be, next to receptacle bins that looked like they might have once held medical equipment, though it was hard to figure out what would have been stored there as they were empty. It was as if we had stepped back in time to a world war with ramshackle vehicles, rationing in full force, and low supplies.

Bizarrely, after only a few metres, the ambulance turned right, and we almost instantly found ourselves outside a large villa with faded letters that read Noonu Atoll Hospital. As we were to later find out, this was the main hospital for all the islands in the Noonu Atoll group, not just for Manadhoo Island.

Island life was a different beast in many ways from life where there was a main body of land. We were in in the Maldives atolls, a collection of coral islands all dotted around in a rough circle in the ocean and connected by a single lagoon. Our hotel was on its own island and where we now stood was also an island, inhabited only by fisherman and their families. In fact, there is no mainland to speak of in the Maldives; even the capital city, Malé, is itself a small island not connected to anything other than a body of water.

Typically, each atoll in the Maldives has their own local government and they can be bureaucratic places. On many of the islands in the atolls, the only buildings are hotels to accommodate the holiday maker. Islands with only local inhabitants are sometimes wary of outsiders like us.

The medical centre was there to administer basic medical services to the resident population of each and every island in the North Noonu Atoll. Interestingly, we learned that most of the islands were uninhabited. Without exception all maternity cases were referred to Malé, the capital city of the Maldives, which was 180 kilometres from there; that's less than an hour by plane in normal circumstances but as far away as a distant planet on a night like tonight. Furthermore, as we were also to discover, being surrounded by a lagoon and located in the Indian Ocean came with its own logistical complications.

Clare was then put in a waiting wheelchair and whisked into the hospital. The gynaecologist, a Nepalese physician assigned to the Maldives, was quite short in stature and somewhat prickly by nature.

He told me to wait outside while they examined Clare. Being familiar with Middle Eastern, Muslim culture, I understood their attitude in matters concerning female modesty, but I also knew Clare would far prefer me to stay. Not least the fact that Clare had an uncanny ability to forget what doctors had said, plus she was in a strange and unknown place. I was going to stay with her at any cost and refused to move.

'You are staying with me?' she asked. It was both a question and a cry for help as they tried to continue the examination, while trying to shoo me away.

'It's okay, I'm right here,' I said. 'I'll stay with you.'

To our surprise, the ultrasound machine at their disposal was state-of-the-art and the gynaecologist obviously know his way around it very well. This gave us a desperately needed modicum of confidence.

Apparently satisfied that all was well with mum and baby, the prickly gynaecologist then gleefully announced, 'Your baby is alive, although he is in the breech position. I need to do another examination in the labour room, and we will give Mrs Curtis an injection of steroids to hopefully stop the contractions and the onset of labour, as long as the cervix is closed.'

Steroids are commonly given to mothers at the onset of early labour in order to safely delay the birth as much as possible. From what we were led to believe the mother is given the first injection, then if all goes well, and her heart rate remains under a certain number of beats per minute, and most importantly the cervix hasn't begun to open, a second injection is administered that stops the labour.

{Clare}

I felt relief wash over me for the first time since the ordeal had begun. Finally, things were slowing down and there was time to consider our next decision with a bit more deliberation. I had felt sure that I was not having contractions in the first place. What was more, I felt no differently now although, looking back, I obviously had no benchmark to compare anything with. All my focus was homed in on the large doses of constant discomfort, and bouts of terror during the initial panic and subsequent boat ride. But at least I knew that I was in a hospital and in safe hands. Well, safer hands.

From there they wheeled me up the corridor and past the baby intensive care room. The door was open a crack revealing a large room that was empty apart from a few boxes piled in the corner. As we entered the labour room, I saw it was clean, but very, very basic. There was a toilet in the corner, which to my western eyes looked freakishly out of place. That gave me cause for concern as I stepped up on the bed and Jeff was, once again, ushered out of the room.

Not one to give in easily, Jeff stayed right outside the room, refusing to go any further. From where I lay, I saw him pull the curtain back a smidgen so he could see and hear what was going on with me. Again, I relaxed just a little more, knowing he was as close as possible.

In the middle of the vaginal exam the gynaecologist said to me, 'Your cervix is closed and now that you have your steroids, I would like to give you a second injection that should delay the onset of labour. But first you must get your heart rate down, under 120 BPM. And, don't worry. Nothing will happen right this moment.' This was excellent news and I started to calm down inside. But, most of all, I wanted Jeff to be at my side.

{Jeff}

I could barely hear, but I hung on every word, and finally it was my turn to feel a wave of relief. If I understood the gynaecologist correctly, nothing would happen tonight. Clare would be given the other injection and then get some rest and, hopefully, we would return to our hotel on Randheli Island in the morning. *Perfect. That is good,* I thought to myself. Back to where we were before this nightmare. From Randheli Island we could fly back to Dubai via the capital Malé and, once home in Dubai, would enjoy some of the best medical care in the world.

It was almost 1am. I was dead tired, and I wondered how Clare was feeling, just a few steps away from me as I stood in the doorway to the labour room, at the Noonu Atoll Hospital, on Manadhoo Island. She must have been worried and, though I desperately wanted to go to her, I realised I would have to bide my time as I did not want to find myself at war with the hospital staff.

Just then, the prickly gynaecologist exited the labour room and walked straight up to me. Totally deadpan, he said, 'Your wife is three centimetres dilated. The baby will come tonight. I *might* be able to save your wife, but you must accept that we *will lose* your baby.'

Chapter 2

The Team

10 days earlier…

{Clare}

I remember sitting in the meeting room of my Dubai office, looking down at my stomach. By that point it had blossomed into a nice-shaped bump that preceded me. I was six-and-a-half months pregnant, and I had started to like my new rotund shape but also hoped I wouldn't gain too much more weight during the rest of my pregnancy. It was a normal pregnancy; no complications, no abnormalities. But the sickness! That was something else. Beginning in the first trimester, the wretched morning sickness hadn't stopped, as it should have. It only intensified. Whoever had termed it that had obviously been a man because it never subsided throughout the whole day.

'Clare, do you have an answer?' a male voice called over to me, pausing. 'The question was directed at you, Clare.' When I did not answer, my managing director looked at me with concern, wondering where my attention had gone.

As I came back to reality, everyone in the meeting room was looking directly at me – my MD, my assistant, and our four important clients – all sitting at the conference table, all looking painfully in my direction.

I had drifted off; this had become an all too frequent occurrence at that stage of my pregnancy, and not something I was used to after so many years in business. So I opted for the old-fashioned approach: the truth.

'Sorry, I am a little bit baby-brained today.'

I struggled to my feet to shift the weight that preceded me to try to relieve the pressure on my ribs. Everyone smiled of course, thankfully they were sympathetic rather than trying to hide any annoyance. The women at the table seemed to understand, and the men, I can only assume, were astonished at the enormity of my bump on such a small frame and as such forgave me. Frankly it was wondrous that I could in fact stand without tilting over.

Approaching forty-one, I was eager to stay in great shape by eating well and working out regularly. Indeed, since becoming pregnant, I made a conscious effort to totally refrain from alcohol and even stem my workaholic ways – a condition I was, and likely still am, often accused of -– so as to avoid getting overtired.

I still loved to have fun, but somewhere in my late thirties I temporarily hung up my party shoes in favour of a more mature approach to life's social engagements and challenges. We both had – my husband, Jeff, and I – in order to help us conceive. Actually, I don't like the word workaholic but let it pass when friends joked about it. With my tendency to work a little too much, I must admit that even after becoming pregnant it was hard for me to realise that I needed to slow down. And for that, my body made me pay the price, shutting down periodically for the benefit of mother and baby, whether I liked it or not.

After arriving in Dubai some ten years earlier, Jeff and I quickly fell for the exotic and exciting lifestyle of the "Manhattan of the Orient". Fine dining overlooking the azure Persian Gulf; feeling the spray of the dancing fountains outside the Burj Khalifa; and generally enjoying what Dubai had to offer. Before we knew it, the three years we originally planned for Dubai turned into five years, and then one day we woke up and it had been a decade. The place we once expected to treat as an extended vacation became our adopted home. We dearly missed our family and close friends from home, yet work had taken us to the Middle East, where time simply melted away.

Jeff and I did a great deal together. We were far from home and so relied on each other perhaps more than we would have if we'd been in the UK with our family close by. Like all married couples we had our ups and downs, but whenever they arose, we always tried to remain positive and battle on. Even though we had an amazing group of friends around us, Jeff and I always seemed to work as a team; if one of us struggled the other would instinctively take some of the load, until both were running at full steam again. This trait led our friends to call us 'Team Curtis'.

Originally it was their banter of course; however, we loved our collective nickname. In an expatriate society so far from family it meant a great deal to us to be thought of in that way. For some it may sound strange or even aloof, but for us it's not trivial, and as the events that were about to unfold around us began to mount it also became our mantra, our trigger word in order to keep us sane. Without teamwork I simply would not be here to help write this story today.

My concentration wasn't improving, so I was relieved to see that the meeting was adjourning for the day. As people stood to leave, I felt the baby twist inside me and experienced a sudden yearning for Jeff's emotional and physical support. My stomach pressed against the table, keeping me balanced, and I wished Jeff were not out of town on business again, as was so often the case. Sadly, I would be going home to our empty house again.

{Jeff}

As Clare yearned for a night with her husband, I was busy navigating my own meeting at the government offices of the Ministry of Oil and Gas in a neighbouring oil-producing country. It was a common place for me to be found back then, dissecting the latest trading data in the world energy markets. I was seconded by my then employer, one of the world's largest oil companies, to a joint venture in the region. I was immersed in the regional culture and had a great circle of close friends as well as a couple of personal ventures that kept me busy.

A mathematician by nature rather than nurture, I would meticulously recount reams of numbers and equations that would make most people's heads spin, including mine at times, although I would never have admitted that openly.

{Clare}

I thought I noticed a light red mark as I shifted where I was sitting in the meeting room. I looked closer, trying to focus. I remember thinking to myself, *Is that blood? No, no way, I must be paranoid!* Although this current pregnancy was conceived naturally, after four years of trying for a baby, five rounds of IVF that consumed a great deal of what we had managed to save while living in Dubai, and a miscarriage, who could have blamed me for feeling a wave of alarm?

I stared at the spot on the office chair, thinking that if it was blood, something must be wrong. I began to feel giddy. I just wanted to leave the room and to get to the bathroom to check what was happening. *Was it just a spot of blood or was it more than that?* I hurriedly excused myself to the bathroom, leaving my MD to complete the pleasantries.

Once inside, I locked the bathroom door to give myself privacy and told myself it was probably nothing. I had heard about spotting and that this could sometimes happen during a pregnancy; though behind all that logic I started to panic. Not for the first time; I had been petrified for pretty much the whole pregnancy. A previous miscarriage had really scared me, and the red spot reminded me of the amount of blood I passed after the first pregnancy was lost.

My logic by then was trying to kick in. Perhaps I had cut myself? It was difficult to check as I couldn't twist myself around to see everything and I couldn't just come out of the toilet to look in the mirror. I was, after all, still at work. I remember feeling confused and a bit stupid as no definitive explanation could be offered. What I really needed was Jeff to reassure me there was nothing wrong. But he was not even in Dubai.

{Jeff}

Nearly finished for the day, hundreds of miles away from Clare, I was trying to contemplate my next day's schedule. I was sitting in the most important meeting of my trip, the main reason for me being so far from my wife at this late stage in her pregnancy. Although I found it difficult to concentrate on the conversation as I was happily distracted by the thought of Clare's blossoming belly, which we started to affectionately call Balthazar. Just then my phone started to vibrate, and to my surprise it was Clare. I didn't pick up at first out of courtesy to those around me. Still, I couldn't help wondering why she was calling me. As the meeting continued, my curiosity niggled me, though my British resolve stuck to protocol.

Then the phone rang again. This stopped me dead in my tracks. We had an unwritten rule between us that if the other called twice it was urgent, really urgent, and couldn't wait. And with Clare being pregnant second calls were certainly cause for alarm. I immediately answered it.

'Talk of the devil,' I said into the receiver, keeping it light and, excusing myself from the deliberations that had followed my explanations to my colleagues, as I left the conference room and stepped onto the exterior stairway.

'Jeff!' Clare interjected in a panicked tone. 'There's blood!'

I heard the genuine strain and worry in her voice, something very rare for Clare. She would normally be cool, calm and collected; a woman in a man's world, always demonstrating good logic and precision-thinking. Despite this, inside I wrestled with what to do for the best. I almost never put personal needs ahead of work.

'I'm coming home,' I said finally

With that I could feel Clare's panic subside. Of course I would have to reschedule the meetings, but I also knew that in the Middle Eastern culture family always came first. So, I returned to the hotel in order to check out and collect my belongings, before making a mad dash to the airport to catch the last plane home.

Before long, I heard, 'Ladies and gentlemen, we have started our descent into Dubai International Airport. Please ensure your tray tables…'

As I absentmindedly gazed out of the window of the plane, I saw the sun was setting on the horizon of the Bedouin desert. Dubai sparkled brilliantly in the twilight, the golden light dancing off the city's striking, ingeniously crafted glass buildings. The magnificent 828-metre obelisk of the Burj Khalifa pierced the Arabian sky and towered over my plane as we descended toward this most amazing and vibrant city, until the wheels touched down smoothly on the tarmac.

{Clare}

Waiting at home, I curled up with Patch, our cat, in Jeff's armchair, sleepy and ready for bed. Though he had covered a considerable distance in barely more than a few hours door-to-door, by the time he walked through the door I was exhausted from my earlier ordeal and barely able to keep my eyes open.

'You made it,' I mumbled as I fought back a yawn. 'I'm so sorry to have dragged you all the way back.'

'It's fine, there are more important things in life than work.' When the words came out, I knew he meant them. I knew he loved me with all of his heart of course, nothing would change that, but work for Jeff was, well, work. It was for both of us really. It defined us.

Two days later we attended an appointment to see my gynaecologist, Doctor Amir. We had decided to take a so called 'babymoon', a holiday before the delivery of our baby-to-be and at thirty weeks pregnant we wanted to make sure I was safe to travel. I also needed a certificate from the doctor for the airline to this effect.

After years of visiting Doctor Amir, I felt a strong bond with him and felt fortunate he was my gynaecologist. Years earlier Doctor Amir had developed a passion for card playing, becoming so good at it that he retired from his position as head gynaecologist in a respected US hospital and moved to Las Vegas, where gambling became his main source of income. Finding life as a retired doctor didn't suit him, he switched strategies again, opening up his practice in Dubai following calls from former colleagues, who valued his incredible work ethic and bedside manner.

For Team Curtis, getting pregnant had taken such a long time that when we walked into Doctor Amir's clinic it was like walking into an environment of friends; all the nurses and staff would greet us like family.

Unbeknown to anyone apart from the medical staff and our close circle of friends, I had suffered a miscarriage two years earlier. It was discovered at the eight-week scan when they couldn't find a heartbeat. When Doctor Amir broke the news, he told me it was okay to cry, but I couldn't in front of him. Instead I went home and only then did I let the tears flow. I had to wait an agonising few days before the foetus could be removed and in that time I clung to the hope that the baby was just a late starter and that the heartbeat would miraculously appear on the screen. It never did.

So I was nervous from day one of this pregnancy. Before every scan I worried they would find something wrong and any time I couldn't feel the baby moving inside me for an hour or more I would go and lie down in a dark place and concentrate on my tummy until I felt a little kick or a wriggle.

So, it was natural that before we made any final travel decisions, we would go and gain the reassurance from the good doctor that we were okay to go. This need was somewhat amplified because of the recent blood spotting. I just wanted the visit over with and be told everything was ok.

Interestingly, when I look back, my concern before this scan was that something could be wrong with the baby rather than the possibility of miscarriage so late in the pregnancy. I knew it was possible but for some reason the notion it could be a reality for us at this stage never crossed either of our minds.

{Jeff}

Doctor Amir was different to most physicians. Although he would gamble in his personal time, his vocation required him to make informed medical decisions at work. He exuded a sense of quiet that was infectious. We felt very close to the doctor, maybe because of what Clare and I had been through with him; the journey of trying for a child together, the loss of a pregnancy together, and then finally after so long trying for a baby Clare managed to carry the pregnancy seven-months, with the medical and emotional support of Doctor Amir. There was a trusting confidence, so the lavishing of a warm greeting felt natural, even comforting.

Previously we had found that Clare had fibroids, but the doctor felt they were small enough not to impede the growth of the baby, although he did make a note for the future birthing team, to consider the option of a caesarean should the fibroids warrant it. If Clare could go through to natural birth, which is what we were all hoping for, then there was a risk that one or all of the fibroids could rupture, which could in turn leave her needing a blood transfusion. Without the right treatment the outcome could be fatal for her and almost certainly for baby too. All of this, Doctor Amir had meticulously logged in Clare's pregnancy notes.

Clare had been extremely sick for the whole of the pregnancy, including projectile vomiting without warning. She even managed to be sick over Patch, the cat, on her way to the bathroom once. However, she never complained. She had always felt that, after such a long wait to be pregnant, a little sickness for nine months was bearable. It was a small price to pay but it would have been nice for her if it had stopped at some point, so that she could actually enjoy the pregnancy a little as so many other expectant mothers seemed to.

Meanwhile, her attitude was, *'That's life!'* It was Clare's gift to her baby in order to gain the best chance of a good life, even if it was at the detriment of her own well-being, she would do it. It was not just her aim; she had felt it was also her duty as an expectant mother.

As Doctor Amir finished the ultrasound, he suddenly went quiet, and his demeanour mirrored that of twenty-four months earlier when he could not find the heartbeat of our first baby, and we learned that Clare had suffered a miscarriage. We froze, waiting for his next words.

Eventually Doctor Amir smiled. 'Everything looks fine and there is absolutely no reason for you not to travel, but–' then he broke off.

{Clare}

I stared at Jeff, I was actually in deep thought and becoming anxious about what Doctor Amir might say next. I didn't have to wait long as his sudden intake of breath brought me back to reality, followed by an unexpected statement.

'Although, I do want to state for the record that I would prefer you to take your holiday somewhere less remote, like London or even Singapore. I don't want to scare you, but I have delivered many babies and so often I have been witness to people giving birth when they least expect it.'

'It's fine,' I interjected. 'I've called the private hospital in Malé, the capital of the Maldives. They know Jeff and I are coming and if anything happens, they have the facilities to help, including an operating theatre. I've also checked all the escape routes, and the ability of the airlines to get us out quickly should anything go wrong.'

Famous last words. I had made full enquiries and checked every possible detail to an infinitesimal degree, or so I thought. If anything were to go wrong with the pregnancy, we would be able to get medical help, and quickly.

Anyway, what were the chances of something going wrong? I thought to myself. I still cringe over that thought today. Doctor Amir alerted us in our previous visit to some low-level worries about taking a vacation prior to the birth, which was what had sparked me to thoroughly research the Maldives, I also spoke to my friend Natalie, who had vacationed in the Maldives when she was 34 weeks into her pregnancy (almost full term) without incident, and she assured me that doctors always over-worry. 'Go have fun!' she urged me. Besides, I was only thirty weeks along, with no signs of a baby coming early, so there was plenty of time, wasn't there?

'What's the worst that can happen?' I exclaimed.

{Jeff}

As we left the clinic, we had a certain aura about us. 'Life's good sometimes, huh?' I remarked to Clare, feeling her mood matching mine. Right then we could have walked on water or leapt tall buildings.

Everything that was bad in life at that point was masked by the fact we were finally going to have a baby after so many years of trying.

As I pressed for the lift to whisk us down to the car park, I felt almost carefree, smiling inanely at anyone we passed like a lovesick teenager. I wanted to let everybody know we were going to have a baby. Not only this but we were finally going on holiday to get some much-needed rest. I was so unbelievably excited. I managed to suppress my emotions inside of course, but only just.

'*What's the worst that can happen, indeed?*' I remember mumbling to myself as we left.

Chapter 3

10:23pm

{Clare}

A few days later we flew to our island resort in the Maldives. Jeff and I saved very hard for this one spot of luxury before our life as parents began, a small respite away from the world as we were sure everything would change. We intended to savour every moment of this holiday. We both needed to rest and to have some relaxation, not least because we knew it would unlikely happen again for some time.

The hotel staff were amazing and upgraded us to their very best villa – their special treat for 'the expectant couple' – and we would have been in paradise had it not been for the weather, which was not as expected. It rained all day, every day with more on the forecast and, to add insult to injury, the seas were unseasonably rough in the usually calm lagoons, which meant I did not dare to go swimming.

By the middle of the week, unable to leave our villa without getting soaked, I was feeling ever more isolated and home sick. Jeff made arrangements to leave the very next day and get me home but, anxious not to seem foolish and over dramatic, I put on a brave face and convinced Jeff that we should stay. We would be home in a few days anyway and would then have two months to complete everything before our bundle of joy arrived.

{Jeff}

Clare let her fork fall onto her plate in an act of submission. It was 10:23pm, a time frozen in my mind. There was a break in the weather, and we were on the beach outside our private villa on the penultimate day of our long-awaited, one-week babymoon.

The meal consisted of freshly caught barbequed fish and luscious home-grown vegetables, all cooked up right in front of us into an amazingly decorative and tasty array of food. But Clare wasn't able to do anything but pick at it; all that day she had seemed to have no appetite.

'Are you okay?' I asked, noticing her discomfort. She was thirty-one weeks pregnant, but tonight she was looking more distressed than usual. After deciding to stay on the island a couple of days before I had become ever more concerned about her, cooped up as the rain hammered down. This was different though, now she was looking physically uncomfortable.

'I'm fine. It was lovely of the manager to offer us this complimentary dinner and big screen to watch the film on the beach, but I'm just not feeling right. I'm hot and can't quite get comfortable. Balthazar must be lying in a strange position.'

She wasn't complaining. She just told it the way it was. She shifted in her chair again, but it looked as though this only made it worse.

'You have felt Balthazar move today though, right?' I remember asking with an edge of concern. It wasn't uncommon for him to move less than the prescribed minimum throughout the day, although we were never sure if it was just Clare's baby brain! Something we joked about as Clare's body redirected resources away from her brain, to the baby.

{Clare}

The name Balthazar became our term of affection for my bump at the time, it originated on one of Jeff's business trips to London. He'd been sitting with half a dozen industry colleagues in a famous seafood restaurant called Balthazar. I was twelve weeks pregnant and we were just starting to tell people we were going to have a baby. The marauding drunkards with him at the table that night, who to this day swear blind Jeff was almost certainly the ringleader, got it into their heads that 'Balthazar,' the eatery's namesake, would be a perfect name for our baby. He then proceeded to drunkenly message eight or ten of our friends to announce the future new member of Team Curtis.

I had awoken back in Dubai with a barrage of congratulatory messages. On opening my phone, however, I had only one question in my mind:

'Who the hell is *Baby Balthazar?'*

{Jeff}

'Yes,' Clare had exclaimed. 'He was quite active earlier. He was doing some gymnastics, but he's settled down. I'm just not feeling right.'

She continued to shift in her chair without much success, while she looked at the staff out the corner of her eye. 'They are looking over at us again, you know,' she told me, as she nodded her head toward them. 'I'm not sure whether it's my huge belly or the film we're watching.'

Our choice of film amused the staff, who were watching us, as we watched our film on their big projector screen on the beach. It was an animated children's comedy called Inside Out, that personified five emotions of a new-born child as imaginary characters. I had absentmindedly watched part of it over someone's shoulder on the plane returning from my recent cancelled business trip. The staff couldn't see the irony in the choice that we could, due to the pending arrival of our bundle of joy. To me at least, it seemed quite an apt choice, but maybe that was lost outside the privacy of Team Curtis.

Suddenly a huge fork of lightning streaked across the sky directly above us, causing everyone to jump and look up. The clouds darkened as they rolled toward us in the twilight sky and the wind rose, which brought a sense of foreboding. Neither of us could quite have said why, but it felt almost spiritual, as the heavens above were lit from darkness and flashes forked across the sky.

{Clare}

The chef had been hovering nearby, then he suddenly turned to us and said. 'A storm is coming in. It's natural for rain this time of year but this will likely be much worse than usual. Enjoy the electric fireworks, finish the film, but you'd best make sure you are inside straight after. By all accounts it's supposed to be a big storm.'

It sent a shiver down my spine as I looked at Jeff for some reassurance. The chef probably hadn't intended it, but his ominous words increased my sense of disquiet, especially given that we were eating alone on the beach, some distance from the main reception. That feeling, coupled with a larger sense of being cut off from civilisation and the odd looks from the staff, made me feel just a little exposed and uncomfortable on our penultimate evening in paradise.

We both wrenched our heads to the sky as the gods unleashed yet another enormous flash of light – this one illuminating the heavens like daylight. Though I would argue we were both level headed and rarely got spooked by old houses or ghost stories, I shivered as the chef's words resonated in the air. I realised that very shortly a huge storm would hit the island and all we could do was ride it out in the shelter of our thatch-roofed abode.

{Jeff}

The film soon finished and by then it was time to retire for the evening. I was glad as, although our private BBQ was an exquisite way to finish the holiday, Clare looked quite visibly distressed. She obviously needed to get some rest. The chef had inadvertently spooked her and, as we left the table, I started to curse myself for not listening to my instincts and leaving Randheli island to return home to Dubai a few days earlier.

'Come on,' I motioned to her. 'Let's get you back to the room and into bed where you belong. I'll give your feet a rub. Would you like to walk down the beach to the villa, or we could get a buggy along the path? It's your call.'

The villa was only a hundred feet away. It was an enormous, open-plan, thatched beach cottage, with the most sumptuous décor and furnishings, including its own stand-alone, roll-top bath, full-size outdoor swimming pool and private beach. Inviting to say the least, especially now.

Clare had grown enormously in the last five days on the island. Neither she nor I were sure quite by how much, but it was obvious that walking was difficult. Still, she fancied she might try the beach walk, in hopes Balthazar would move into a more comfortable position.

We thanked the chef and waiter for an incredible meal and for setting up the projector screen, adding further thanks for the chef's weather warning. I then took Clare around the waist and proceeded to move her slowly down the beach, checking every step in front of her to avoid any mishaps that late in the holiday.

{Clare}

Once inside, my discomfort continued, and I felt I needed to go to the toilet. As I sat, strange feelings began to emerge from inside of me and the worry was starting to build once more. Whatever this was it just didn't feel right. I asked Jeff for some water. As he passed it to me he suggested that, once I re-emerged from the toilet, maybe a rest on the couch for ten to fifteen minutes before going to bed might help.

As the chef had predicted, the weather turned progressively worse; accompanying the clapping thunder and vivid flashes of lightning, a torrential downpour of rain then blanketed the island. A fully-fledged tropical storm descended upon us. The howling winds were bending palm trees and blowing the crystal-clear water out of the pool. In fact, the rain was pounding so hard on the windows that we started to worry. Most frightening was that the storm seemed to be raging harder and harder, without any sign of dissipating.

We listened to the shaking and howling around us, and I was grateful for our decision to come straight back inside. As I sat on cold porcelain in the bathroom, the thought now ran through my mind that I must be constipated, as nothing was happening even as my body signalled its discomfort. Eventually I gave up and re-joined Jeff in the lounge where I tried lying on the huge couch, hoping that might relieve some pressure. It didn't, so Jeff helped haul me off the sofa and guided me as I waddled toward the bedroom.

Moving off the sofa, something seemed to catch my eye as I looked back at where I had been sitting. *Is that a spot of blood?* I thought. *Can it be? Oh no, not again!* Blood rushed to my head as I fought back the rising panic. *Should I say something? Jeff will most certainly play it down. No, it's fine. I will just go to bed.*

Then I saw another spot and I became fixated on the red mark. I shuffled over to where I had been sitting and leaned in to get a better look. The spot was not dry. I mustered as much resolve as possible to keep my tone light, then said to Jeff, 'Don't be mad. But can you just look at the sofa?'

Caught off guard by the question, Jeff did exactly as requested and immediately saw what I was referring to. My eyes were riveted to it, leading him to look at the same place although, as predicted, he immediately dismissed it, presumably in the hope that it was nothing.

{Jeff}

'Seriously, I don't think it is anything,' I offered, but I saw it too and I was just wishing at that point that I hadn't.

My response was exactly as Clare expected it would be, so she held her ground. 'It's still wet, don't you see? It's definitely blood.'

Ice-cold worry shot through my veins, but I tried above all else to keep calm. 'It's all fine. Let's not get ahead of ourselves here,' I said, not really knowing where I was going with that line of conversation. Truthfully, I was stalling, trying to think of a solution as fast as possible and coming up blank. The situation was already beyond anything in my understanding or experience.

Clare gathered some clean white tissue and dabbed the spot to double check that it was blood. We quickly concluded that it was. Both of us began to panic; a nervous sense of urgency had suddenly filled the room, exacerbated by the fact neither of us could find the words of explanation or comfort for the other. We just stood there dumbfounded and glued to the spot. I clung onto logic, in the hope Clare would follow my lead. 'Okay, there is a little blood. Let's check you out to make sure you don't have a cut on your leg or something.'

We did a quick once over of both of her legs, but we found nothing. From there we feverishly looked for other possible sources for the red mark and, finding none, it finally pointed on the obvious; it was a spot of blood. Nothing more. Nothing less. It didn't mean anything. A mere spot. But it was likely in relation to the pregnancy, though neither of us wanted to admit that.

Uncertainty then mixed with our barely contained panic, because we were still unsure what was causing the bleeding. In the meantime, no more blood was to be found and as much as I wanted to check further, Clare felt she wanted to follow logical reasoning, no more blood, no more problem. She decided to go to bed and check again in the morning.

I wasn't so sure; however, I also could not find the words to argue the situation, allowing myself in that instant to be drawn into Clare's charade for the sake of my own sanity as opposed to facing the alternative: that we had a real problem! In the few feet before we reached the bed, Clare changed her mind. Out of an abundance of caution she decided to call Doctor Amir for advice. Unfortunately, he did not answer his phone.

Next, we thought of Clare's midwife, named Nicky, who had been assigned for the forthcoming birth. Nicky was of course a professional, trained in childbirth. Moreover, due to most pregnant couples being expatriate in Dubai, there was sometimes a lack of family support that might be expected at home, so midwives would commonly provide emotional, physical and educational support for an expectant mother to bridge the gap.

I'm not sure she would ever have expected the telephone call she was about to receive. However, we thought that any reassurance or any advice she could give might help until the good doctor could be reached.

'Hi Nicky, it's Clare and Jeff here calling from the Maldives,' Clare said. 'Can I pick your brain for a minute?'

She kept her voice light, trying not to expose any worry unnecessarily. Nicky was very reassuring. She told Clare to lie down and put her feet up a bit. Occasionally a woman in her condition at thirty-one weeks might experience a small discharge of blood.

'Knowing you,' Nicky said, 'you might be overdoing it a bit.'

Although reassured, Clare decided to go back to the bathroom and check once more before getting into bed. This time there was more blood on the tissue, less than from a nosebleed, but more than just a spot. Despite Nicky's reassurance, whatever the cause, it was getting worse!

'Jeff!' Clare frantically called me, 'There's more blood!'

{Clare}

I hadn't meant to sound panicked; but it just come out that way. Because I realised that my worst nightmare might be coming true, again. Another miscarriage!

I had carried the baby to 31 weeks, so it had never entered my mind that I might suffer a miscarriage again; it was so late in the pregnancy.

Responding more to the elevated pitch of my voice than the words themselves, Jeff came running. He had only been standing feet away, but I saw that the instant panic had sent his heart pounding and made him out of breath as adrenaline kicked in. This made me panic even more than before. With no words of encouragement coming from Jeff, we started to feel lost.

Blood rushed to my brain and we stood thinking of our next move. *What should we do now?* Being the twenty-first century, Jeff's initial suggestion was to do what any normal couple would have done in the same situation, 'Okay, let's Google it,' he said.

We were isolated with no help or literature to hand, but we had Wi-Fi, so we improvised, I guess that's the modern age for you. We both grabbed our iPhones and punched away. Quickly we managed to find reams of information that all seemed to lead in circles. The problem was, there was no way of telling what was causing the bleeding. As we sifted through the websites and articles, we started to realise that it was probably a condition called Braxton Hicks, not a miscarriage. One site even stated, reassuringly, 'Don't panic, you're probably having false labour pains, known as Braxton Hicks.'

Unfortunately, we hadn't started our pre-natal classes yet – they were scheduled for the days in which we arrived back in Dubai – so we were unaware what to do when hit by the inevitable false alarms.

Our preferred website on pregnancy, which tended to be less dramatic than many of the others, also offered other advice that assuaged our worry somewhat, corralling most of our early concerns into the category of 'false alarms'.

Jeff read through the lists of false alarms – there were so many. He learned more about what could or would happen and when, and also of course about Braxton Hicks. Our final self-diagnosis; I was undergoing early false labour. 'It's just the body going through the motions of readiness, practising to allow the baby safe passage into the world,' Jeff read aloud to me as the pressure alleviated a little.

{Jeff}

Just then I realised that there was more to that particular paragraph. It was hidden under an advert, for contraception of all things. As I read further, I started to panic. 'If the mother is having a bloody discharge,' it stated, 'it is not Braxton Hicks. It is more likely not to be a false alarm.'

'Shit,' I mumbled to myself under my breath. I tried to be careful so as to not unnecessarily alarm Clare. Then I heard a scream from inside the bathroom. I was standing just outside the door, so pushed it slowly open. I found Clare standing there, her white nightie drenched in blood. My eyes followed hers as she slowly looked down into a toilet bowl that was also stained red. Her blood was flowing heavily, it was like a scene from a murder rather than the inside of a bathroom.

Clare was frantically wiping the blood from her thighs and lining the soaked tissues on the side to show me exactly how much blood was flooding out. I didn't need to see the tissues; I could very plainly see the blood trickling rapidly down her legs.

I fought the urge to panic while Clare frantically told me about a friend who had bled during her pregnancy and then continued to full term without any complications, as though it held some bearing on the situation we found ourselves in.

'Look,' she cried out to me, her calm demeanour collapsing. 'This amount of blood must mean a problem.' She motioned to the line of blood-soaked tissues and looked into the bowl again.

I searched for a solution; my brain constantly processing what to do next and how we could save this situation; save our baby.

'I'll get the doctor,' I offered finally. Clare stood there motionless, her legs wide with blood flowing down her thighs.

{Clare}

Maybe this was a miscarriage? I remember just thinking over and over again. It was on both of our minds, but still neither Jeff nor I dare say it out loud. *Was this the sign of the foetus dying, even after surviving the first trimester danger period?*

Whatever was happening, we both knew one thing; that amount of blood wasn't a good sign.

{Jeff}

In her own bid for survival, Clare then pushed past me and moved to the bed to lie down. She felt the need to relax. It's what her midwife had advised her to do. Bizarrely, she intuitively grabbed a towel to bring with her so as not to mess up the bed sheet for the hotel.

I could sense Clare fighting back a growing sense of panic, although it seemed to be becoming increasingly impossible. The blood in the bathroom, the blood on her clothes, and now the blood on the bed, everything that surrounded her turned red; a universal sign of alarm. No matter which way either of us turned, we couldn't get away from the awful sight.

Responding to my call, within minutes a female doctor arrived at the door, shepherded by Mauroof, our butler; and Arjun, the resort's male nurse, coupled with a small entourage of helpers they seemed to have brought with them. It's not uncommon in countries such as the Maldives for a lot of people turn up to tend to the most menial task, and this was no exception, though even to this day we have no idea who everybody was. The sheer size of the villa, oddly, swallowed them all up. It didn't feel like there were nearly a dozen people in that room.

I stood motionless, if not helpless, in the lounge of the villa with Mauroof and Arjun, accompanied by their entourage, as a gaggle of men all stared wide eyed at my bloodied, pregnant wife being attended to by the female doctor on our bed not so far away.

Clare was examined on the bed, only about fifteen feet away but all I could do was watch; I felt helpless. I looked through the window at the enormity that was laying siege to us outside. Even as I did so I realised that I was probably experiencing the largest storm of my life. But at least, my mind told me, all of that commotion was taking place outside. We were safe as long as we stayed indoors.

I could see Clare look up at the doctor with a weak smile, her British politeness ever shining through. The doctor put a stethoscope to Clare's chest and then to her enormous belly, and with that she had completed the examination in short order. Seeming satisfied, or at least not displaying any evidence of alarm, she proceeded to read through Clare's pregnancy notes that we had brought along for the trip... just in case!

If it were even possible, with all that was happening, Clare's belly seemed, to me at least, to be protruding even more than it had earlier that day. As I walked to Clare's side the doctor seemed to smile and frown at the same time, and then she continued to ask more questions to which a pale Clare replied as factually as possible. I knew Clare wanted the doctor to make an informed decision. And then with just the sweep of her head, the doctor looked back at Clare, then again at me, and then over to the others who still stood in the living room.

'Get help!' she yelled.

I went straight into business mode; this as I found out, was my survival mode. Having travelled to various difficult and often war-torn third-world countries with my old job as a trader in the oil industry, I had been warned to watch for coups, uprisings or any reason to leave at a moment's notice. I suddenly remembered words of advice given to me years before. *Always have your passport, phone and wallet nearby, and always move quickly. Move as fast as you can to the British Consulate [neutral ground worldwide] if necessary.*

So my first reaction was to make a beeline for the room safe where I proceeded to pull out both my and Clare's essentials; passports, phones, wallets.

Of course, there was no compulsion, at that point at least, to run to the consulate to escape a military coup or uprising. But I did pick up the pregnancy notes, glad that we had thought to bring them along. We almost left them behind due to the bulk and weight of the folder. At least we had got that much right.

When no one moved, as they all stood like statues digesting the magnitude of her last statement, the doctor raised her voice an octave. 'Get a boat ready and inform the management we need to get Mrs Curtis to another island.'

I immediately saw a shocked look emerge on Clare's face. I was in no doubt the same was on mine. The hairs on the back of my neck stood up as I started to feel dizzy, rather like motion sickness, due to the magnitude of thoughts filling my mind all at once, the room span in front of me as the realisation sunk in. We were in serious trouble!

'My dears,' the doctor said, turning her attention back to us, 'there are two islands with medical facilities close by. The better-equipped one is normally forty minutes away, but in this storm it's risky and could take hours. Assuming you can even make it. There is a clinic on the neighbouring island. It's basic but they have a gynaecologist who I know is working tonight. It might take some time to get there, but you can't stay here.'

'What?!' was my only manageable rebuttal, as the implications of her intentions took hold. 'Nobody is going anywhere in this storm. It would be madness to get on a boat in weather like this, and at this time of night.' I continued as I looked at my watch. It was 11:30pm, only one hour and seven minutes since it had all started, and people were already losing their minds.

Despite the chaos around me I was racking my brains for a plan of action. *What did all this mean? What was wrong with Clare? What was wrong with our baby?*

The doctor changed tack and spoke calmly. 'Your wife is about to have a baby. We have no medical facilities to cope with a premature delivery here on Randheli Island. The notes say that your baby is breech, so we must move you to better facilities. The options in this weather are limited. It's very dangerous, but we have no choice.'

'Having a baby?!' I blurted, almost incredulously, I think my only line of defence was denial or even disbelief, I didn't want to subject

Clare to an unnecessary boat ride in her condition, in that weather. 'You mean to say you think my wife might go into labour, right here, tonight?'

'Mr Curtis!' The doctor exclaimed. 'Your wife is already in labour and could give birth at any minute!'

Chapter 4

Seaplanes Don't Fly at Night

{Jeff}

Back on Manadhoo Island…

I continued to stand in the doorway to the labour room, at the Noonu Atoll Hospital. Our hotel's female doctor had shepherded us off from Randheli Island by boat while a storm raged, to a destination originally unknown to us. When we arrived on the almost-uninhabited island of Manadhoo, Clare had been prodded, poked, and…

What had the gynaecologist just said?

'I might be able to save your wife, but you must accept that we will lose your baby.'

His last statement hung in the air. I felt like I had been struck by a thunderbolt from the electrical storm battering the island outside, almost as if hit by a lightning rod which had passed through the roof and entered my brain.

Might save wife, will lose baby!

It swam around in my head while I tried to make sense of the whole situation. Thirty seconds ago, the gynaecologist told Clare everything was going to be fine. I had heard him; there was no mistake in what I heard. With that one statement everything totally reversed, everything dear to me in this life seemed to hang in the balance.

Stunned, but never one to be discarded to the wayside when times get tough, I forced myself to digest the terrifying words the gynaecologist had just spoken. I was confronted with the prospect that my unborn child may suffer his demise before ever having the chance to live.

What have we done? I asked myself.

We had been so damned tired; could our desire for one last slice of respite away from Dubai prior to the birth of Balthazar be our undoing? Had we foolishly dismissed the advice of our friend Doctor Amir as trivial, just because we wanted a piece of deserved luxury in the form of an island paradise holiday?

I struggled to comprehend our decision. We caused this catastrophe; our undoing was purely brought on by us, with no one else to blame. Tortured, I looked at Clare through the curtains only a few feet away. She was caressing and talking to her enormous bump with a smile on her face, blissfully unaware that her life and that of her baby were in serious jeopardy.

'But didn't you just tell my wife that everything would be fine?' I enquired urgently of the gynaecologist. 'Did I hear you incorrectly?' I was confused as to why he would tell Clare one thing and me another.

'There is no point worrying her,' the gynaecologist replied evenly. 'She may die tonight and if she doesn't then her son will, so either way we may as well keep her in blissful ignorance until such time as we know what the outcome will be. At least it will keep her heart rate down.'

The gynaecologist imparted the information with zero emotion and seemingly no care in the world. I wondered about his social skills; his manner was so blatant and his tone so callous as to be mind-boggling.

'Right!' I replied with indignation. I could feel my adrenaline rising and taking control. 'Doctor, you need to listen to me. We need to get serious about this. If she really is in that much danger, and the baby is almost certainly going to suffer consequences that might not be survivable, let's get a seaplane in here and evacuate her as an emergency. Damn it, we need to get to the capital island, Malé, right away.'

The moment that I said it, I felt better. It put me back in control, and at the same time it countered the bad hand I had been dealt – or had dealt myself. We had insurance and credit cards and had considered the possibility of an emergency before we arrived, so we could activate our well-thought-out evacuation strategy right then. The strategy was simple; get a seaplane, get to Malé and get into the private hospital that would have modern medical facilities and the ability to deal with any situation at the highest level. Job done.

'But sir,' the gynaecologist pleaded, his voice finally showing some stress. 'There are no seaplanes moving in the area tonight.'

It was a counterpunch that forced me to pause for a split second and reconsider my options. I'd be damned if I'd be trumped out of the game so quickly.

'Well,' I said, as thoughts formulated, 'planes are parked at the resorts ready for very early-morning operations, are they not? Surely one of those could be used in an emergency. If my wife and child are in grave danger, I'm sure someone will redeploy and fly us to Malé.'

'Sir, I am sure that the pilots would graciously do it without hesitation, but there is something you must know. The problem you have is that seaplanes don't fly at night.'

As the gynaecologist said this, he remained his normal, serene self. I couldn't believe that our fate suddenly fell into the pessimistic hands of our prickly gynaecologist, who didn't seem to have a care.

'Seaplanes don't fly at night,' the gynaecologist reiterated. I heard him, but I wasn't willing to accept his pessimism for face value. How did I not know this seemingly absolute nautical fact? I was a private pilot with ten years' experience, a night rating and two-thirds of the way through my instrument rating. But apparently there was an answer to my question. Landing on a solid surface of a tarmac runway and landing on the open sea were entirely different matters, because at sea there were no landing lights. That made it impossible for commercial seaplanes to land, even in emergencies. How could this simple and obvious fact not have come up in any of the many phone calls that took place prior to going there? Why did nobody ever impart this crucial piece of information?

Emotionally, I felt an enormous void open beneath me. Circumstance was clearly laughing at me directly in the face, the law of percentages had changed the risk profile of the situation.

Ignorant of the situation facing us, Clare looked over at me and smiled. When our eyes connected, she beamed at me, effusing all of her natural beauty, not just generally, but as a soon-to-be mother.

I smiled back, but inside I felt sick. Not only had I earlier concealed from Clare that blood spotting almost certainly meant full-term labour, I now concealed from her that the gynaecologist had given our baby a death sentence; one that she potentially faced too. I so desperately wanted to tell her this fatal prognosis, but the truth was that the only person on this earth that I could not possibly tell at that moment was her.

To manifest my refusal to accept that fate, I gently laid my hands on the gynaecologist's shoulders. Even at only five feet nine inches, I actually towered over the gynaecologist and with the girth and shoulders of a former rugby player, I presented a formidable presence to the much smaller man. I stared him straight in the eyes and said in a firm, deep voice, 'This is not how we will start the evening together. Right now, I need you to be positive. If you are positive, everybody around you will act in the same way.'

I knew my words carried the power of truth. Call it the power of positive thinking or collaborative intuition, or call it what you will, I had witnessed it first hand. Often enough I had been part of teams that succeeded in their business ventures despite strong odds against them when all seemed lost. Put another way, success often came down to the effort and energy employed by the participants, with super-hard teamwork often reaping big dividends.

'There is no glass half-empty in this room tonight,' I continued firmly. 'There is not even a glass half-full. Our glass is overflowing, and I need you to have so much positive thought that it would be impossible for anything to go wrong.'

The gynaecologist just looked at me sceptically, which only energised me further. 'I realise we started this night with a long road ahead, but I am not letting my family go tonight. Tonight is the night we make miracles happen – miracles we can tell our children and grandchildren about for years to come.' I honestly didn't know what the outcome would be, even with the gynaecologist on my side, but I had to know he believed it could be a good one, if only for my own sanity.

'Mr Curtis,' the gynaecologist said in a firmer voice and with more urgency than before. 'Your baby is breech, in the worse possible position, he is almost nine weeks early, and your wife has unknown complications causing her to bleed. We have no proper medical supplies here. Even if we can deliver him alive, we have no facilities for premature infants to enable us to keep him alive. You should have gone to the other medical facility on the other island.'

I would not take no for an answer. 'Doctor,' I urged, 'promise me you will do whatever medically you can do and have to do before we leave this hospital, whenever that is. I'll sort the logistics.'

As the gynaecologist nodded his head meekly, I realised Arjun and Mauroof were standing directly behind me and had heard everything.

'We're here and able to help,' Arjun told me. 'I know a lot of the medical staff and Mauroof comes from quite a distinguished family, so we can help make arrangements.'

It was obvious that both Arjun and Mauroof genuinely wanted to help. And theirs was not a concern borne out of need to assist the clientele of the hotel. They were two sincere gentlemen who saw a family in trouble, and they would muck in wherever and however possible. After all, they had risked their lives without any hesitation just by boarding the boat to get us all there in a horrible storm.

As I managed the crisis around me, I realised I was reverting to work mode again. My line of business has countless moving parts, with many people involved doing many things, which inevitably led to mistakes. Having the ability to solve problems quickly and efficiently was a crucial skill to obtaining an optimal outcome. Only at that time I wasn't saving money for the trading book; I was trying to save the lives of my family.

I looked at Arjun and Mauroof; the thought arose that those two could easily be my old team at work by proxy, as I was at my best and in my element when I had a resourceful team to bounce off. I also needed Clare and though she was only running on half-steam in her current condition, it would be enough for Team Curtis to form a foundation; we complimented each other so well that we could function at nearly full force even if one of us was incapacitated, as the other would simply pick up the slack.

'That's excellent,' I exclaimed.

Clare's job was to take care of our unborn child. This was not something I could do, other than being there for support. Although she was about to give birth, she could still use her brain and logic.

The gynaecologist had stepped away and suddenly he returned from wherever he had gone. Somehow, he seemed different, as if he wanted to be more useful than earlier. The seed of hope was planted.

Mauroof, who had apologised a number of times about the gynaecologist's bedside manner earlier, noticed the change in his demeanour. I agreed with him that apparently my impromptu pep talk had not fallen on deaf ears. So there was hope after all.

'We need to give Clare the second injection,' the gynaecologist said in a much more positive tone than before, 'to see if we can stop the contractions. If she can maintain her heart rate lower than 120 BPM, then she has a chance to slow things down and then we may be able to move her to the main island at first light.'

Okay, I thought, *we have a plan to slow things down and then medical evacuation to a better hospital. Brilliant!*

{Clare}

Jeff marched up to me, apparently with a plan in mind, but he did not know exactly what to say or how to say it. To give my baby and I the best chance, I needed to try and keep my heart rate down, so his words and delivery of what I needed to do had to be perfect.

'You gotta work with me tonight, babe. It's you and me together. We have to be strong together and do whatever it takes to get through this.'

I could see in his eyes he was dead serious. I also knew the baby was breech and how dangerous that was. I didn't ask him to elaborate, as I didn't have to. I knew our baby was in trouble but resolved to leave my thoughts there. I didn't need to know how much trouble exactly, I trusted Jeff implicitly, I trusted him with my life.

'I need your brain too, please,' Jeff continued. 'You may not be allowed to get up and walk around right now, but while you are lying there doing nothing,' he said ironically, trying to ease the moment, 'could you get some blood to that brain of yours.'

'Teamwork, right!' I agreed, I also wondered what the weather was like outside. 'Has it got any better?

'Yes, much better, but it's still too bad if we need to travel.'

'Can we get to the other island then?' I asked with desperation. 'Maybe it's better to get to the other island and if they have a paediatrician over there, and an operating theatre, surely we will improve our chances?'

My thoughts were locked onto a mercy dash in another speedboat to a bigger island with better facilities; it had to be a definite option. By now it was 1:30am and the weather had apparently improved slightly, so maybe it would be less dangerous to attempt it. Why hadn't Jeff or someone thought of that option before? I managed to take a deep breath, in order to clear my mind. Maybe we had finally been dealt a card that would trump circumstance. We were not out of the woods yet, but at least we had a fighting chance and something specific to aim for. Moving my brain into gear, I looked over my left side and out of the door, over to where Mauroof and Arjun were standing just outside the room. 'That boat we came over in is still outside, right?' I called over.

Mauroof nodded.

'Could it take us to the other island, with more advanced medical facilities? And is there a paediatrician on this other island?' I continued, as I let the plan formulate.

'Yes, we can certainly try and use it in order get you off this island and to better medical facilities,' Mauroof repeated, boosted with confidence at this great idea that apparently the gynaecologist's pessimism had precluded him from even considering.

With a clear and immediate plan, Jeff and I then set about the business of assembling a small evacuation team. The boat was ready, and the boat drivers less concerned about being at sea in the prevailing conditions than before, as the weather had improved, slightly. Arjun and Mauroof and one nurse agreed to go along in an effort to help, which gave us comfort. But just then the ever-bleak gynaecologist walked over to us and said, 'I hate to be the one to tell you, but I gave Mrs Curtis a steroid injection to calm her. It would be ill-advised to move her presently. If she can get her heart rate down to under 120 BPM, I can then give her a second injection that may slow things down enough for you to move her. If she gives birth on the boat, with no resources of any kind at your disposal, it's certain death for both.'

Though his manner had become less prickly, the gynaecologist remained as direct as a speeding bullet. *What am I to do?* I thought, with a small tinge of despair. If we stayed, almost certain death for baby would follow, with the possibility of the same for me. If we went, the facilities at the next island would be better but the baby and I could die on the boat. We were facing Hobson's choice: damned if we do, damned if we don't.

Jeff and I built a head of steam and between the two of us we'd built up enough adrenaline to make the decision; we were going! In fact, we had almost become gung-ho about it, bravado emitting from our chests because we were going to save our baby. The entourage formed an improvised evacuation team that moved in unison down the corridor, supporting me under my shoulders as I valiantly struggled to walk, our optimism infectious. We all felt the refreshed energy brought on by the hope of the new plan. However, suddenly Mauroof stopped us at the door.

'It would normally only take forty minutes to get to the island,' Mauroof said, 'but islanders always under-estimate. I think it will be more likely an hour, maybe even longer with the weather and high seas. And I'm also not sure about the medical facilities at the other island. I have not seen it myself, and although it's considered a better facility, we might in fact be transferring you to the same situation.'

Jeff and I looked at each other as the new revelation sunk in. We were in unfamiliar territory, and our plan would only be as good as the information given to us. With Mauroof openly questioning the validity of the information, the plan was then in doubt. Perhaps we had been foolhardy to mobilise based on information they couldn't be confident about, but really, what choice did we have? The less risky plan was to sit tight and wait it out until the next morning even though we all knew the baby and I may not make it through the night!

Chapter 5

Monte Carlo or Bust!

{Clare}

I reluctantly clambered back up onto the bed. In doing so it did feel like I had taken a backwards step, which only added to my apprehension. I knew this was the best place for me to be at that point, waiting calmly and getting the second injection. Although the gynaecologist had lied to me about how far dilated I was; I knew because Jeff quietly revealed it to me soon after we had decided to stay.

I hadn't really noticed before, but there was another gentleman sitting quietly in the corner of the room, just staring and taking it all in. He was dressed like someone you might see in a film from the 1980s – large, square-rimmed glasses, striped shirt, corduroy trousers – for some reason I had an uncanny sense that he was Russian. He suddenly moved toward me, handing me a mask and gesturing for me to put it over my face and I obediently did so, because of the confidence of his gesture.

'Thank you,' I said, understanding the general purpose of the mask but not yet knowing what I might be breathing in. It had been a long night and I felt these people were there to help me, causing me to trust that they would not do me any harm.

'What is this?' I lightly asked from behind the mask.

'Oxygen,' the gynaecologist replied from behind me. So not the gas and air that I had heard about, which at least could send me to a happy place.

I noticed him fiddling with some apparatus and untangling wires and tubes that looked like they may have not been used for a while, unknotting and tugging free what seemed to be a mess of spaghetti.

'I'm afraid we have nothing stronger on the island,' he added. He was somewhat distracted with what he was untangling. 'Medical supplies are scarce, and anaesthetic is simply not available right now. The oxygen isn't going to relieve the pain, but it might help get your heart rate lower and give you some energy or even clarity.'

Meanwhile the Russian-looking man had returned to the same position on his chair and just watched. I assumed he could in fact speak, but that maybe he didn’t understand English. After all we were the foreigners, although I was still unsure of his exact purpose, other than observing everyone.

I breathed deeply and took in a good gulp of O2. I wasn’t sure whether it was a placebo effect or perhaps the action of taking the breath itself, but it did do some good as I instantly started to relax, and my heart rate registered lower numbers on the monitor beeping away beside me.

{Jeff}

I immediately saw Clare’s heart rate drop and jumped to my feet. ‘That’s it!’ I yelled, rather too enthusiastically as if we were at a sporting event. ‘You just dropped five points. I know we haven’t really started our birthing classes, but let’s try and breathe deeply and calm ourselves so that your heart rate drops below 120 BPM. Then you can get that second injection and hopefully we can ride this out until morning and be off on a seaplane ASAP!’

If Clare could have her second injection and pause the labour, I figured we had a chance of getting on a plane at first light, when a seaplane could land. With everything hanging in the balance, this was now the sole aim for Team Curtis; to survive until daylight. I was watching the monitor like a hawk; it gave me purpose.

‘That’s it!’ I exclaimed. ‘We’re down to one-twenty-six, one-twenty-five now. Keep breathing with me,’ – I inhaled deeply and exhaled – ‘and try and relax your mind.’

Finding a rhythm, we breathed together for a few minutes and I suddenly knew that we were going to do this. It was just a feeling, but for some reason I knew that together we could get Clare’s heart rate to the required numbers. And I knew that by encouraging and talking to her, she would relax even more, and before long we could get that second injection.

{Clare}

I was getting annoyed. I knew Jeff meant well, but he talked about ‘our heart rate’ and ‘our second injection’ as though he was somehow involved in that breathing, injection-receiving and delivery process. I knew what to do and didn’t need to be told, but I didn’t have the heart to tell him to shut up and give me some space, because he was only trying his best in a very tough situation to do everything possible to help.

I also started to notice that an anger was building inside me and wondered whether it was something to do with the initial injection or maybe even my hormones. Though I couldn't put a finger on it, I felt my emotional and physical self changing, not to any monstrous degree, but enough for me to be aware of it. Just as I felt another pang of anger, my heart rate shot up to 160.

'Okay, we lost it,' Jeff said resolutely, as if our team had conceded a score against them. 'It's okay, it's okay, we'll get it back down in no time.'

'Jeff, can we take a minute?' I asked. 'I feel overwhelmed and just need to stop thinking for a while.'

'Sure,' he replied instantly. 'Whatever you feel most comfortable with.'

{Jeff}

I was relieved in a way, as I was already starting to feel like I wasn't being much help. I thought it best to give Clare the space she requested, so I went outside to check the logistics out there and see how things had developed. When we had announced we were staying, Mauroof suggested that he take the boat by himself and went to pick up the paediatrician and bring him back to the island. It would be quicker than waiting until daylight. I had thought the idea ingenious and wished him Godspeed. Before I knew it, I looked at the back of Mauroof's head as he rushed out the door at full speed. That had been over an hour ago, so Mauroof should have reached the other island by now.

'Any word from Mauroof or the paediatrician?' I enquired as I walked up to Arjun. He sat on a bank of interconnected hospital chairs directly facing the door to our makeshift labour room, a perfect spot to be close enough to help if and when needed, but far enough away so as not to hinder.

'No,' Arjun replied, 'no word as yet, but he should have made it by now.'

'I do hope nothing bad has happened.' I pondered Arjun's statement, wondering whether Mauroof had been a bit hasty to chase off into the unknown weather conditions. However, the seas seemed far calmer than before, although still rougher than usual, Mauroof was a local and would have certainly been used to the weather. I put my worries to the back of my mind and went about trying to find some bottled water. I was parched and was sure Clare would be too. I excused myself, turned left and only then with the nurse's station mere metres in front of me did I realise how tiny the island hospital was where we had been riding out the night. I also noticed for the first time several other facts that stood out as odd. First, the only hospital ward seemed to be an extension of the corridor, not a separate room or proper ward. Second, all the lights seemed to be on at that time of night. And third, all the patients seemed to be wide-awake in the middle of the night. Some of them lay there looking and watching blankly, while others seemed to be moaning in pain, the cause of which was not immediately obvious. I wondered if this was a normal occurrence but suspected it was the result of the arrival of Team Curtis and the three-ring circus that accompanied us, with everyone in the hospital being woken up by all the noise, hollering and clattering. It also occurred to me that some of the patients might have contagious illnesses, causing me to add one more worry to the odds already stacked against us. I decided that the best course of action was to just not think about it and stay clear.

{Clare}

In the labour room, I felt that I needed to refocus, take in what had just happened, and where exactly we were, but there were far too many people for the room to be quiet or for me to feel alone. Everyone seemed to be making some kind of noise – banging or just being unnecessarily noisy in some fashion – and what they were all doing I had no clue. If I was to generalise, they seemed to be packing things into trays and then taking the trays to the other side of the room and unpacking them, rather like soldiers digging a hole and then filling it back up again. No matter what they were in fact doing, it seemed like an endless if not pointless task and my logical side was questioning their purpose and reason for being there. After a few minutes I managed to attain some stillness by turning my head away and actively deciding not to watch, as the curiosity seemed to spike my brain activity, which in turn increased my heart rate to over 120 BPM. I wondered where Jeff was, but knew he was planning and thinking and working out different scenarios in his head for every eventuality. I knew this for a certainty because that was him; he was always thinking about something.

Then suddenly amid my maudlin reflection I felt a pang of despair, not for being left alone – I enjoyed the respite Jeff had given me

– but because I wanted physical affirmation he was nearby. Then I told myself not to worry. Wherever he was couldn't be too far away, as the place was so tiny. Then I heard his voice and at that precise moment, Jeff walked through the door. 'Wow,' he exclaimed, 'I hadn't appreciated how small this place is, but I guess it's only an island hospital so major cases must go to Malé. Which is what we'll be doing at first light, when the seaplanes can fly,' Jeff mused, with a half smile.

I smiled as I savoured that thought for a while. Then it seemed that both of us almost suffocated at the same time from an overwhelming sense that something was missing from this scenario.

'Where on earth is Mauroof with the paediatrician?' I asked in a bit of a panic. 'He's been gone for hours and we keep being told they'll be here any minute.'

'I honestly don't know,' Jeff replied. 'Nobody's heard a word from him. And though nobody thinks the weather is quite as bad now, there are no working phones and it seems there is nobody answering the radio from the boat right now.'

{Jeff}

No Mauroof, no paediatrician, I thought desperately to myself. So, if the baby came, how would it survive at thirty-one weeks without special and immediate care? I saw Clare was starting to panic as well, which sent her heart rate soaring. Instead of reacting to the spike, I willed myself to suppress my concerns and continued to talk to Clare calmly. 'Calls have been placed to the other medical facility, but they are not going through, probably because the storm knocked out the phone lines earlier and maybe the mobile masts are affected in some way too. I'm sure he has the paediatrician and they are returning together now.'

'Okay, but I need a paediatrician,' Clare barked back at me.

However, in her present condition a paediatrician could do nothing for Clare, she already had her prickly gynaecologist standing close by and the Russian anaesthetist, or whatever he was, who sat quietly in the corner.

If only the paediatrician would just get here, I thought to myself privately. Not only would that help Clare relax, he could help if the baby was born early and we needed specialist help to keep him alive until seaplane arrived, and evacuations took place to the capital.

Just then Clare's phone rang. It was Doctor Amir, returning her phone call from what seemed like an eternity ago, although the reality was only a few hours. I grabbed it and offered it to Clare, as I knew she and the doctor were fond of each other.

'Would you mind taking it?' she asked to my surprise. 'I can't think clearly right now.' Without hesitation I swiped my finger across the iPhone screen and answered the call,

'Doctor Amir, how are you?'

We forewent the small talk; I fast-forwarded to Clare going into labour and that she was presently on a remote island, lying in a hospital bed (of sorts) and as she was trying to get her heart rate under 120 BPM, so that we could stop the labour and she could be moved to a better hospital. Doctor Amir asked me to recount what had happened and I did so as concisely as I could with as much information as I could remember. The doctor was obviously out for the evening, as in the background I heard the noise of people shouting and milling about.

'Can you get to City Hospital?' Dr Amir asked. Obviously he thought we were already back in Dubai. 'I can call through and have one of the other gynaecologists take a look at Clare.'

'Doctor Amir,' I gasped, 'we're still in the Maldives.' Struggling to control my emotions, I managed to add, 'On a very small, almost-uninhabited island.'

For the longest time there was total silence on the other end. Then the doctor's voice erupted, 'Oh my God! I thought you came back yesterday.'

Obviously, without the benefit of his patient notes in front of him he remembered our return date incorrectly by one day. Even though Doctor Amir had an immense agility in the cerebral department, he mistakenly thought Team Curtis were back in Dubai, where there was an abundance of medical facilities and some of the best physicians in the world.

'Oh my God,' he exclaimed a second time, as the helplessness of our predicament sank in. I felt a pang of guilt for distracting the fine doctor from his evening's engagement – after all what could he do from so far away? – and just hoped I hadn't spoilt his evening, or his deck in hand at the table.

'Doctor, where exactly are you?' I enquired; I was also genuinely interested in where he was, and what the commotion was behind him. Thinking back maybe I just needed to visualise being somewhere but there in our isolation, just for that moment.

'I'm at the Casino in Monte Carlo.'

Clare was listening to the call with a desperate hope that she would hear from me any moment that Doctor Amir had come up with a miraculous plan to solve all our problems, or just an answer as to what to do next. But she was out of luck. There was no answer, apart from continuing to do what we were already doing.

{Clare}

Just then I felt something enormous burst inside of me. Initially I really wasn't sure what it was. Jeff was still on the phone with Doctor Amir as realisation dawned.

'Oh, fuck!' I heard myself shout from the bed.

Jeff stopped dead and swung his head round to see what was wrong, nearly wrenching his neck in the process. When his eyes found mine, he immediately saw I was totally panic-stricken.

'I think my waters just broke!'

Chapter 6

The Birth of Baby Balthazar

{Jeff}

'What did she just say?' Doctor Amir anxiously asked me from thousands of miles away. It was apparent that he had heard some version of that statement many times before, but I doubt he ever expected to hear it when he made that phone call, from the balcony of the high rollers room at the Casino in Monte Carlo.

'She said her waters just broke,' I said in great confusion. Although I'd always thought the movies exaggerated the scenes of water gushing from the woman just before the hot water and towels arrived, I was nevertheless surprised that I saw nothing, not a drop. Holding the phone in total silence the good doctor and I contemplated the situation, dumbfounded. And then it hit, a tidal wave, as if Clare was initially holding back and then released, a huge torrent of water gushed from under her and soaked everything on the bed and in the immediate vicinity.

'Her waters have broken,' I managed after a long pause. 'It's definitely happening.'

Inside, I felt sick to my stomach. All that work and planning and trying to delay the labour until we could get proper medical attention, or even an evacuation to Malé by plane, all of it was in vain, as there was no stopping the baby from coming. At any moment, our baby was entering into the world on this small island in the Maldives with full disregard for his own safety.

{Clare}

I lay motionless on my back in shock. I wasn't completely sure of what had just happened, though I was relatively certain my waters had broken, so instinctively I knew the baby would soon be on his way. It had been such an explosive feeling; I was now concerned that it might even be something more. With that thought, my mind started to panic. Maybe my placenta had been dislodged, maybe the baby had twisted too hard, who knew? But one thing I was 100 percent certain of; all preventative medicine to delay the onset of labour had proven ineffective and this was the point of no return.

'Well, you're not moving her now,' our prickly gynaecologist observed, deadpan. 'This baby is coming now whether you like it or not.'

He could have been reading my mind, I thought. And if he'd tried to weave any pleasantries into his voice, he failed miserably. But at least he was making an effort, and at least he had listened to Jeff, because he seemed to have adopted a new, less abrupt, bedside manner in what was now a fully-fledged labour room. As the gynaecologist, he become the one in charge by default, as he was the only one with the necessary experience. Jeff looked over just as Doctor Amir's voice came alive at the other end of the phone.

'Get her to the OR, stat!' he yelled.

{Jeff}

I had seen enough movies to understand what he meant, but firstly I was no doctor and secondly there was no operating theatre. We were on a nearly uninhabited, remote island, 180 kilometres from the nearest urbanisation and surrounded by a body of water consisting of sea and lagoons. 'Doctor Amir, there is no operating theatre,' I barked into the phone.

'But Clare told me before you left that Malé had a private hospital capable of caesarean section, should the need arise.' I could hear the strain in Doctor Amir's voice. 'She needs one and now the odds are too high against you. Where exactly are you?' he tried to clarify.

'We were still at the hotel when the labour started, but they evacuated us by boat in the dead of night to this island, which is almost uninhabited. The weather was too bad, and it was too dark to move from here to Malé, where they have better medical facilities. So, we were caught completely off guard, despite all of our planning,' I garbled down the phone like a scolded teenager.

Just telling the story to Doctor Amir made me go numb. On hearing my own words, I just couldn't believe what had happened. Why on earth had I taken my pregnant wife to the Maldives, to such a remote place? I had to quickly snap out of it, there was no time to dwell; it was done. Right then I needed to solve a problem, which was my forte for all my working life, solving problems for the company, so I should have been equipped. That said, I did wait for Doctor Amir before I took my next step. At that moment, almost as if he was reading my mind, he said in a low, balanced and calm voice, 'Jeff, your family needs you tonight. I cannot predict the outcome, but be there for Clare, be there for your baby, do everything you can to help and make sure you take control of yourself and if necessary, take control of the situation around you as well.'

There was nothing more our friend could do. Despite his expertise, he was too far away and too disconnected to do anything effective. Still, he asked me to hand the phone to the gynaecologist in charge. I told Doctor Amir to hold as I looked at the gynaecologist quietly going about his business around Clare. I passed the phone to him with Doctor Amir waiting on the line. He took it without looking and lodged it between his ear and shoulder, so he could continue prepping Clare as he listened.

It was an odd sight; the gynaecologist shaved Clare's vaginal area in preparation for the premature birth. There was no delicacy about his business; he hadn't even asked Clare if he could start. He just took it upon himself that this baby was coming, and he needed to be prepared. Nor did he make any sounds back into the phone that was lodged in his neck. If he listened to whatever Doctor Amir was saying, it wasn't obvious.

Doctors are renowned for discounting other doctors' diagnoses, so I was afraid he wasn't listening. I knew Dr Amir held an impressive memory; thus he could have been imparting Clare's patient notes by rote, however my concern was that that might agitate our prickly gynaecologist by denting his ego. Although I was in no doubt that Dr Amir would use his best bedside manner to convey his message.

Eventually the gynaecologist handed the phone back to me without a single word or even looking up as he simply continued to do his work. I put the phone back to my own ear and found that Doctor Amir had hung up, having no doubt gone back to his business of playing cards. He was, after all, on holiday at the Casino in Monte Carlo and there was nothing more he could do from there.

{Clare}

I, meantime, lay on the bed feeling exposed but that would have been the same in any normal childbirth scenario. *Normal*, I pondered over that word as I thought of it. I was not sure if I even knew what that felt like anymore, or if I would ever feel that way again. In such a short space of time, my life dramatically turned inside out. I had my gynaecologist, who would be there for me, but what about the little one? Who did he have to help him when he inevitably entered the world two months early?

'I still don't know,' Jeff whispered to me as much as himself, as if he was considering the same thing, 'what's happened to Mauroof and the paediatrician?'

I must confess, in my panic I was honestly not so much thinking of Mauroof but of the paediatrician. I was racking my brain as to how I could prevent the baby from being born until I knew we had some form of medical care for him. In fact, in my mind I made the decision not to push until the paediatrician arrived. Keep him inside, I said to myself. Keep him inside, no matter how hard that would be; that's the safest place for him until we have expert help.

'I won't push until the paediatrician arrives,' I finally blurted out, as uncertainty crept in and I realised I needed information before making any decision. I needed to know what to do to help my baby and I needed to know right then and there.

'No,' gasped the gynaecologist, completely scuppering my plan. 'That would be very dangerous. If this baby wants to come, you must let it. You should know from your birthing classes that you must listen to your body first and then your doctor. So when I say push, you must push. If I say stop, then you must stop. Because your baby is not in the correct position, your only chance is to do exactly as I say.'

On these words, Jeff cupped my hand between his and said, 'It's okay! He's the boss now. When he speaks, I'll tell you what to do. I can be the conduit so you just need to listen to my voice and maybe we can try some breathing techniques.'

We hadn't had enough practice or learned any technique by that point, apart from reading the leaflets provided, but we understood the process and general idea of what we needed to do. We would have to improvise on the rest, and if that were wrong, it would have still been better than doing nothing.

The words of the gynaecologist were still rolling in my mind. *'There's no anaesthetic on this island.'* Which meant no pain relief whatsoever: not even gas and air. I had wanted to try and give birth naturally without pain relief and always wondered if I would be able to handle it and not have to call on the epidural – right at that moment, as it turned out, I had no choice!

'I am going to cut her,' I caught the gynaecologist whispering to Jeff in his inimitably direct way, as he brushed past him to get the surgical instruments from the countertop. The instruments were contained within a metal kidney dish, which I only hoped came from a sterile location.

Jeff put his head next to mine and explained what the gynaecologist was about do. I didn't expect it would be pleasant, but it was necessary to allow the baby a wider passage, whichever part of his body came out first.

'I'm going to sterilise the area,' the gynaecologist said next, as he proceeded to slap what looked like wood varnish all over the birthing area. Realisation that it was iodine sank in. I hadn't seen iodine since chemistry lessons at school. It was an old remedy, not exactly modern medicine, but it would serve the same purpose.

The incision was made. I felt it, but at that point, surprisingly there was no pain; my body somehow self-managed and protected me from the feeling and I only hoped the same was true for my baby. Without speaking, the nurses helped me into a sitting position and removed the rest of my clothing. Before I knew it, the hospital gown was removed, and I was wearing nothing but the weak smile on my face and a small hospital sheet to protect my modesty. Not that I cared about any of that right at that moment. As far as I could tell, everything was done carefully and professionally. It instilled a certain level of confidence, despite my worry about the lack of medical facilities and the desperately needed paediatrician, who was still yet to arrive.

Then metal poles appeared from nowhere. They were inserted vertically in purpose-made holes on either side of the bedstead, with leather straps halfway up. I gaped at the sight and failed miserably to conceptualise exactly what they would be for. But I didn't have to wait long, as the nurses, still moving quietly and gently, proceeded to pull my legs apart, tethering each to a pole. This served to immobilise me, preventing me from moving in certain directions and forcing open the birth canal. There seemed something quite barbaric about it all as I lay there exposed to the elements with no ability to move, but there was no time or reason to complain and obviously it had worked millions of times in the past, before modern day medicine, so I just had to trust it.

Just then I started to feel enormous pain. This pain was far worse than anything I had ever felt before. I tried to suppress it, but it was too big. 'Arrrgh!' I screamed, as Jeff held on tight to my hand and provided whatever support he could.

'The baby is coming; okay, push now,' said the gynaecologist to me, looking up from between my legs. Jeff relayed the command and I did exactly as I was told. I gritted my teeth and pushed from my stomach, exerting great force from a muscle group that I had never used before. I could only assume that this was a pretty standard feeling for all mothers giving birth for the first time.

'Arrrgghh!' I screamed as the pain became worse still, but I was determined it would not beat me. There had been no possibility of administering an epidural anyway, and I refused to even think of the notion that I would need one. To do so would have been to concede to the pain, which I point blank refused to do.

'Stop,' ordered the gynaecologist. Jeff looked at me. I must have been wide-eyed by then. I dripped in my own sweat as I lay back, perched on my elbows for support. Jeff relayed the message and I fully complied.

'Okay, so we need to try and find some sort of breathing pattern,' I cried. I was in pain and I wasn't sure if it was normal or because of the breech position of the baby. 'I'm just looking and listening to you and I'm trying to shut out the world and concentrate on breathing,' I told Jeff, in the hope this might alleviate some of the pain. In truth it wasn't the physical pain that bothered me, I could deal with that, it was the emotional side I was struggling with: the not knowing what to expect next and whether in fact my baby was alive or dead.

I looked directly at Jeff, knowing at that exact moment I was the only one who could control the outcome as I progressed through the next few stages of the birthing process. Of course, the gynaecologist was directing things, but I knew I had to obey my body to give my unborn child the best chance of survival.

'Okay, push,' the gynaecologist instructed once more.

I didn't know how the gynaecologist knew when to push and when not to; maybe he was making an educated guess, but I couldn't argue with that, so as a team Jeff and I worked together as we always did. While I was pushing, I started to enter a desperate state. I was in such great pain and right then I needed to say something I felt was vitally important to Jeff. I looked him square in the eye, poised to tell him what I needed.

{Jeff}

Clare suddenly looked at me, she looked as though she needed to tell me something really important and through gritted teeth she managed to growl, 'Whatever happens tonight, tell my personal trainer Danielle that this pain is nowhere near as bad as her 'lean legs' programme. Arrrggh!' And then she screamed again.

In the middle of Clare's howls of pain while giving birth on an almost-uninhabited island, hundreds of miles from anywhere, her coping mechanism surfaced as it always did, and it made us both laugh. Hysteria maybe? Who knew, and who cared?

So there we were, in a basic hospital with basic facilities, lacking one butler and a paediatrician, surrounded by culturally different people who were simply helping us because they could. Our world was so far upside down that neither of us was sure we'd ever see right side up again.

'You're not pushing hard enough,' cried the gynaecologist, who seemed a little distracted by the sight of us laughing, almost hysterically, at each other. Clare gritted her teeth once more almost in defiance of him and pushed as hard as she was capable.

Then the gynaecologist stopped us once more. I could see Clare was exhausted but there was nothing I could do for her except comfort her and counsel her at that point, so I was grateful right then for her rest. A little respite. That's when the gynaecologist excitedly shouted, 'That's it, the baby is coming. Push hard, keep pushing, and don't stop!'.

Clare looked at me and whispered, 'I'm not sure I can push any more. I don't know if I can do this.' That scared me, but all I could do was tell her she *could* do this, and I would be with her every step of the way. She nodded, perhaps not completely convinced but determined to keep going.

Unable to control myself, I quickly looked toward the action end. This violated our agreement in advance that I would not watch the delivery in order to better preserve the all-important, post-pregnancy sex life. As I looked down, I saw something pushing through the birth canal and materialising into the world through Clare's vagina. But the more it emerged, the more that something didn't seem right. Of course, to me it resembled something from the National Geographic channel, as television was the only place I had ever seen births before that day. For the life of me I could not identify the part of the anatomy that was poking through, though I knew that it was almost certainly stuck.

The gynaecologist continued his war cry to push, and suddenly something gave way and out popped a leg. It was buttocks first and, before I knew it, a third of the baby was through and sticking out in plain sight. With one more push, most of the rest of the body was out. But there was concern showing on the gynaecologist‘s face – serious concern; the baby's head was stuck and there was a fair amount of manipulation happening with the torso, which applied pressure to the baby's neck.

'Don't look,' I pleaded to Clare, because I feared the gynaecologist was about to break the neck of our half-born child. There followed more frantic manipulation of the baby, with its head seemingly stuck between Clare's legs.

{Clare}

I was exhausted and emotionally drained; I had been cut, split, shouted at, pushed and pulled from one end to the other. I could see and hear Jeff yelling something at me, but I couldn't quite focus on what he was saying and so didn't understand a word as I stared out blankly, trying to regain my composure.

I felt nausea wash over me and just wanted it to stop; I needed my child to be freed from within me. The rollercoaster of emotions had got too much, and I needed to know one way or another if my baby, my son, would survive. Just then I felt the baby pop free. As a wave of relief washed over me, I smiled, but as the gynaecologist lay our newborn baby on my chest, we both realised it together:

There was no sign of life!

Chapter 7

No Sign of Life

{Clare}

A motionless body that resembled a baby marsupial lay on my chest. Its skin was all purple and wrinkled, yet – most disturbing of all – big, black pupils stared lifelessly back at us, its frantic parents, who barely recognised it as their longed-for son.

Time stood still. For what seemed like an eternity, neither of us could take our eyes off those big, black pupils. There was no sign of life from the baby and suddenly the gynaecologist whipped him up with the placenta still tugging inside my womb. The medical staff quickly cut the umbilical cord and took the baby away behind a curtain.

Jeff held up his arm in protest at the umbilical cord being cut, I instinctively knew he remembered the numerous conversations he and I had had about stem cell collection and delayed cord cutting, but then – instantly realising the gravitas of the situation – he immediately put it back down by his side. I saw he was bathed in a sea of confusion, stuck helplessly in the middle of nowhere, with the lifeless body of his newborn before him. Not knowing what to do next, Jeff just watched, helpless to do anything. I wanted to call out to him and say to my husband, 'It's okay.' But I couldn't.

I closed my eyes and all I could see was the image of those large, black, dilated pupils. The darkness that emitted from my baby's unseeing eyes would be imprinted on my brain forever, like a retina burn from staring at the sun. Nothing made sense. There was numbness in the room and desolation all around us.

Had we really come this far just to lose everything? I looked at Jeff; my eyes pleaded for help. He always had a solution; he was the problem-solver of Team Curtis. 'There is never a problem too big,' he would say confidently. 'It's just how much it is going to cost you.' But it was different, because no amount of money could buy the solution we needed, and for this we hadn't planned.

Where is the paediatrician? I screamed; but it was only inside my own head, and nobody could have heard my silent cry of anguish.

Why couldn't I keep the baby inside longer, to keep him safe? I asked myself frantically. *Why did the gynaecologist make me push?*

It had been all too surreal. As I opened my eyes, I saw Jeff step back – three then four steps – I could see the tears in his eyes. He appeared lost, which made me feel that all hope was lost too.

{Jeff}

I couldn't breathe, I couldn't see, I couldn't hear. My life stood still and at the same time flashed in front of me. I had no idea how Clare was. She was motionless on the bed; I couldn't see her clearly as my eyes blurred and stung with tears. *Would I lose both Clare and my son tonight?* I wondered. The two things I cherished more than life itself. For the first and only time in my long and educated years on this earth, I didn't know what to do. I just stood there, suspended in the turmoil around me, disorientated by the events I had just witnessed.

Out the corner of my eye I could see that the Russian, who had been forgotten until that point, had taken the body of our son from the gynaecologist over to the resuscitation table. Both men rubbed the limp and lifeless baby vigorously with a towel. They had not given up, and seeing that, I knew I must pull myself together.

Clare was lying catatonic on the bed. My tears had stopped so I could clearly see that she was alive at least. From the look on her face, I could tell she was still struggling to comprehend the events that had just passed, too. I knew that image would be burned into her soul for the rest of eternity, as the only memory of her son. This was not how it was supposed to have been and for the whole period of the preceding events that evening we had never even given a thought to it ending with no living son. Even after what we had been told, it had never crossed our minds that we would lose him.

{Clare}

Where is the paediatrician? I thought again. *Where is my son?* He had been taken from us and was now out of sight. My mind spun into a panic. *Where have they taken him?* I wanted to see my newborn baby. I wanted to help and nurture him, do anything and everything in a mother's power to ensure his survival. I wanted to see him again, and I also wanted to purge my memory of the only sight I had of him.

Suddenly I found the energy and called out to Jeff. 'What is happening? What are they doing?' My legs were still raised into the air, tethered to the poles. Blood was still oozing from my birth canal.

Then suddenly, after what felt like an eternity, a baby cried out. And after the first cry, it cried out again and continued to cry, fighting for air. It was the most amazing sound I had ever heard. And it was the cutest cry I could have ever imagined.

OUR SON WAS ALIVE.

I couldn't believe it. Even to this day I wouldn't be able to begin to tell you the elation I felt, the energy it conjured or the determination it fed. The gynaecologist and the Russian had worked together to resuscitate our baby. Somehow, they did this without any verbal communication, which had been the same for most of the night. The how, the what, the why – those questions could be answered later. Right at that point, the most joyous thing happened. With virtually no medical supplies, these two people came together symbiotically with our child, squeezing out every drop of their skills and fortitude to save our baby boy.

'Hahhh!' Jeff gushed, releasing a cathartic roar.

{Jeff}

Could it be true? Could our son still be alive? Could the gynaecologist's razzmatazz and hot-shoe shuffle to the resuscitation table have worked? I thought to myself. It certainly seemed so. I desperately wanted to go and hug Clare to say, 'We've done it!' But at that same time, I wanted to see and touch the living being behind those cries. I wanted to be near our son and offer any sort of help that I could. I just didn't know where to direct my feet first: left for Clare or right for baby.

Clare just looked at me from her precarious, tethered position. 'Don't worry about me, just look after Cameron!' her voice elevated with a visceral urgency.

I made for the table where Cameron lay. He looked human with his vibrant blond hair and mesmerising, bright-blue eyes – eyes that were consciously starring back at me already. Clare had inadvertently taken the final step and chosen the name. Cameron. It was the right fit, it suited him, and he was the newest member of Team Curtis!

What a beautiful baby! I remember thinking to myself. Then a smile formed on my face. *How can a baby that cute and good-looking possibly be mine?* As I looked on, the Russian was going about his business with a sense of familiarity. That was good. It gave me reassurance that the outcome that night may well, after all, be a good one.

Cameron had been wrapped in a towel, presumably to keep him warm. The Russian held in his hand what looked like a tiny hose. He used it to vacuum out Cameron's airways, which seemed to be full of mucus. A sense of normality began to fill the room. Both doctors stayed busy, analysing and checking Cameron all over. Because of his prematurity, they were especially careful, manipulating every joint and part of his tiny body to see if there were any breakages or abnormalities. From what I could see, and judging from the calm, confident actions of the doctors, there were no fractures. They both carried on busily, which in the main meant continuing to vacuum the airways with the tiny hose.

{Clare}

Meanwhile I remained on the bed, feet still tethered, with only the nurses for company. They were kind-hearted and pleasant but were unable to give me any solace. I had heard the cry and watched as Jeff leapt toward the other side of room with the look of shock on his face, only to feel helpless because I couldn't see what was happening. But I had heard the cry, that miraculous melody of a baby's crying that told me all, in fact, was not lost and that the task then was to keep Cameron alive.

'What's happening?' I asked, in the vain hope that either of the doctors or Jeff would hear me from the other side of the curtained partition. The curtains were pulled across the delivery room on purpose; providing a visual barrier between mother and child, should the unthinkable have transpired.

'They are checking Cameron over and ensuring that his airways are clear of mucus,' Jeff said from the other side of the curtain before he poked his head around with wide eyes. 'It's quite a lengthy process by the look of it, but he seems to be coping with it well; he is breathing with difficulty.'

I could hardly believe it. And it was then I realised both of us had been using his name, Cameron, rather than just 'the baby', and already it felt natural. Jeff shuffled back and forth between Cameron and me, poking his head around the curtain to give me a running commentary of what I couldn't see.

'He looks like a Cameron,' he whispered to me. 'It fits him so perfectly. In fact, he fits perfectly into our team.' A big smile suddenly beamed from Jeff's face, as he was unable to hold onto his deadpan look, the look of not wanting to jinx the situation with false optimism.

'There is a scale with which we rate the progress of premature babies,' the gynaecologist said to Jeff, after he went back behind the curtain again. I struggled to hear. 'It's a numerical scale from zero to twelve.' The tone of the gynaecologist's voice caused me to pause. It wasn't as optimistic as I had initially expected. 'We have only given Cameron five out of twelve. His breathing is clearly laboured. Your baby is struggling to breathe.'

{Jeff}

It was true. I could see and hear it clearly from my side of the curtain. Cameron was wheezing and gasping big gulps of air. As Cameron's eyes remained closed, the Russian diligently vacuumed mucus from his airways. Although he was definitely alive, one thing was for sure; he was in urgent need of specialised medical care right away.

'What do we do now?' I asked. I needed to know how we could solve this, and I knew Clare would ask me the same.

'Now we pray,' replied the gynaecologist, but that wasn't enough for me. I felt that there was a dimension other than spiritual, a practical one. I hoped to offer common sense to that conundrum where it might have been lacking from time to time. I wasn't about to leave Cameron in the hands of the gods; I was going to do as much as humanly possible to keep my son here on earth.

{Clare}

Just then the gynaecologist crossed around the curtains, stood next to my bed, smiled, and then, to my total and utter surprise, high-fived me. I was stunned by this unexpected outburst of emotion from one of the most impassive people I had ever encountered. He congratulated me in what seemed a most unusual way considering the circumstances and Cameron's unknown condition; yet moments before he scored Cameron a five out of twelve, less then fifty-fifty in other words, which made Cameron's prognosis very high risk. The night had been surreal anyway, but that was just plain bizarre.

'My job was to save *you* tonight, not your baby,' the gynaecologist explained, which only added to the shock I already knew would have been visible across my face.

'Thanks,' I said. *Thanks!* I thought, indignantly to myself.

The gynaecologist had been nothing but a pain, truth be told. He was rude and his bedside manner lacking. I wanted to hate him, yet I also felt the tinge of guilt coming from the fact he had just saved our child from suffocation when his head was stuck within the structure of my pelvic area. Not to mention, he saved me too.

'Now we have to give birth to your placenta,' added the gynaecologist as the nurse came over to join him.

We have to do what!? I thought.

The gynaecologist and nurse started to work on me, but I was still very confused. *What do they mean, give birth? Haven't I already done that?*

As the gynaecologist worked between my legs, I couldn't help but notice how he all but forgot Cameron's existence. He was manipulating my stomach in order to release the placenta – the afterbirth – while our newborn struggled to survive not three metres away. I looked helplessly at the curtain separating me from my family, hardly believing that I actually hadn't seen my son alive yet. Despite all the people in the room, oddly I felt lonely; even though I had firmly directed Jeff to help Cameron first, I missed his presence. It was so bizarre.

{Jeff}

On the other side of the curtain, I was standing beside the Russian, who suddenly and without warning laid down the vacuum and started to leave the room. Not willing to wait to learn why, I caught him gently by his shirtsleeve.

'Where are you going?' I asked. 'You're leaving when Cameron needs your help the most?'

'He'll be back shortly,' came the gynaecologist's answer through the curtain, as he grunted from a push on Clare's stomach.

It hadn't been a question as much as a statement of fact, but since the Russian was leaving, I asked, 'Shouldn't someone be vacuuming while he's gone?'

'You are capable of doing it,' the gynaecologist replied, again deadpan. 'Just be gentle and don't push too far down.'

So that's exactly what I did. I picked up the tiny hose and started offering it up to each minuscule nostril and then Cameron's tiny mouth; one, then the other. And, once I realised I wouldn't accidentally vacuum up a lung, I accepted that the vacuuming task wasn't as hard as I had initially thought it might be. All of this just added to the unconventional nature of the last few hours. In fact, I even commented through the curtain to Clare that the vacuuming process actually felt quite therapeutic.

{Clare}

'As he was born before thirty-four weeks, his lungs aren't fully developed,' the gynaecologist said with a reflective tone; he talked about one thing while he completed his other task, sewing up the incision he had made in me just before Cameron's delivery. 'We will need the nebuliser and we will get some oxygen into him. This will help with his own breathing. We don't have a ventilator here, so we have to hope that he has enough strength to breathe on his own a little while longer. He is using a large amount of energy, breathing in such a laboured way, so he will need help, and soon.'

A shot of worry coursed through my veins, because I had no idea when that help might arrive.

'What's happening?' I asked urgently, I couldn't see Cameron or Jeff because of the curtain; I couldn't see what the gynaecologist was doing either, with my legs tethered up. Now that my baby was born, it was as if the mother was no longer needed.

How daft, I thought. *Why can't I see my son? He has been given less than a fifty-fifty chance of survival, so aren't I at least as entitled as everyone else to see what is going on?*

Just then, as if he read my mind, Jeff whipped back the curtain and revealed Cameron to me for the first time since I'd seen those big black eyes looking back at me with the stillness of death not so long ago. Jeff was poking the tiny hoover inside Cameron's airways and Cameron was breathing. I could see my son's little nostrils flare and his chest moving up and down as he breathed life into his under-developed lungs. For the longest time, I just looked at the two of them; father and son. Jeff looked so natural, but instead of normal fatherly duties and the celebratory cigar, he was busy keeping Cameron alive. It was a strange sight, yet with all that had happened that night, it also felt oddly normal. I struggled to see Cameron properly, as Jeff worked around him and in so doing blocked my view. Just then he moved to his left and Cameron came into full view. He was so tiny and helpless; I glimpsed his vibrant blond hair and blue eyes, and it was only then that I saw with my own two eyes that Cameron was truly alive.

Of course, it wasn't how I had envisaged the birth of my first offspring; with a romantic and heart-rending image of my newborn son being presented to me, then lying together with him on my chest like any other new mother. Alas, this vision of normality wasn't to be, I knew that. I felt helpless, I was still being administered to and tethered to those barbaric metal poles, but I realised it would be only a short time before I could go to him and hold him close, nurse him and love him like only a mother could.

'He's a survivor!' I just looked at Jeff; it almost surprised me to hear my own words of prophesy.

'He's strong,' Jeff agreed. I wasn't sure if I'd seen something to spark the comment, whether it was just a mother's instinct, or if I'd just said it to make myself believe it, but I could see Jeff felt it too.

Cameron's breathing might be laboured, I thought, *but it is with purpose, intent.* He fought for life and gulped in air with conscious determination. His body seemed to instinctively know that survival meant getting oxygen into his blood stream. Of course, what Cameron couldn't have known was the science behind his precarious, life-threatening situation. In reality, despite his determined efforts, at only thirty-one weeks his lungs were too immature to properly convey the oxygen into the blood stream, which is what made his breathing long, deep, and strained.

Just then, the Russian returned to the room in great haste. He wheeled a huge well-used cylinder that looked like a torpedo. When he stood it up on its end, it towered over us. It was an oxygen cylinder and it was for Cameron. Since the hospital lacked any modern equipment for childbirth, much less premature births, that huge device was connected to a tiny pipe to aid Cameron. The Russian took back the vacuum hose from Jeff's hand and continued. I could see the pang of disappointment on

Jeff's face, from his demotion as he returned to his status as only the observer, the father, whose job was to stay out of the way.

The cylinder blew oxygen through another tiny pipe. The Russian placed it gently under Cameron's nose, and it provided a makeshift oxygen flow. I noticed that Cameron's skin had started to turn pink. Capillaries emerged on his tiny face that was not much larger than an apple, and then on his body too. The pumping of pure oxygen into Cameron's system had instantly made a difference.

Life hangs from the tiniest of threads, I thought.

'Jeff, we really need that paediatrician right now.' I reiterated the very the same words that had been on everyone's mind, as still no one had heard from Mauroof for hours. Jeff had occasionally left the room pre-birth to check with Arjun on the status of a number of things, but the birth had superseded everything for the last hour. Whether Mauroof had capsized in stormy seas or was soon to arrive safely was anyone's guess.

'What happens now?' I asked no one in particular, although I needed to know for myself, so I added a certain urgency to my question.

'I'm going to find Arjun and see if there is any news at all, on anything.' Jeff said this as he strode out of the room with purpose. You could see by his posture that adrenaline was flowing through his veins now that Cameron had a fighting chance. Jeff was on a mission; when I saw him disappear out the room, I knew he'd be back with answers. That was his way. I looked hard at my son a few metres away; he was a survivor, I knew it. My eyes were glued to him as if his life depended on it. I so wanted to go over to him, but I had been told to lie still for some time.

{Jeff}

I sat next to Arjun on one of the interconnected chairs outside the delivery room and spoke to him about the plight of Mauroof.

'Where are we? Give me the news.' I pitched questions like I was in the office awaiting quality information on the next trade. I knew I needed to ask a lot more questions to ensure the legitimacy of the information, upon which my son's life depended.

'So, as we discussed,' Arjun started, 'we have another speed boat that has gone out from the hotel to try and get another paediatrician from a different island a few hours away. Once the boat gets there, if there is still no word from Mauroof, the doctor there has promised to get on the boat and come and help. Then we have a third boat going out to try and get some premature baby medical supplies and we have a spare that is waiting at the hotel in case we need it. All client boat trips have been cancelled today.'

Just ninety minutes before, when I discussed with Arjun what to do, he had found logistical flaws in a number of my ideas using his local knowledge, so I quickly responded with numerous other suggestions until we found something workable. But by then it was only 4:30am island time, so the daylight options were still a good few hours away.

With no word from Mauroof or the paediatrician, and nobody able to work out what had happened, all we could do was continue to be positive and hope they'd come walking through that door at any moment.

Arjun also mentioned that the reception manager at our hotel, the Cheval Blanc, had called him to say that she was on duty early to coordinate details from her side. Among other things, she was busy ringing all the local pilots to see how quickly they might mobilise a seaplane to get Cameron out before his little lungs succumbed.

'Thank you,' I said to Arjun with genuine appreciation as I walked back toward the labour room to impart the limited but welcome information to Clare. At least there was something for her to digest, even if there was nothing from the one specialist person we desperately needed more than anything else; the paediatrician!

{Clare}

I still lay on the bed with my ankles in the straps as the gynaecologist finished stitching me back together again. I was aware of the doctors and nurses, who buzzed around me, but as they went about their tailoring, I felt nothing; everything was a blur. I saw my newborn son when I looked over at the resuscitation table, where the Russian continued to hold the tiny tube blowing oxygen under his nose. It seemed the vacuum pipe was being used less, with only the occasional wipe round to remove any slow build up.

Other than the Russian repeating his same routine on Cameron, there seemed to be an air of disquiet. Although on the surface people busied themselves, there was definitely an undertone of what exactly should they do next? In the eerie aftermath, the gynaecologist hunched over finished his stitching, oxygen pulsed into baby and the nurses drifted idly around busying themselves by unnecessarily packing and repacking surgical equipment on different counters. People started to look out of the corner of their eyes at each other, a flick here and a glance there, as if to ask who should be directing them.

I started to gather my thoughts and wondered where Jeff was. I couldn't see or hear him again and couldn't quite remember what he'd said only few moments ago before he hurriedly left the room. For that matter, where was the bloody paediatrician? It seemed nobody could give me any concrete answers.

I started to rationalise things in my head; I tried to pull myself together. There was a different situation to deal with. As the mental fog that had enveloped me during the birth started to lift, little by little I began to realise that the operation of military precision that Jeff had created in the room and continued to direct was starting to come apart in his absence. Right at that moment no one seemed to be doing anything essential for Cameron's survival.

Sod this for a game of soldiers, I remember thinking that I should kick back at the seeming futility of the situation. I needed to be more involved. I needed to take back my full part in Team Curtis. That was the logical side of my brain taking over. Maybe it was protectiveness or just the ease of switching into business mode; but no matter which, it was less about becoming a mother and more about saving a life right now.

'Nurse!' I shouted, startling everyone.

'Could you stop what you are doing and help me off the bed? I need to go to the toilet.' Although that was true, I also needed an excuse to get off the bed before anyone realised my true intentions. I had made the decision to go against medical advice and stand. I dressed in a hospital surgical gown, the only thing in reach, and slid off the bed. I also felt the awkward pull of a stitch, like claws pulling between my legs, but I had entered my business mode, so my mental toughness kicked in and I quickly erased the pain and discomfort from my mind.

'Let me help you, ma'am,' said an observant and respectful nurse as she came to my rescue. I was happy to take the assistance.

'I need to go over to my son, please.' I tried to steady myself on my feet; a certain confidence surged up, as I didn't feel too bad despite lacking any pain medication and just giving birth only moments earlier. 'And then let's make the room ready for whatever medical supplies they manage to find, here in the hospital or what they bring by boat. Okay?'

Orders given, I shuffled over to my son. I had not been that close to him since his birth and not yet seen his tiny features from the point of view of standing and looking down on my vigorous bundle of new life. I yearned to touch him and hold him to my bosom, to nurse him, but the silent Russian did not move away or give me this option, as one might have expected. He just continued about his job. I wasn't sure, but I feared intervening might be medically unwise at that point. But the very act of being there, and of asking questions, made me feel more in charge. And by feeling more in charge, I knew Cameron's chances for survival had improved.

{Jeff}

As I walked back up the short corridor to the room, I saw the gynaecologist resting behind the nurse's station, apparently uninterested in helping any further, now that his patient was stitched. I wasn't surprised to find, when I returned to the room, that Clare seemed to be directing things in my absence.

'Tell me,' she said, looking directly at me with a new sense of determination. I sensed she was ready for action. She awaited any news from outside the room, and I imparted the small amount I had managed to gather.

I looked down and saw that Cameron was breathing in his same laboured fashion, but he was with us still: still alive. I noticed that one eye was cracked open, viewing a fuzzy world no doubt but there was something conscious behind it. Whether or not it was focused, I couldn't tell. I felt Cameron looking at me and it made me smile, inside and out.

I looked up as I continued to hum the same two lines over and over, I had read somewhere that it was therapeutic for an unborn baby and supposed it couldn't hurt to try now.

'When Cameron was in Egypt's land, let my Cameron gooo…' I sang. This was to be the first song to enter Cameron's ears. It was a song from *Ferris Bueller's Day Off*, my beloved go-to film in tough times and it was sung by the best friend in the film, whose name was also Cameron! I had sung it to Clare's bump, Balthazar, when she was heavily pregnant in the hope the baby would hear. In hindsight, and also for that reason, maybe we had always known his name would be Cameron.

I was undeterred by the strange looks I received from the onlookers, who likely asked to themselves why I was singing half a song, to a half-unconscious newborn. I really couldn't hold a tune, but I didn't care.

Just then reality hit me with a jolt, I think I may have had an epiphany…

Chapter 8

The Man in the Purple Shirt

{Jeff}

'We need an incubator!' I shot across the room like a splatter gun, at no one in particular. *Why hadn't anyone thought of this before now?*

'We don't have one,' came the reply from a younger doctor, whom I had not seen up until that point. His name was Dr Mehedi and he was the general practitioner. The new doctor seemed intelligent. He went about his medicine methodically and without fuss, quietly imparting his requests to the nurses in a very humane way. And his English was impeccable, as was his demeanour. Turning to us, he explained that he had just finished a call, in which he hoped to get some help via the telephone from any other paediatrician that he might raise at that time of night in the islands.

'You have an intensive care unit for children,' I said. 'Surely there will be an incubator in there somewhere?'

'It's empty. All of our premature birth cases get sent to the capital, Malé,' came the answer, while he continued to search for a number in his phone.

'Surely,' I continued, and then hesitated to further formulate my thought more succinctly. 'Surely it's worth having a look around the hospital to see if we can find something. Isn't keeping him warm of paramount importance now?'

'Yes, well, certainly one of the priorities. We also need to get an IV line into him so that we can give him nutrients through a drip, but we don't have any supplies for a premature baby, and with him being so small…' Dr Mehedi trailed off, his hand pointing in Cameron's general direction.

Okay, I thought. 'I'll try to find anything to keep him warm. Dr Mehedi, can you find other medical supplies that can be adapted to fit?' I looked over at Clare, who looked back, in wait of my next words. 'Shall I go and search the hospital and see what I can find?' I said directly to her, as if she held full authority to allow me to do just that.

'Why not? Anything you find is a bonus,' she replied. So off I went.

{Clare}

With Jeff off on another treasure hunt, I was intent on not getting back on that bed at any cost. I had enough bed rest for one pregnancy. One of the nurses moved silently and swiftly away and found me a chair to sit on. She put it close to Cameron. I then sat and started to take in my surroundings, I noticed the people busying around me but also noticed how eerily quiet it had become. I looked at my helpless little baby and wanted with all of my heart to do something more to help him, but what could I do? I'm not sure what I was looking for, but I looked around the room in the hope an idea would emerge from the silence. It was then that I noticed a large bloody mass on a silver tray. It had literally been lying in a heap on the side of the counter near to the toilet I had just used.

What the hell is that? I wondered.

'It's your placenta,' an observant nurse said, as she noticed the look of incredulity in my eyes.

Despite knowing what a placenta was, I had no idea that it could be that size. It wasn't the flat disk I envisaged but more like a small football and with my baby scrunched up in his frog-like breech pose, it seemed easily twice the size of Cameron.

'That's enormous,' I gasped, but no one seemed to hear or care, everyone quietly went about his or her business, whatever that was, as it didn't seem that anyone was doing anything essential.

It dawned on me that only two days earlier I had been watching a webcast of what to expect in pregnancy at the stage of thirty-one weeks. And though I had been waiting for the antenatal classes to learn the intricacies of childbirth, it still never occurred to me that the placenta could be so impressively large. All of a sudden, I felt like I had been really ill-prepared for what had just happened; I had given birth and didn't even know what size to expect the placenta to be. It then occurred to me that the placenta's unusual shape and size might have contributed to the premature labour, but I had no real idea and would have to worry about that later.

{Jeff}

To my horror, as I walked through the halls, I realised that the facility simply wasn't big enough to house much at all. Then I noticed I was being trailed closely by some of the nurses, and as I carried on, the entourage seemed to grow. Trying to think prudently, my strategy was to start my search away from the ward housing the sick-looking patients. I didn't want to disturb anyone and frankly I was unsure exactly what ailed each of them, so preferred to keep my distance. In particular, I was careful to avoid getting contaminated with germs I might take back into the labour room, which was now our makeshift nursery.

I initially looked in the adjacent room, marked NICU, which seemed the most logical place to start my search, but found a room that was pretty much empty, except for a pile of junk in the corner. I then walked out past Arjun, who was still sitting on the interconnecting chairs, and then down the corridor that led back to the initial consultation room where our journey had started on arrival. Along the way I spotted a series of doors that actually turned out to be cupboards. I opened and closed each one in turn; but there didn't been much to find. What had I expected to find? I had been told that there was neither incubator nor the medical supplies in the hospital. *So why*, I thought to myself, would I expect to find them stacked in normal cupboards?

Dejected, I then hurried back to the nursery to share with Clare the ineffectuality of my search, and by the look on her face when I did push through the door, she expected nothing less.

'Is there any way that we can improvise?' I asked and heard an edge of distress in my own voice. I was having difficulty comprehending or accepting the inadequacy of medical supplies on hand. 'Can't we wrap him in blankets, or maybe wrap a box in blankets so that he can keep warm?' I searched for a creative solution and begun to blurt out anything that might spark a thought for someone else to finish. But everyone looked back at me blankly. Rather than succumb to the silence, my brain instead went into overdrive. I tried to work through the problem in multiple threads of thought, I conjured up and everyone rejected options as fast as my brain would allow. Unfortunately, no matter how hard I tried, there just didn't seem to be a workable solution. At that time, Cameron was stuck on the resuscitation table, being held in place by the hand of the Russian. We desperately needed proper medical help.

Just then, out of the corner of my eye, through the nursery room door that someone left wide open, I saw one of the younger nurses wheeling something out of the room marked NICU and through the door where we were standing. As she tore off the cover, I was astonished to see that it was an incubator.

I stood and Clare sat in her chair, both dumbfounded at how on earth I had missed it in the near-empty room next door. Although it was under a cover, and not completely set up, for the life of me I didn't understand why nobody directed me to it earlier.

'But–,' I started.

'–That's an incubator,' Clare finished.

We then looked at each other as if the other would answer all of the questions we both had to ask, such as, why on earth was it not here from the start? Clare shrugged, looking at me and then asked, 'Well, we have it now. Can you do something with it?'

Good question, I thought. I'd never assembled an incubator before and certainly never thought I'd need to learn how to do so on a remote island to save the life of my newborn son. But how hard could it be?

'It's broken,' one of the doctors lamented. Nobody seemed to agree or contradict him.

'How do you know?!' I almost shouted. 'Twenty minutes ago, when I was running around the hospital, you didn't have one.' I was angry by that point, but I knew it was futile to argue.

'It's not built,' someone said in a panic. 'We are not sure how to do it. There are no instructions.'

I turned to Doctor Mehedi and tried to defuse the pressure in the room with a jovial comment, 'Well, we are men, aren't we? We don't use or need instructions. We can just fiddle and build!' I then smiled at the doctor, and he smiled back.

I thought, *When was the last time a family brought a TV home and the father said, 'Hold on, let's look at the instructions?'* Normal circumstances invoked images of excited kids and daddy holding things this way and that to see how they fit. Sure, a few screws might be left over at the end, but instructions were overrated in the male world, well, at least in my world, and in the end the TV always worked.

So that's what we did. In unison we started piecing it all together and quickly realised that it could be assembled with a few snaps and a couple of hammer fists for encouragement. In no time we had managed to piece the incubator together. Then a nurse picked up the plug and to everyone's amazement she unplugged the resuscitation table where Cameron had been tended and then plugged in the incubator.

Almost instantaneously, I switched the plugs back. I was incredulous, reeling, at what I had just witnessed. Why on earth had this woman, who previously had been such a great help, unplugged the only piece of apparatus that we knew worked? Especially since there were five or six other sockets empty on the wall.

Just at that moment, as if the incident seconds earlier had not happened, the nurse did exactly the same thing, unplugged the resuscitation table again. Though my back was to her, I heard Clare audibly gasp. Without having to turn around, I knew she had seen the same thing. It was an amazing if not preposterous thing to have done; yet she had done it, twice. I immediately switched them back and held up my hands, fingers splayed, giving the universal signal to STOP.

'But the incubator won't reach the other plugs,' she simply said.

When I asked for an extension lead or anything that might be able to keep the incubator in the position, mild hysteria enveloped them all, causing me to feel they were missing the whole point; it was not an exercise in hospital logistics. It was simply to keep our baby alive.

Without saying a word, I flicked the footbrake positioned on the wheels of the incubator to the 'off' position. Then I pushed the incubator, which was now in one piece and standing on its own wheels, several feet toward the nearest empty socket. It was not the most convenient position, but once Cameron was transferred to the incubator, we could simply and easily move it to any desired location.

I had the distinct impression that the staff had known all along that there was an incubator in the adjoining room but they either didn't want the hassle of putting it together or were disinclined to share it with an outsider. The nurse who produced it may have gone against the wishes of her peers, and just then she was standing at the door holding an extension lead so that they could put it back into the desired location.

'Where did you find that?' I enquired with an exasperation that I unsuccessfully attempted to suppress.

'The room next-door,' she replied.

{Clare}

'Didn't you just go in there?' I enquired of Jeff, who looked equally as bemused as I felt. It seemed that room was a veritable treasure trove of medical and technical supplies that no one had been able to find earlier. Given the fact there wasn't anywhere to hide a large piece of apparatus, I wondered where all the stuff was when Jeff entered earlier and why he failed to see it before.

'Okay, let's use it,' I said excitedly. 'Jeff, can you get the incubator up and running?'

Jeff nodded, indicating he would give it a go. He flicked the brake off and pushed it back, thanked the nurse for her resourcefulness, and plugged it in, with the help of the extension lead. But putting electricity to the incubator presented a whole new set of problems to be solved. Red lights blinked in different areas, while an audible alarm got louder and more infuriating. It worked, but barely. Bewildered by the mass of warning signals, it seemed better to try and solve the issues one by one.

Before Cameron could be transferred into the apparatus, a gaggle of nurses scooped him up and carried him off. Witnessing this, and immediately concerned, Jeff followed in hot pursuit. Although apparently they were just moving him across the room, Jeff wanted to ensure that no new local custom or idiosyncrasy was forced upon our child. They arrived all together with an abrupt halt at a set of baby scales. Because their experience hadn't included much in the way of premature babies, there was a mad panic about the whole process.

'What are you doing?' enquired Jeff calmly. Although it was quite obvious that they were going to weigh him, it was the panic in their voices and actions that raised his concern.

'We are going to weigh him,' one of the older nurses replied. Then six hands presented tiny Cameron to the scales. The hands were gentle and kind. Once on the scales, they turned the scale on, but no weight displayed, and they promptly took the baby off and turned the machine off. Then they put the baby back on the scales for a second try and turned the scales back on. This happened another three or four times with all the women showing a look of failure. Realising that the scales needed to be turned on first and calibrated to zero before the baby could be set down on it and properly weighed, Jeff found he needed to intervene before it went on any longer.

'Ladies, you need to wait until the scales are on and zeroed,' he said, as he tried to keep his voice helpful, as opposed to frustrated. Then, with nothing he said having sunk in, they did exactly the same thing yet again, all while Cameron was lying there, his fate in the wind. Jeff knew he needed to try a different approach. 'Why don't you leave him there, turn the machine on, and then zero it. Once you take him off, whatever weight is shown in minus numbers will be his weight.' He said calmly and matter-of-factly. They didn't comprehend him. He continued. 'So, if he is 1.5 kg, the scales will show him at minus 1.5 kg.'

In response, the nurses scribbled something down and transferred Cameron to the incubator. We had no idea what they wrote down but as Cameron was now in the safest place for him, I breathed a sigh of relief. Even though the incubator was only intermittently working, it seemed a better place for him to be than being held precariously, albeit professionally, by the Russian on the table. They found a Plexiglas cuboid that went over Cameron's head and the oxygen pipe was fixed so his whole head was enveloped in the oxygen. It wasn't ideal, but it was much better than before, despite Jeff still struggling to fathom how the damn thing worked.

'See, it doesn't work,' Doctor Mehedi offered. 'We have not tried it before as far as I recall, but I was sure it wouldn't work, I'm sorry, there is only so much we can do.'

'I don't think it's time to give up yet,' countered Jeff as he studied the contraption. 'Let's fiddle with it as much as possible until we get it working. We have to. If you can work out how to get an adult-sized cannula into Cameron, I can continue trying to figure this out.' Jeff said in the vain hope that his intuition and problem solving was as good as Dr Mehedi's seemed to be.

As Jeff thought about the problem, I noticed through the still-open door that Arjun was not in his usual seat, the one he had been sitting in for hours. Maybe he had taken a break from the hard seat and gone for a quick breath of fresh air outside, as he'd been awake for hours.

In place of Arjun at that point was a smaller gentleman. I couldn't really make him out properly as I was only partly conscious of him out of my peripheral vision, and frankly, my only concerns were for Jeff to get the incubator operational and to ensure that nobody did anything to endanger Cameron. They were all there to help and they displayed good knowledge of what they needed to do medically in a general sense; however, at times it seemed that common sense was not always so common, when pressure was at its highest.

My eye kept going back to the small gentleman who replaced Arjun in the seat. He was young and looked like a local, but he didn't seem to be visiting anyone or have any business at all in the hospital; it was more like he was just looking on, an interested observer. He wore a distinctive vibrant pink shirt but everything else about him seemed normal and nondescript.

'Damn!' Jeff said with exasperation. 'It won't work. It starts, but then the alarms sound and it cuts out, no matter what I do!' He said this directly to me with hands on his hips, his mind already considering new ways to solve the puzzle.

{Jeff}

I just could not get the incubator working and as hard as I tried, something always seemed to prevent it from functioning properly. Out of the corner of my eye I saw a man in a dark purple shirt: there was no mistaking it, the shirt was a very noticeable purple colour. He was sitting in the seat Arjun had occupied just moments before.

I wondered who he was as he stared intently and directly at me without breaking focus. It didn't feel uncomfortable, in fact his presence felt normal, even comforting, almost as if he should have been there.

{Clare}

Then, something quite unexpected happened. The man in the distinctive shirt quietly and without commotion got up, walked from the interconnecting hospital chairs along the short corridor, and entered the nursery. He seemed quiet and unassuming. I didn't feel threatened by his presence one bit, which was strange as we were in an unfamiliar place and heaven only knew who could have walked in. There was just that one distinguishing feature that I had noticed almost immediately; the pink shirt that look slightly out of place for the uniformed staff around us.

Just then I realised that the room was quite empty. In all the chaos and aftermath, I had not been cognizant of people slowly exiting the room. Except for a single busy nurse, it was just Jeff, me, and the unknown man who pointed vaguely at the incubator.

'It needs water,' he said with a soft, assured tone. 'There is a tray there that's almost hidden. Pull it out and fill it with water. Then it should work.'

I watched while Jeff pulled out the tray and gave it to the nurse, who filled it with water to the line indicated. He then slipped the full tray back into the slot and stood back. Almost immediately the alarms were silenced and all of the previously flashing red lights turned green.

'Thank—' Jeff started to thank the young gentleman, just as both of us realised he had gone.

'Where did he go?' The words came to us at the same time. It was like the man had disappeared into thin air. Jeff raced out into the corridor to find him. The hospital was quite small with only two ways to leave the building, but he was nowhere to be seen.

Then Dr Mehedi returned to the nursery with some of the other nurses, all of who had gone off to find some instruments in order to improvise getting a cannula into Cameron, so they could administer much-needed sugars and nutrients.

'Where did the man go?' Jeff asked the doctor. Then, through the open door, I saw him look in the other direction where normally four or five people would have been milling about behind the nurse's station, including the gynaecologist; but oddly right at that moment there was nobody there either.

'Where did who go?' Dr Mehedi replied, confused.

'The guy in the dark purple shirt,' Jeff said, assuming Dr Mehedi must have seen him as he'd come from the same direction, where all the entrances and exits converged. It was strange, Jeff was referring to the same man I had also seen, but he was insistent he wore a dark purple shirt, I had definitely seen him wear a light pink one, not two colours that could easily be confused.

'Sorry, I didn't see anyone, but I was in a world of my own.' He said as he looked up at the incubator. 'Oh, you got the incubator to work properly, that's amazing, how did you do that?'

'The guy in the purple shirt. He told us about the water tray.'

Dr Mehedi took a fleeting glance at the part of the incubator that Jeff indicated. 'Well, it is an old machine, so I am not surprised it has some quirks.'

'Well, it was the guy in the purple shirt, he was sitting over there.' Jeff pointed in the direction of the interconnecting chairs. 'And he simply came over and told me what I needed to do.'

'Purple shirt? Are you sure?' enquired Dr Mehedi. 'The hotel nurse, Arjun, has been sitting there all night.' By his tone, the doctor sounded simultaneously surprised and intrigued.

As my eyes moved over to the interconnecting hospital chairs, I saw Arjun again, sitting in the same seat as he had been virtually all night long. It seemed that nobody else apart from Jeff and I had seen the gentleman come into the room, not even the nurse who was with us in the room had noticed him particularly. How strange, as we both quite clearly saw him. Though, what seemed most bizarre, whoever that man had been, I clearly saw him wearing a light pink shirt, whereas Jeff had seen him wear a dark purple colour!

It was as if he had appeared, dispensed his advice and then simply vanished without a trace. Without him we may have never got the incubator working, yet who, or what, he was remains a mystery, even today.

Chapter 9

The Prodigal Son Returns

{Jeff}

'So, any news from Mauroof?' I asked Arjun, who was propped up in the same interconnecting chairs. I looked up and down the corridor, still with the expectation of seeing a missing purple shirt.

'No nothing, and everybody is starting to get a little worried to be honest,' Arjun replied, bleary-eyed. He looked exhausted.

Mauroof left four hours ago, in the middle of the night, during a storm. I began to wonder if he had fallen into harm's way. I also felt a pang of guilt, though it was Mauroof who insisted on making the journey alone. Of course, there could have been a simple explanation. We were marooned on a collection of small islands surrounded by vast areas of water after a violent storm, which meant communications may have gone down so as to hinder or delay his progress.

'How about the other boats that have been sent? Have they reached their destinations yet?' I continued to press.

'The boat that went for the other paediatrician has yet to return,' Arjun replied. 'It did make it, but it was further away, and the sea is still quite rough. And the one that went for medical supplies has not only reached its destination, but it will be back here in a few hours.'

I nodded my head to show that I understood and thought intently of our next move; my brain went into overdrive once more.

'Our hotel coordinator is in constant contact with the seaplane operations teams as well, but as yet it has not been possible to raise one. It's likely we will need some paperwork,' said Arjun, completing his assessment of the current situation.

Paperwork, I thought privately myself. *It's a bloody emergency. Just fly the damn plane in and pick us up.*

'What's the problem with getting a seaplane?' I asked slightly confused. 'Now it's almost light out. Isn't it close to their opening time?'

'Well, yes, although don't forget that we are on island time, so there is another hour to add to that,' Arjun explained as he looked at his wristwatch.

It was not for the first time that night that I'd forgotten we were one hour ahead of Malé, the Maldivian capital island. The outer islands adopted the time change unofficially to give their patrons more evening light. Right then, for Cameron, however, it only served as a penalty because every time we looked at the clock, we needed to add another hour of delay.

'There's also another complication,' Arjun then told me.

'What's that?' I replied, I started to feel my nerves fray.

'Manadhoo Island doesn't have a licence to dock a seaplane. We need to work out how we will get you all from here at the hospital onto the seaplane.'

What? I thought. *What did he just say?* 'Really, no licence? You must be kidding!' We were in the middle of the Indian Ocean in a life or death situation and people were worried about a piece of paper. However, I'd lived in the Middle East long enough to understand how these things worked. We would have to get the necessary documentation completed before we could move; or find someone high enough in government to grant us free passage.

{Clare}

In the meantime, I continued to perch next to Cameron's incubator, talking to him. When Jeff stepped into the room, which he did intermittently, he sung the same two verses over and over from the same song. While normally that might have made me mad, with the way things were going, I actually found that it soothed me too.

Just at that point, Mauroof suddenly strode meaningfully through the door and announced, 'This is the paediatrician.' Most people just stared or let out a long-held breath, because there, in tow, appeared a rather large, thickset woman with a gait like a roman centurion. Mauroof later confided that he'd had a similar reaction some hours earlier when the paediatrician turned out to be woman, not that it would be rare to have a woman high up in the medical profession these days. It was just uncommon in that region of the world.

The paediatrician is finally here, I thought. I almost cheered. I barely believed it.

Meanwhile Cameron continued with his laboured breathing, with one eye open as if observing everything going on around him. Though I knew that was medically impossible, he certainly looked as though he was looking on.

When the paediatrician walked in, she threw her bag aggressively on the desk, and everybody was rather taken aback by her deliberate show of anger toward the situation. As first impressions went, one thing was for sure; the paediatrician's love for her profession and for helping babies wasn't evident. If anything, it was just the opposite.

'Perhaps you would like to borrow my stethoscope,' suggested Dr Mehedi, timidly.

'No,' came the stern and unforgiving reply. 'Why do I need to see this baby?' she questioned in her broken English.

'Okay,' said Dr Mehedi, somewhat astounded.

The paediatrician looked at Cameron and she said, 'It's a baby, he's breathing, what do you need from me?'

I felt my eyebrows raise; I was unclear what to do. I had waited hours for this woman to arrive, she was the paediatrician we prayed for, and Mauroof had risked life and limb to bring her here. Not to mention, as I came to learn, another reason for Mauroof's delay had been the length of time it took him to convince her to come.

Apparently, at first, she had been adamant she was not getting on a boat in the dark during a storm, especially with him. Her attitude, he said, had been less than friendly at first. So how did Mauroof manage to get her there? He had taken his time and used his pleasant island temperament to slowly wear her down. After some time at her doorstep, even in light of the fact she was tired and that it was the middle of the night, she had finally succumbed and agreed to go with him.

'Maybe you would like to look at my son,' I asked as I extended my hand like an olive branch. 'Hi, I'm Clare, the mother. We understand that you have had a long journey, but maybe you could look at him and let us know he is okay and medically fit to travel as soon as we can get a seaplane to help us.'

As I finished my sentence, I deliberately looked at Cameron, hoping my appeal would direct the paediatrician’s eyes to the incubator since, as yet, she had been so obstinate as to not allow herself to look at the baby.

‘No,’ she said again.

What is wrong with this woman? I thought. I understood that having your door beaten in at some ungodly hour of the morning might not be the best way to start the day, but surely she had heard of the Hippocratic oath? Certainly, now that she had arrived there, she could take that small extra effort to tend to Cameron.

Listening from the side, Dr Mehedi had already rung another paediatrician and continued to take instructions over the phone on what to do next. It was better than nothing.

A cannula was then fitted to Cameron, courtesy of Dr Mehedi and the mystery caller. There were already bruises on Cameron’s two wrists and an ankle from the initial failed attempts, but at least he had nutrients and sugars going into him now.

‘They have attached a finger monitor to his foot, look,’ I feigned happily to Jeff.

‘Oh yes! That’s clever, how did they know how to do that?’

It was another brilliant suggestion that came from Dr Mehedi’s mystery caller. Whoever it was suggested an unbelievably simple solution to measure Cameron’s heart rate, oxygen saturation rate, and temperature. Simply to connect an adult’s fingertip clamp to Cameron’s whole foot. He was so small it fit perfectly.

Just then one of the nurses pulled out the oxygen pipe from the huge bottle. I couldn’t believe my eyes. Not only had a nurse pulled the plug out of the resuscitation table earlier, but after all that she pulled out the oxygen pipe that supplied Cameron.

‘What are you doing?’ Jeff shouted from across the room.

‘We’re changing the oxygen bottle,’ she told him. ‘I need to get the other one.’

Trying to keep the situation calm and both of us wishing she would use a modicum of sense, he replied, 'Why don't you keep the current oxygen flowing, while you get the other bottle?'

'It's nearly finished,' she replied stubbornly, to which Jeff then responded without words by simply helping her turn the oxygen back on and plug the pipe back in so that Cameron was still fed his much-needed additional O2.

'I'll keep an eye on this bottle while you find the other,' Jeff offered as a distraction. The nurse seemed satisfied with that and strode off triumphantly to get a new bottle.

When she returned, we could see it was just as huge as the last, though we were uncertain as to how much gas it actually contained.

I watched on, somewhat perplexed, as oxygen bottles were rolled in and out, and the valves opened and closed. I did find myself wondering, *If they were in such short supply, why was I given oxygen earlier in the night. Why,* I thought, *had they not saved these bottles for when Cameron was born?* Obviously, it had not entered their mind or been a priority at the time. Or perhaps a more likely reason, sadly; they wouldn't want to waste the limited supply of oxygen on a baby whose initial chances of survival were so slim.

If Jeff was thinking the same as me at that point, then we would have both been astounded over the mix of medical ingenuousness and mishaps that were helping Cameron stay alive long enough so we could leave the island. Before I could speak, my phone rang. But it was in Jeff's pocket, so it startled him out of his deep thought.

{Jeff}

I loved the ingenuity and resourcefulness of a few of the people around me but felt I could not switch off even for one minute.

I answered the call. 'Dr Amir, how are you, are you winning?' As I spoke, I took the phone call out to the corridor so as not to disturb Cameron. With my son on a good flow of oxygen, my mood had lightened slightly, even though the paediatrician still refused to look at Cameron, which was bewildering.

'Not really,' came Dr Amir's delayed reply. Unbeknown to us, at that point when we had originally called Dr Amir he had been €1.7m up, while sitting at the high rollers table. However, after our initial call with us he was completely unable to focus due to the fear that his friend and patient, Clare, could die. It had been impossible to concentrate. When he finally could bear it no longer, he left the table for the night and called us back. At that point he was €2.5m in the red.

Dr Amir continued without interruption, 'Jeff, what has happened? Was the baby born? How's Clare? Are they okay?'

I downloaded as much as I could, as concisely as I could, and with enough detail to give Dr Amir an accurate assessment of the situation without overloading him with unnecessary facts. I wanted him to have a clear picture of the whole process so that he might possibly put his brilliant mind to work on it. Though I am not naturally concise, a personality trait that I know needs polishing, somehow that time I managed to convey the message beautifully and succinctly.

'This is great news, Jeff, really great news,' Dr Amir said. Then, to my complete surprise, he added, 'Now you need to call your insurance company, let them know you are there, and explain the situation.'

Although it was for his medical expertise that we had originally contacted him, Dr Amir had reminded me of a crucial, practical, missing element. In truth, with Cameron's life in the balance, I hadn't given insurance a second thought. I had been focused entirely on getting my wife and son safely to the hospital in Malé, then from there to Dubai.

'It's okay, doctor ,I have it covered. We have funds and we can claim some back when we get home,' I said.

'No, that's not it, your insurance company will have a partnership with an international rescue company. These are the experts, Jeff. They will ensure that you are all moved from where you are to proper medical facilities and then back home. They can help make sure the baby is in fact safe to travel.'

I had never been in that situation before, never needed an emergency evacuation, and had no experience with accessing medical assistance outside my home neighbourhood in Dubai.

'Oh my God,' I stammered. 'So, my insurance company will help get us out of this mess?' Apart from getting the incubator started, this had been our first break since hearing Cameron cry.

'Yes,' Dr Amir stated firmly. 'Now go and talk with them and let's get you out of there. Dubai is only a few hours away, so we should have you home in half a day. I will arrange to have my guys waiting for you at City Hospital. The lead consultant is a personal friend and he also runs the NICU there.'

I hung up and went for my wallet. Immediately I found my insurance card with the emergency numbers on the back. As I dialled my hands shook; I realised that something so easy as a phone call to my insurance company might be the way out. Certainly, with diving being so popular in the Maldives, they would have to have experience with evacuations.

'Hello, this is James from the emergency team. How can I help?'

Salvation.

'Hi,' I started and then stopped. I realised I didn't know where to start, what to say, or how to elaborate on my story. 'I have an interesting story that ends in needing an emergency evacuation,' was all I could muster.

'Okay, why don't you start from the beginning?' the insurance rep said. 'Firstly, please give me your membership number so I can get a clearer picture of who you are, and then you can explain what has happened.'

I quickly gave him the insurance information, and everything was authenticated. They then registered 'Cameron Curtis' on my insurance policy. I recounted the story as I had done for Dr Amir only a few minutes earlier. Then the insurance company took over, well-versed and well-practised in getting the most information out of distraught family members in dire need of help.

'Okay,' said the rep. 'Before I can sanction an evacuation, I need to bring our doctor on the phone call so that he can medically evaluate Cameron's situation. We will only evacuate if the medical facilities at any new location will be substantially more effective than your present location.'

Though I felt a qualm of worry, I felt that I divulged the information well in establishing the need for better facilities. While I waited for the doctor to join the call, I further racked my brain trying to remember any information that might be of help and that I might have missed, but nothing came to mind.

'Hello, my name is Doctor Michael Stone,' a new voice said at the end of the telephone.

'Hi,' I said.

'James has filled me in on the details so far, and my part is to make a medical decision on whether Cameron should be moved or left in the current facility. It's simply a matter of what's best for the patient.'

I nodded my head and listened intently. I certainly hoped that's what the insurance company intended.

'I have some questions and want you to give me answers to the best of your ability. I know you have been through a lot, but hopefully we can start to help you from now and evacuate you very soon, if that's called for.'

Though I was tired, dog-tired, I answered all of the questions as best I could, I kept my business head screwed on tight as I hadn't wanted to appear overly emotional or distraught. I wanted the doctor to trust my information, as I knew it warranted an evacuation.

'Okay,' the doctor said and then, after a short pause, continued, 'It is quite obvious that you need to be moved as quickly as possible. I will make the necessary file here and we can start to alert the right people. I will give you all my contact details at the end of this call and you can call me day or night. We shall be in contact every day to ensure that the patient is receiving the best medical care in your local vicinity.'

Then James came back on to the line and said, 'There is only one consideration, Mr Curtis. In your area we are much more versed in evacuating casualties from diving accidents. We do not have the contacts or experience to evacuate a premature birth from such a remote island.'

With that last information, my heart rate doubled.

James continued to explain. 'It will take two to three days for us to send someone and for them to make the necessary arrangements to get you off the island. The easier part comes from when you are in Malé. Is there anything you or someone with you can do to get you to Malé?'

I was disappointed at the news, I hoped to pass the responsibility for getting my family to safety to the insurance company, but I accepted my fate. As before, I would have to continue to source my own rescue with the help of the colourful characters around me.

'We will pay directly for all of the costs,' James finished. 'But you just need to arrange yourself the most expeditious removal from your present situation.'

'Okay,' I replied. 'Believe me we are working on it.'

'That's fine,' said James. 'If you continue now, we will arrange pick-up after Cameron and your wife receive their medical clearances to fly, once you are in Malé.'

Okay, not the best news, I thought, but at least we had got somewhere. We had a plan of action and surely it wouldn't be long before our seaplane arrived. Then International SOS could do the rest and get us back home!

After the swapping of contact details, I felt less alone than I had all that night. And although there still was an immense amount to do, my own plans were already in motion so I could proceed with the assurance that more help was close by. I felt, for the first time that night, that momentum was on our side.

Right at that moment, right as I took a life-assuring deep breath, Dr Mehedi left the nursery. He looked at me and stated, 'Cameron's breathing is still too fast, but he is responding well, plus his blood oxygen saturation has always been 97% or above. We have raised his chance of survival from five out of twelve, which we told you before, to seven.'

I smiled to myself; Cameron had been given better than fifty-fifty odds of survival. I wished it were more, much more; it was disconcerting to rely on the black or red odds of the roulette wheel while referring to the chance of survival of my newborn son, however Cameron was a survivor, Clare was right!

I made haste and went to tell her some good news.

Chapter 10

Telephone Vortex

{Jeff}

Clare's reaction summed up just how dire things were, 'Wow. That's the best news all night. Our son has a better than fifty percent chance of surviving. It's small, but it's something!'

'I know. It's true. A little respite, even some light at the end of the tunnel,' I replied.

Between us the unspoken notion was shared that, in the circumstances, that was great news, but it was by no means time to get excited and rest on our laurels. We still needed to be on full alert.

Then Clare beamed at me, her husband, 'You are doing brilliantly, Jeff. I am not surprised as this is you all over. It appeals to your obsessive-compulsive personality.' She smirked wickedly at her own sarcasm. There was just a little more hope at that point, as people outside the small island had now began to work to help us solve our predicament. It felt refreshing to know people were aware we were stuck on a small island. *Where were we, anyway?* I thought. Manadhoo Island, one of an archipelago of islands in the North Noonu Atoll. You couldn't find it on a map without a magnifying glass.

{Clare}

It started with the fear of a miscarriage, then the fear of losing mother and child, and now – presently – mother felt fine and baby was stable, but in urgent need of proper medical assistance. Maybe the burden of giving birth had fallen to me and the burden of organisation fallen to Jeff but in the main we held it together as a team. Yet there were also other people who, without knowing it, had played a significant if brief role in the 'Babymoon Birth of Baby Balthazar.' Without their help it would have been very difficult or impossible, to have got that far at all.

'Hey, you haven't done so bad yourself, Mrs C,' Jeff beamed at me. His compliment made me radiate; it gave me energy to fight on for the life of our son, as we were a family. The realisation sank in then that I had managed to hold it all together and given birth naturally, in the most unnatural of circumstances, to our wonderful baby boy. No painkillers, no training, no modern medicine or facilities, yet I had even been able to find humour in the midst of it all.

'Thank you, Mr C,' I replied. 'You know we could never thank these guys around us enough for all of their help, but also without you we wouldn't be in such a strong position. Cameron wouldn't even have an incub--'

'Without us!' Jeff interjected. 'Without us.'

It's true, without the people in that room, and some that had since departed when their shift or duties ended, both mother and child could have already died. And if we had left the hospital against the wishes of my Nepalese gynaecologist, both Cameron and I would almost certainly have died. Fortunately, we had made the right choices and directed a whole host of forces, as much as possible, so that the hospital staff with good general medical knowledge could think creatively to help our premature son.

'Of course, I helped deliver twins the other day, premature,' suddenly stated the paediatrician, who still refused to look at Cameron but felt fine recounting her premature twins story to a captive nurse nearby. Jeff and I just caught the tail end of it.

'They were only four weeks early, they weighed more than this baby here, but they died.' She continued her account very matter-of-factly, as if Cameron and his parents were not there.

I was appalled; I opened my mouth to protest at the ridiculous lack of sensitivity, if only in a belated attempt to stop the words from entering my ears. Jeff stopped me by a wave of dismissal and then got up and whispered in my ear, 'It's not worth it. Let it go. Dr Mehedi has it under control.' He was right of course.

With that he left the room to see how Arjun and Mauroof were getting on with their tasks, as there was an untold amount to prepare before Cameron could be moved. And since International SOS had said they could not move us in a medically acceptable timeframe, the responsibility still fell on Jeff's shoulders to use the resources at hand to get us out.

I had a sudden realisation we had told no one what was going on. As Jeff came back into the room, I looked at him; 'We need to call our parents and let them know what's happening.'

In response, Jeff looked at me sideways with a look that said he wasn't so sure, and replied, 'I guess so, why not?' So he took both phones out of his pocket, held on to his and gave me my own.

{Jeff}

As I stepped into the corridor, I brought my parents' phone number up from the menu and pressed call. It rang a couple of times and then I suddenly thought, *What on earth am I doing? Everyone will have just gone to bed in the UK. What's the point of worrying them until we know more? We should wait!* But before I could hang up, I heard the groggy voice of my mother at the other end.

'Hello? Jeff, is everything okay? Why are you calling in the middle of the night?'

Bugger! I thought. I should have waited. I would only worry my parents sick and likely cause them not to sleep a wink all night. What would be the point of us all losing sleep with them thousands of miles away and unable to help from there?

'Sorry,' I recoiled. 'I should have waited until morning, when we should know more.'

'Oh, dear, Jeff,' my mum replied with concern. 'Is Clare okay? Is the baby okay?'

I began to lightly tell my mother what had happened, as I didn't want to alarm her more than necessary. I was already kicking myself for calling in the first place. In truth, however, there was a selfish aspect to it. I released that I wanted to hear my mother's voice, but from that same place of love I now realised she was the last person on earth I wanted to worry.

'Don't worry,' I told her. 'We'll call you when we get to Malé and update you. Try and get some sleep now.'

She sighed, 'Well, I don't think that's going to happen now. Mind you, your dad is snoring anyway, so I may as well get up and make myself a hot drink.'

I felt guilty that I would deprive my mother of sleep and felt a little stupid, so I said goodbye to her and walked down the corridor to get an update from Arjun and Mauroof, who as luck would have it were now back together again. With the inclusion of Clare we in fact made a formidable team.

{Clare}

Meanwhile, I tried appealing to the paediatrician's maternal side and, to my surprise she picked up the spare stethoscope Dr Mehedi had put on the incubator and started to look Cameron over. It was quite awkward, as the old incubator was of the type that was covered all over with two small portholes on either side. From her dexterity, it was obvious that the paediatrician knew her field. She was delicate with Cameron and it took her only a short time to check him over.

When she finished, she turned to me and said, 'Hmm, the other doctor is doing a good job. The baby seems as fine as can be expected. Not sure what you need me for?' Though her accent was heavy, her words were not harsh. And maybe she had been right in wondering what she could do in the circumstances. I didn't know what I had expected, maybe just confirmation from the specialist that Cameron was stable. The paediatrician also presented a second medical opinion, which I realised was important for me to hear.

Despite my small satisfaction at receiving a good prognosis, I still bore mixed emotions about why the paediatrician had acted in the way she did. This led me more than ever to want to talk to my own mother. I desperately wanted to tell my parents that they had a grandson, but I also didn't want to worry them, not knowing with certainty whether he would make it through the night.

After several rings, my mother picked up. 'Hello?' she said drowsily.

'It's me, mum. The baby has come.'

'What do you mean, the baby has come?' my mother gasped.

'He's been born. I gave birth prematurely tonight while on holiday,' I tearfully replied.

'That's nice dear, that's wonderful news,' My mum said, being upbeat. I heard my father sleepily ask who was on the phone from the other side of their bed, then my mum said, 'It's Clare, dear, she's had the baby.' Mum then came back to the phone, 'What's his name, dear?'

'His name's Cameron, Mum.' I felt a tad bewildered; I had expected a different reaction. My mum obviously didn't realise the gravity of the situation, maybe as a result of me playing it down, so as not to worry her. But I desperately wanted to hear her mother's voice, to tell her we had a son and find the confidence to speak the words.

'But Mum, we are still in the Maldives,' I explained. I surmised that my mum may have thought we were safely at home. 'The baby has come two months early, and he only been given just over fifty percent chance of survival.' As my heart pounded, I could hear my mother tell my father the baby's name.

'They're calling him Cameron, Norm. Isn't that nice?' I didn't hear his response but heard my mum's voice back on the phone to me. 'Congratulations, make sure you say we said the same to Jeff.'

'Mum, did you hear what I said?' I promised to keep them updated on everything and ended the call. I was very confused at the tone of the conversation.

Little did I know that at the moment I hung up, my mother was in a flood of tears. She had tried her best to be strong for her daughter, holding back her profound worries over the potential death of both her grandson and her own daughter. It was the middle of the night in the UK and she sat up in bed, clasping my father's hand for love and support, for in reality there was nothing she could do for me. A few moments later, I received a text on my mobile. It was from my parents and it read, 'Congratulations on the birth of baby Cameron.' I was dumbfounded. All I wanted was to hear my own mother's voice and have her say, *'Everything will be alright.'*

Just then Jeff walked back into the room and saw me staring at the wall.

'Everything okay?' he asked. Given the way things had gone thus far that night, the answer could have been anything, but I still don't think he was expecting the reply I gave him.

'My mum,' I said, bewildered. 'She congratulated us on the birth of Cameron.'

Jeff tried to assess the situation. 'But did you tell her everything, I mean about the blood, the boat, the gynaecologist, no pain killers, etcetera? Or did you try and let them in on the night gently?' He knew my family would always recount a story to another member in such a way that protected the other. It was a very nice trait to have in a family, although it didn't always tell the real story, sometimes leaving out many of the gorier details.

'Well, not everything,' I said thoughtfully. 'Maybe I left a few things out.'

'Do they know we are still in the Maldives?' Jeff pushed.

'I'm not sure. I thought I said so but maybe I didn't. Maybe I only told her half the story.'

'Clare, your mum is one of the most caring people I know. If she knew the whole story she would be worried to death. I just called my own mum and by her reaction I should have told you not to call the parents at all. Now mine are worried sick and, well, at least yours are maybe none-the-wiser and we can tell them the outcome tomorrow without worrying anyone else.' Jeff tried to say it without the tone of an 'I told you so' sentiment, but it didn't work. I scowled at him because I knew he was right. All the calls to our parents had done was make everyone feel terrible.

'Promise me,' Jeff said to me with a wry smile that formed on his face, 'that if we ever find ourselves in a situation like this again, we wait and call the folks when we get to safety.' He chortled, and I smiled, but inwardly, not allowing Jeff to see that I actually agreed.

We both mused over the strange vortex we found ourselves in; it was almost an alternative universe that presented us with infinitely stranger and stranger scenarios. But this last one, we had actually managed to bring on ourselves.

'Well if we ever write a book about all this,' I finally said to Jeff, 'you have to promise me we don't include this bit, as mum would kill me!'

Chapter 11

Preparations for Departure

{Jeff}

I collected my phone that I had left charging on the side by Clare and returned to Mauroof and Arjun to see what the current situation was.

'So,' I said, fully back in business mode, 'how do we get ourselves off this island, as nice as it is?' I smirked at them both. Before either answered, Dr Mehedi and another gentleman I hadn't seen before appeared with quite stern faces. They had obviously been talking about something important but broke off when they saw me walk up to the two hotel staff in preparation for our departure. The other man was introduced to me as the manager of the hospital we were 'trapped' in. After a few moments of conversation, I learned he had been behind some of the phone calls searching for a portable incubator. Unfortunately, it seemed, the manager's role right then was to be the bearer of more bad tidings.

'So, we have been discussing how we get the baby off this island and to the capital, Malé. Sending you all back to the hotel island and onward by seaplane is a good option, but it will take too much time. We need to think of a better way.'

I took a differing view. 'Well, we have been here waiting for hours to get a seaplane. Would another boat journey in daylight and decent weather be that bad? With sea conditions much better, it's only thirty minutes. Surely it would be the safest option, wouldn't it?'

'The problem,' interjected Dr Mehedi, 'is that we do not have a portable incubator, and having a premature baby held in the arms of a nurse or his mother, while on a boat on bumpy seas, may not be the safest option.'

I could see his point, but thought, *Hasn't a normal incubator appeared before? Could there possibly be a portable one that might also appear from nowhere?*

But for that moment, I kept my thoughts to myself because the welfare of our newborn son was at stake and I wanted to consider all the options.

'Is there a portable incubator available anywhere?' I enquired 'Maybe on the hospital island we were trying to go to last night or even in Malé?'

'We believe there are three portable incubators in the atolls,' replied the manager. 'One is in Malé and we are not sure where the other ones are presently, but we are trying to find out.'

I quickly processed. 'Well, can we not have someone like my travel agent fly down on a seaplane with the portable incubator?'

'The person responsible for it would have to go and collect it,' said Dr Mehedi.

'Fine,' I replied, 'get me a mode of transport I can use, and I will go collect it myself. Then I'll return by seaplane and we can put Cameron in it and go to Malé.'

'The paperwork would take weeks,' the manager reacted, brushing off the idea of me doing the job.

'Paperwork?' I shot out. At a time like that, it seemed bureaucracy was set to close off another avenue. 'Surely they would allow it to be used in a situation like this without all the necessary paperwork?' I persisted.

'Unfortunately not,' said Dr Mehedi remorsefully. 'We were just discussing transferring you all from a boat in the open sea. Believe it or not, that would get around the paperwork because it's actually the bringing of the seaplane into harbour here in Manadhoo Island that requires the paperwork. But then, forgetting the paperwork, with no incubator it would be dangerous.'

Too dangerous, I thought. *At least these two nice gentlemen are trying to think of original ways to solve our dilemma. But have they not considered that a newborn baby transferred with all of the wires and tubes from boat to seaplane in choppy ocean waters is a recipe for disaster?* I had to nip that in the bud.

Before I could say anything further, Mauroof looked thoughtfully up at me. 'Well, ten years or so ago a fisherman managed to get a giant hook lodged in his leg.' He continued to look at me, so I eagerly motioned for him to continue.

'He was losing a lot of blood and he needed an air evacuation but, as you know, there is no licensed jetty on this island. Well, someone managed to negotiate with the mayor, and he granted special dispensation for the seaplane to land, and then the fishermen living on this island helped pull it through the harbour walls. They pulled it all the way back up to the beach. From there they loaded him up from the beach on the skids and he was taken to the hospital in Malé, where he made a full recovery. He would have died, if not for the plane.'

I let the words rattle around inside my head for a moment. *It could work*, I thought, *but it still doesn't negate the need for an incubator, which seems to be off-limits to outsiders.* If there were another way to transport Cameron, then I could be the negotiator. We had the necessary tools, just not a means to safely transport Cameron to the hospital.

As if reading my mind, Dr Mehedi interjected, 'I have read somewhere about skin-to-skin. It started not so long ago in South America. It is where the mother and child are touching each other's skin, and this helps regulate the temperature and heart rate of the baby. It mimics the relationship between a joey and its mother, when the young kangaroo is naturally born early and develops enveloped in the warm security of its mum's pouch.'

'How effective is it for humans?' I requested; I wasn't entirely convinced by the theory.

'I need to quickly research it, but I believe I read somewhere it can increase survival rate of premature babies by over 300 percent.' Dr Mehedi seemed energised as his memory of the article returned to him and was able to impart good knowledge that was useful.

Three hundred percent, I thought privately. *That's amazing odds*! We had been living off less than fifty-fifty odds for most of the night. That was certainly worth considering, although there was one more thing to consider,

'How the hell do we get the mayor to agree?' I suddenly shot, 'In fact, who is the mayor and is he even close by?'

'Just as well Mauroof knows the mayor,' Arjun smiled.

Mauroof continued, 'He's close by on another island.'

And so it was, during deliberations in the hospital corridor, the gentleman familiar with island politics and bureaucracy helped hatch one of the best plans of the night.

From there, everyone turned intensely to the business at hand. Mauroof walked off to make his calls to the mayor; Arjun arranged a boat to pick him up, assuming he would agree to come; the manager then reached out to the local fishermen to ask if they would help bring in a seaplane with their fishing ropes; and Dr Mehedi rushed off to further Google how to prepare mother and child for transportation.

This left me to tell Clare the *hopefully* good news, and as I entered the room, she was still at the incubator talking to Cameron. It was a marvellous sight to behold, mother and child alive and well, communicating completely naturally. The room was also much quieter with a sense of calm having taken hold. Now that Cameron was more stable, it was a waiting game.

'Excuse me, Mr Curtis,' a nurse said. She broadsided me and before I had a chance to speak, she held out a form and a pen. 'We need you to fill out your details for the birth.'

I couldn't help but laugh to myself. Of course! We would need to record his birth and start the paperwork in order to get everything ready, which to be honest hadn't yet crossed my mind. I took the pad and filled in all of our names and passport numbers from memory, my father's and grandfather's details, addresses and phone numbers, and so on. As I passed the paperwork back, I noticed that Cameron's weight had been filled out at *1.5kg,* the weight that I had been using figuratively. I rolled my eyes, and only hoped that his actual weight wouldn't be much different.

'You haven't put your marriage certificate number on here.' The nurse broke my thought process again when I absent-mindedly passed it back to her. 'We'll also need copies of your passports and marriage licence before you leave.' From the tone of her voice you could tell that for her it was another normal day at the office, she was deadly serious.

'What?' I said. All I could think was *passport, phone, and wallet.* That's all I had ever been taught, should things go wrong on a business trip in a hostile environment. *Passport, phone, and wallet.* Nobody had ever mentioned marriage certificate and we hadn't brought it with us. In fact, we did have a certified copy back in the safe at home, as we had lost our original in their numerous moves around the world as the years passed by.

'It's the law,' she continued. 'We have to have your marriage certificate number before we can let you get on that seaplane.'

What seaplane?! I thought incredulously. In my mind, the problem was simple; get Cameron in a mobile incubator, get a seaplane and leave. But it seemed that everyone on that island wanted to put some form of obstacle in our way to prevent that from happening. How on earth was I going to overcome that one? Many countries, including where we lived in Dubai, had unbending bureaucratic policies and procedures, particularly when it came to paperwork and identifications. Those at the top made the decisions and those at the bottom didn't think to question them, regardless of the circumstances. There was a need for the 'i's to be dotted and 't's to be crossed, with the right stamps in the correct box. That is what the administration wanted, and right then that was what the nurse would require. The overriding problem, the fact, was that at that exact moment in time there was no way of getting our physical marriage certificate to hand in time. Once again, I needed to think of a way round the problem.

My first thought was to stall. 'I'll get it for you in a while. Before we leave, I will try and find it.' I made a mental note to store copies of our most important documents digitally on our phones or iPad in the future, to prevent anything like that from ever happening again. But stalling, of course, would not solve the problem. Next, I went off to seek advice from my two new best friends.

'It's the way things are here, I am afraid,' Mauroof stated, on hearing my new problem. 'I realise that it's not going to be possible to get your certificate tonight, but we'll need to find a solution, though right now I cannot think of one. Sorry.'

I thanked him, realising there was no way of fighting the system. I needed to find a solution until I could get to our safe at home or have one of our friends go round and get it out.

'Any other news from the outside world?' I asked, as I tried to keep the atmosphere as light as possible.

'The medical supplies are almost here on the other boat,' Mauroof replied, 'and we told the other paediatrician not to come as we have our own; and of course, Dr Mehedi is doing a great job. But we do have a spare boat coming back just in case we need it.' I nodded my head in acknowledgement and Mauroof continued to list off the things that needed to be done in preparation for departure. 'The mayor said he would come, and there's a boat going to pick him up as we speak. He should be here soon, hopefully.'

'Well that's great news. As soon as he is here, let me know and I'll sit with him.'

'Certainly,' replied Mauroof.

I got up and made my way back into the nursery room. Just as I got through the door, I saw the nurse who had exchanged the oxygen bottle last time fiddling with it again. 'What are you doing with that?' I asked.

'It's finished,' she told me.

'But it's only just been put on there, the bottle is massive.' I stared at the battered bottle of oxygen that towered over everyone in the room. She then proceeded to turn off the oxygen that was feeding into Cameron's Plexiglas box and once again seemed to allow an extraordinarily length of time to pass, as she fiddled with the other bottle to get it flowing.

'Let me help you with that,' I said, disbelieving what I was witnessing, and I immediately swapped it back again, so the oxygen continued to flow until the new bottle was ready. Then I helped the nurse open the valve on the new bottle so that oxygen flowed from it too, so she could instantaneously switch between the two bottles. When she was done, I realised I had been holding my own breath as I started breathing normally again.

'This is our last bottle of oxygen,' she said. 'It will need to last you until you get to the hospital in Malé.'

Suddenly I felt like I was being bombarded with problems, the new bottle was quite a lot smaller than the others had been and those had run out quickly. Presumably they had not been full when they were brought in, so there was no way of knowing how much was left in that smaller bottle. We were so close; Cameron had been born, mother and baby were alive, and yet there was one problem after another and all of them took considerable time to solve. Not the least of which was the fact we didn't have a seaplane, and when it eventually did arrive, we would lack a marriage certificate. And all the while we burned up the little remaining oxygen necessary to keep Cameron alive.

'How long will this one last?' I asked, fearing the answer. I was mortified that it might not be big enough to last the journey.

'About three to four hours,' she replied. And there it was. I thought we had overcome the hard part, but it looked like the hard part would continue until we reached Malé.

Just then the door to the nursery burst open and in strode Renato, our hotel manager. Under both arms he carried huge bags overflowing with what looked like gifts. He wore a huge grin across his face and as ever he looked pleased with life. 'Hello, my friends,' he beamed, as he reached out to bear-hug me and then repeated the same greeting to Clare. She had only just given birth, and was bruised and stitched, but she was powerless to prevent his overly vivacious gesture.

'All of the staff in the hotel are so excited!' Renato exclaimed. 'A lot of them have got up early today, just to help if they can.' He showed all the gifts stuffed inside the bags, as if he were Santa Claus. Some had even been donated by the staff. He pulled one out; a fluffy, white, stuffed toy in the shape of a horse with the hotel name written on it, 'Cheval Blanc'.

It was an incredibly nice gesture, the presents and the congratulations and the razzmatazz of his surprise entrance, but Team Curtis didn't feel particularly jolly. Our baby was still in danger. Born two months premature, with no proper medical facilities, he remained alive, but his breathing was still laboured and there was a limited oxygen supply. Something could go wrong at any moment. The main thing we wanted was to get to safety, and from there, home as soon as possible. We also knew how much Renato and his teams were doing to help, so while it was a lovely gesture, we just couldn't bring ourselves to celebrate.

Renato then left in the same fashion that he had arrived, with a flourish, with his big smile, saying hello to all he passed and carrying along with him the whirlwind of his good nature and huge spirit. Renato's departure left a slight malaise in the room but also gave us a brief opportunity to rest. We had been up nearly twenty-four hours and were exhausted. Actually, it was entirely possible that Mauroof and Arjun had been up even longer. All were beleaguered and exhausted.

I looked at Cameron and thought, *Hang in there, buddy!* Cameron looked back out from his Plexiglas helmet through the glass of the incubator, so small and helpless. He was wrapped in a nappy three times his size, and his legs were pulled up like frog's legs, which apparently was normal for a breech birth. Oddly enough, his one open eye still followed everything that went on around the room. I smiled and wondered what on earth would come through that door and present itself next.

Just then Mauroof stuck his head in the door and stated with glee, 'The mayor is here.'

Showtime!

Chapter 12

Escape from Manadhoo Island

{Jeff}

I walked out into the corridor to find yet another entourage approaching me, with some very serious-looking gentlemen, including the mayor. I quickly scanned my mind and prepared it for negotiation, a technique I had adopted in my oil-trading days. Having an outline in my mind, I could focus on the agenda I needed to present while ad-libbing where necessary. It was a technique I had used thousands of times before, and every time my modus operandi was simple; in negotiations, always be prepared to walk away from the table, do not get emotionally attached. But how could I possibly do that here? How could I be emotionally unattached with the life of our son on the line? In my mind, I needed to create a structure to ensure that my delivery was precise and succinct; I hoped to appeal to the mayor's sense of family. I only had one shot.

'Hello, it's a great pleasure to meet you.' I beamed a smile and extended my hand with no pretence, as I had always taken pleasure in meeting new people and understanding who they were; I genuinely cared. But that day I was admittedly very nervous. How my next few sentences were formed and how they were interpreted could make a life-or-death difference.

The mayor was not quite what I was expecting. Looking slightly darker skinned than other Maldivian men, he wore a very colourful, pinstriped shirt that in London may have looked quite flamboyant, but on the islands looked smart.

'Hello, how are you?' the mayor asked, with genuine concern. I realised at once that I was being treated to local pleasantries, very similar to those in the Middle East whereby a number of formalities are naturally afforded anyone who is being greeted properly. I wasn't ready for that, perhaps expecting something more negative.

'I am fine, thank you for asking, how are you?' I enquired in return.

'I am very well, thank you,' replied the mayor. 'How are your family?'

Though I should have expected it, as it was part of the ritual, it caught me a little off guard. Directly behind us down the corridor was my wife, who sat in front of our newborn son, who in turn lay and waited with laboured breath inside the old, unstable incubator.

I was crying out inside, as I just wanted to ask, *How do you think I feel?* But I held back my emotions; there was a process to follow, I knew. The immediate medical care that our child needed was being delayed, due to the game of bureaucracy that had been played already that night, a game I felt compelled to play because here was a man with the capacity to help.

After the introductions finished, I walked the entourage down the hall and presented Clare. I then showed the mayor the incubator and asked that he, the mayor, please be aware of each and every person who had been instrumental that evening in helping Clare and Cameron to stay alive. I wanted to ensure that all involved received some form of local recognition for their efforts.

'Please,' I said, as I gestured with my hand for the mayor and entourage to move outside into the corridor. The hospital contained a small area down the hall with tables and some vending machines and coffee. The mayor and I walked together like we were taking a Sunday stroll around one of London's great parks, while the entourage followed us like chaperones. Not dissimilar to an escort for a courting couple from yesteryear, they kept their distance behind us, the happy pair, while maintaining an ever-watchful eye.

As we approached the chairs, I explained to the mayor that Clare and I had been holidaying in the Maldives nine weeks before the anticipated arrival of our new baby; a babymoon, it was called. The hotel was nice, and we loved the islands. I politely gestured for the mayor to sit and the entourage took up residence close by at the other table.

'Thank you for coming to the island, Mr Mayor. I appreciate your coming by boat and trying to help my family get off the island and to medical help. My son seems strong, but he is premature and is in need of urgent specialised medical attention. We would very much like your help with that.'

I wanted to impart to the mayor that I understood him to be a man with power in the locality, who could make great things happen. Toward that end, I offered him a bit of the story, without elaborating quite yet.

'Of course,' the mayor replied. 'I heard of your family's situation and I wanted to see if I could help. I found a boat waiting for me, which was a pleasant gesture. How can I be of help to you?'

'Well, I understand that a number of years ago a fisherman had an accident and he got a large fishing hook lodged in his leg. Without the use of a seaplane evacuation, he would almost certainly have died.' I let my last words hang in the air.

'Yes, I remember that. He did indeed survive and continues to fish today.'

From the raising of the mayor's brow, I could tell he was already starting to grasp where the conversation was heading.

'So, Mr Mayor, I would like to ask your permission to land a seaplane outside the harbour and, like ten years before, ask for the fishermen to help pull the plane in backwards through the harbour walls with their fishing ropes. We need to get my newborn son to safety as soon as possible. Do you think you could grant permission for that to happen?' I deliberately used the word 'grant,' so as to acknowledge the mayor's position of distinction.

'Yes, I think I can allow that as special dispensation under the circumstances,' replied the mayor.

Excited, I got up from my seat and vigorously shook the mayor's hand and then excitedly proceeded to shake the hands of all the mayor's chaperones just for being there. In fact, I was so effusive that I shook the hand of everyone that sat there at the tables. Even the confused-looking gentleman sitting at an adjacent table, who might have been a visitor himself, his hand was shaken. *To hell with it!* I thought. I made sure everybody in the vicinity received some appreciation.

As we all got up to leave, the mayor said, 'If there is anything else I can help you with, please do not hesitate to ask.'

I found my chance to solve another of the issues that coalesced only an hour before. 'Actually, there is one thing.' I began in earnest. 'As you might be aware, my wife and I were not expecting this, and though we were fastidious enough to bring almost all our documents, we never thought we would need our marriage certificate. Under these unusual circumstances, might we forgo that formality on this one occasion, as it is at home in the safe, in Dubai?' I finished with bated breath.

The mayor smiled. 'Yes, of course. Would you be so kind as to send it through, once you have a chance? It just helps with the paperwork.' And with that, the mayor was gone, followed by the long string of chaperones.

To my amazement, I had just killed two of the proverbial birds with one stone. I would of course send through the details, even though I was fully aware that once filed, the document would never see the light of day again.

Mauroof was standing just out of the main crowd but heard every word. By the time I got back to the room, Mauroof had already told everyone in the room and was on the phone to the hotel to get the seaplane there at the very earliest opportunity. Though a tad disappointed my thunder had been stolen by Mauroof announcing the amazing news, it was fleeting. After so many hours of waiting and wanting, we gained the permission and could check both the seaplane and marriage certificate off the list. Now it was time to re-focus on the portable incubator.

{Clare}

'Did you hear that?' Jeff beamed at me. 'Job done.'

'Good work, Mr C!' I smiled. 'Now we can get him to Malé and from there home!' As I said that, I felt a wave of relief wash over me for the first time since it had all started. Getting to Malé was the first step toward getting our baby proper medical care, and for that I radiated happiness. Before coming on our babymoon, I had done a lot of research on the hospitals in Malé and there was at least one private hospital that could deal with a premature baby, which is the same one that could have helped with an emergency caesarean had we managed to get there in time. So I knew better medical facilities were on hand, but still a short flight away. I also knew deep down that we were not out of the woods yet.

'How long will it take to get the seaplane?' I asked the same question Jeff had been asking the others all night.

'I'm trying to get that ETA myself,' Jeff replied. Then he moved closer to me. 'I need to talk to you,' he said hesitantly. 'There is no portable incubator that is close enough for us to use.'

I looked at him blankly, and my newfound relief dissipated instantly. 'How do we–' I started to say.

Jeff interjected, 'We have been talking about skin-to-skin. It's where the mother holds the baby naked on her chest and the skin contact regulates the baby's vitals. So you will have to hold him that way on the plane.'

'What?!' I exclaimed, shocked at this new revelation. 'What does that mean?' How can I carry Cameron all the way to Malé? Surely on the plane he needs to be shielded from the world in an incubator?'

The look on my face must have said it all, and though inside I was petrified, I would of course do anything to save our baby.

Dr Mehedi appeared in the room with a look of determination on his face amid the beehive of activity. He obviously had something serious to discuss.

'Skin-to-skin is definitely the way to travel,' he proclaimed. 'It's recommended even if we did have a portable incubator. At this stage of life, only seven hours old, the fact that he needs specialised help, skin-to-skin would help regulate his temperature and breathing. These of course are essential.' He looked expectantly at us and we looked back at him and then at each other. We knew that might be the only way to get Cameron out in those next few hours, maybe even the next few days. Dr Mehedi had not only displayed an immense knowledge of his craft, but also proven that he was to be trusted. We made the decision instantaneously, with just that one glance at each other, we would take Cameron skin-to-skin.

'Okay,' I said, although inside I was petrified of this whole idea. I suddenly felt like the room had closed in on me. We were getting out, but it would be at some risk. My body felt cold and I developed a prickly feeling on my face. I was panicking but pulled myself together, I was prepared to follow instructions as I had done all night.

'Ok let's go through what is necessary from us all and how we will get him to Malé as safely and quickly as possible,' I said, as I tried to push my fears to the back of my mind. My expression was stern as I looked directly at the doctor, but the look was created by fear still: fear of getting something wrong that would affect Cameron, fear that it could be my fault if something was to go wrong. Team Curtis had two very logical brains with limited specialised medical experience, apart from what we had picked up in those last hours, but I believed we could do it as long as a proper plan in place.

'I agree,' Jeff concurred. I suspected that he also felt my fear resonating through me. 'Let's go through who and what will come with us. And once the plane is available, we only do this if we are happy everyone understands their part implicitly.' He meant it, too. This would be a daring escape from Manadhoo Island. We knew the risks, but staying wasn't an option, as oxygen would only be available for the next few hours and meaningful supplies of both medicines and equipment were already almost depleted.

The clock was ticking!

'We need to get him a blanket to travel in, to ensure that not too much sun gets on him and that he is kept warm,' Dr Mehedi said. 'But most importantly, he needs his mother's touch, so they will travel chest-to-chest.' He continued to run down who and what would be going and how. He elaborated a division of duties and responsibilities, with individual actions often blending into teamwork, not just by Team Curtis, but everyone involved:

Dr Mehedi would come along to oversee the whole evacuation and would be the one carrying the monitor screen.

A new, younger nurse would be in charge of holding Cameron when not on the plane, as she had experience of handling newborns.

Mauroof and Arjun would come to ensure that Cameron received proper medical treatment on arrival at the hospital in Malé. They would help me onto and off the plane and, as locals, could provide a counterbalance to any fears from the local populous of us as outsiders.

Jeff would carry the oxygen bottle and hold the mask (that was four sizes too big) over Cameron's face to ensure adequate supply for his still-laboured breathing. We would also need to disconnect all of the cables and tubes from Cameron while he was carried between modes of transport, moving as quickly but safely as possible from one to the other.

I would sit, and Cameron would be handed to me; Dr Mehedi and the nurse would plug the drip and monitor back in, and Jeff would operate the oxygen and mask.

It was like military precision in its design.

Arjun immediately went off to the only shop on the island and purchased a blanket. Mauroof was to be in command of operation evacuation and also in charge of communications back to the hotel, whose staff would coordinate efforts as it was light at this point. The nurses made a swaddle for Cameron, using bandages, muslins and anything else that would ensure warmth.

Cameron through the entirety of the planning still lay quietly, as he experienced life with his one open eye and laborious breathing. Nobody had been quite sure, but everyone felt he was somehow aware that if he held on for a bit longer, he would finally receive the specialised treatment he so desperately needed.

Arjun reappeared with a blanket. The island was so small that the shop was very close by but only held limited supplies. And as he pulled it out an odd look of expectancy formed on his face; the only blanket he could find was pink. Privately, both Jeff and I rolled our eyes, thinking to ourselves that the first clothing that our baby boy would wear in his life would be pink. Obviously, we were ever thankful to Arjun for buying it and felt of course that pink was better than nothing, we just hoped that we could laugh about it one day, when we looked back on the whole ordeal.

'There is just the matter of the hospital bill,' Arjun then stated.

Jeff was at first taken aback. In honesty, we hadn't even considered the matter of a bill until Arjun mentioned it.

{Jeff}

'Can't the insurance company settle direct?' I asked, suspecting the answer would be 'no'. Arjun took me to the front desk where an abundance of ladies sat. All looked up and smiled, almost giggling.

One of them presented me with a sheet of paper that was a mixture of English, Maldivian and numbers that were not really possible to work out. In response to my obvious confusion, she pointed to the last figure and expressed that it was USD. It only totalled a few hundred dollars. *Easy, get it paid and go,* I thought.

'Can I use a credit card?' I asked, as I removed the card from my wallet.

She took the card and tried it in the machine, but it didn't work, so she tried it again and of course, it still didn't work. Immediately Arjun withdrew his wallet and luckily had just enough local currency to cover the bill. I was insistent that I could just go to the cash machine, but it seemed that international bankcards were not readily accepted outside of the five-star hotels in the Maldives. I made a mental note to pay Arjun back as soon as possible, but at that point I could only thank him profusely for his help. Without it, there could have been another sticky situation.

I trudged back to the room and as I did, realised I was starting to get weary. The night had presented me with more problems to solve in such a short space of time than ever before. Indeed, I had taken a sabbatical from work recently due to a health issue relating to energy levels depleting too quickly, because I'd lived on adrenaline for too many years. That one night felt like a year in itself, as I rode on a mountainous wave of adrenaline. But that wasn't enough to stop me, it had never done so before, and it certainly wouldn't that night either. Even though I was so dog-tired, there was still the prospect of a small mountain to scale and I was determined to achieve it; to get my family out of there and home safely to Dubai. Sleep would have to follow.

I mustered all of my resolve and positive energy as I marched back to Clare and Cameron. In their room, preparations were well underway for the departure. Swaddling was prepared and medical supplies were cleaned, inspected and assembled as though the SAS was preparing to storm a stronghold. Dr Mehedi had taken complete control, which allowed me to take some mental rest while still watching everything like a hawk.

Then Mauroof poked his head in the door and said, 'The plane has arrived. In ten minutes it should be on the beach waiting for us!' He beamed. 'The fishermen are pulling it in as we speak!'

Outside, the pilots of the long-awaited seaplane shut the engines down as the fishermen attached ropes to the back of the floats. There was an almighty concerted effort from all who arrived at the harbour to help those European strangers and their newborn baby. The plane then made its way safely backwards and through the harbour wall that was barely wide enough for the fuselage. As they pulled the plane backwards, it moved slowly toward the sand until, with one last superhuman effort, the craft was beached and readied for the arrival and embarkation of its newest passengers. Us.

{Clare}

Inside the building still, we were at the point of collapse. It had been eight hours since Cameron's birth and eleven hours since the start of labour. The not knowing, the anticipation, the worry and the fear had taken its toll on Jeff and me. The plane had finally arrived, and it was already on the beach waiting!

It was as if everything went from slow motion into fast-forward. Everything happened quickly from then on. Cameron was scooped up out of the incubator and put into the swaddle, but it was quickly realised the swaddling was too much and the baby needed to be in contact with his mother's skin. All of that work to prepare the immense and intricate swaddle to cover Cameron was for nothing, as it was dispensed with in favour of that pink blanket.

A rucksack appeared, courtesy of the young nurse, and all of the medical supplies that had been collected were meticulously packed; spare nutrients for the drip, extra finger clamps for the monitor, and so on, but we all knew that there was only one canister of oxygen left.

'Is everybody ready?' Dr Mehedi yelled.

Everyone nodded in affirmation as the sense of readiness was quickly overcome by the fear of the unknown. The initial elation of our impending freedom had brought more doubts, even though the hospital had formed a kind of prison for us for the last eleven hours. All of the hopes and efforts had depended on Jeff securing a seaplane and on me holding myself together, so I could carry my child to safety. But now it was finally happening, and we were ready to roll, a sense of institutionalisation hit us, as if we were inmates being freed to a world where time had advanced without us.

'Is it really happening?' I asked Jeff with a sense of uncertainty. 'Are we going home?' I was breathless, and my heart was racing. I was supposed to be there to regulate Cameron's breathing and heart rate, while I could not even control my own. It made me even more fearful, but I kept my worries to myself. I looked down at myself. I was still dressed in some form of hospital gown and maternity pad for the afterbirth bleeding. I became aware that a nurse was holding something up in front of me. It was the nightie I wore when I arrived on the island, covered in blood.

'Madam,' said the nurse, 'would you like this back?'

I stared at all the bloodstains that conjured so many painful memories and created unanswered questions of whether Cameron would still be alive at the end. I was almost speechless but managed to reply, 'No thank you, I think it can be thrown in the bin.' I looked around, but there was nothing else to wear except that thick, towelling dressing gown Jeff had grabbed from the villa eleven hours earlier. Though I preferred the lightweight gown, Jeff had taken the heavier one, incorrectly, but understandably, assuming we would return to the villa that night. By then it was mid-morning of the day after and the heat was searing. Nevertheless, it would have to suffice.

The nurse was holding Cameron as we begun to run the gauntlet, which felt strange for me. Neither Jeff nor I were in charge now; we were going along for the ride and doing as we were told.

'Let's hope this is it,' Jeff gasped. After so many false starts and seemingly impassable obstacles he looked numb as we made for the exit; we were finally leaving.

Sunlight hit us as we stepped outside for the first time since nightfall the day before. The old, white ambulance waited to take us a few hundred yards up the beach. Without argument Jeff and I simply climbed aboard, followed by the nurse holding Cameron, and the doctor holding the rucksack and monitor. Then Arjun and Mauroof, who carried things on board with phones to their ears, juggling calls essential for our escape. The sheer effort that went into the symphony of movement was breath-taking and, as far as Jeff and I saw it, those responsible could never be thanked fully.

The ambulance trip was painfully short but necessary. We stopped inches from the beach, where we all disembarked, very carefully and very uniformly. Everything was about Cameron's safety and absolutely nothing else mattered. The nurse who held Cameron gently in her arms took the first step, and only when she was happy and secure in her footing did we all move.

The doctor followed behind her until everyone was ready to embark the plane. As I walked across that beach, I was suddenly struck by the fact that we were not alone. Almost the entire population of that very small island were on hand at the beach for the spectacle, watching on and wondering. All the fishermen, none of whom could be thanked for their role in securing the seaplane, looked on, as did the nurses, the mayor, and the mayor's entourage. They were all on hand to witness our departure. It must have been truly a peculiar sight to behold.

I looked back at the crowds, and the crowds looked back at me. 'Are you okay?' Jeff called up to me. 'You've gone white!' I was a little in front of him, trudging through the sand. I started to feel a little disorientated. Feeling dizzy, I was aware that there were noises around me, but they all started to disappear into the background, images became blurry as I found myself smiling at figures of faceless people and thanking them as I was helped toward the plane.

I hadn't until this point appreciated that the plane would be on the beach, rather than the water. Also, I suddenly felt slightly embarrassed. I felt like I was a television reality star on display while only wearing a dressing gown, disposable underwear that only loosely secured a rather large sanitary pad, and the hotel slippers that I'd worn when we first set out. We trod carefully so as not to step on some old, abandoned fishing tackle, fishhooks or weights that might injure us or get entangled in our feet or even worse the feet of the nurse carrying Cameron.

Mauroof and Arjun were, as always, helping anyone who needed it and right then that was me, as they acted as my crutch and supported me as I stumbled precariously across the sand. The nurse had already gone in front and held Cameron securely but not too tight, the doctor was right next to her and overseeing the journey. Jeff brought the bottle of oxygen up from the rear.

As we arrived at the seaplane, the nurse climbed inside in an instant. I was helped in and put in the middle seat beside her and Cameron was handed to me. It was the first time I had really held him. I could feel him, I could feel my baby's skin on mine. I felt such an overpowering emotion, an emotion that I can't begin to describe, but I could attest that Cameron was alive. His breathing was still laboured, but as I put his bare chest against mine, I was sure I felt his breathing stabilise slightly. The waves of emotions were plenty and they almost overpowered me, but for some reason tears did not come.

Jeff sat in the row in front, as we watched doctor and nurse systematically hook Cameron back into the IV line, followed by oxygen and then the monitor. When all vitals were stable, the co-pilot improvised a place to hang the IV bag. Everyone was strapped in. Everyone was ready.

'Are you okay?' the doctor shouted to me over the revving engines.

'Yes, thank you' I said, raising my voice and I hoped that I would not disturb Cameron, which was ironic because even over those bellowing sound of the exhausts, he was snuggled into Mummy's chest and sound asleep with both eyes closed. Incredibly, contentment showed visibly on Cameron's face.

'The nurse will do some last checks,' the doctor said, 'and if we are happy, the pilots will take us out.'

Jeff overheard this and I could see in his face he was just itching to get airborne. As a private pilot himself, he was half-watching the pilots cycle through their start-up checks, in a futile effort to somehow speed up time. Finally thumbs up from the nurse to the pilots, engines at idle throttle, and the pilots squeezed a little avgas into the engine cylinders to dislodge the plane from the beach. Just like that, we were floating. The pilots then carefully negotiated a path through the harbour entrance, expertly manoeuvring the fuselage back through the narrow opening to ensure the propellers did not strike the harbour wall beneath us. For a few minutes we bobbed about like a cork in the water, as final checks were made.

'All good, all clear,' stated the captain.

Throttles were pushed full and the enormous might of the engines pulled the floats through the water faster and faster as we broke friction and became airborne. And just like that, we felt freedom! Not just the freedom of flight but also because we had just escaped from Manadhoo Island.

Yet, little did we know, our real journey had only just begun!

PART 2

Chapter 13

The Plane Ride

{Clare}

'We're off, we're free!' Jeff cried jubilantly to me. It was almost inaudible over the sheer noise of those engines. His hands were cupped over an oversized oxygen mask covering Cameron's face, and he leant over his front-row seat, as the entourage were all seated behind and next to us.

'Next stop, home,' I replied, and then added, 'after a quick stop at the hospital.' I took a long look at Jeff for reassurance. We knew by then that the first forty-eight hours post-birth were critical, and we had already used up a number of them. I looked down at Cameron, and as opposed to earlier when he had been separated from me, now he lay naked – apart from an oversized nappy – and cuddled up into my chest. That gave me an overwhelming sense of responsibility as, without my physical presence, Cameron's survival was at grave risk.

'It's going to be fine, Clare,' Jeff confirmed as he saw my face and recognised my fears. I appreciated the positivity, though I knew the strain hadn't left my face and it was obvious to everyone on the plane. 'Don't worry, you're doing a great job.' Jeff smiled, but his kind words may have been met by my unconvinced eyes.

'How are his vitals?' Jeff called to the doctor and nurse. He yelled to be heard over the continuing roar of the plane, which at last found an even balance as we had levelled out. The doctor held up the screen to Jeff, though I think it had mainly been for my benefit, to give me the reassurance I needed as I sat worrying.

'Still good,' the doctor had replied. 'His heart rate is stable, although a little high, and the oxygen saturation in his blood is still 97%, which is very good. He is of course breathing the additional oxygen from the mask you are holding, but he seems strong right now, given the circumstances.'

I noticed the doctor's even tone. He called out the information quite naturally, as if discussing it with other medical staff. 'As long as we get him to the medical facilities quickly without any delays, we should be fine,' the doctor continued. 'There is a team in the NICU waiting for us the minute we arrive, so there will be no delay. It is imperative that we go straight to the NICU. It's on the top floor.'

Both Jeff and I nodded. It eased my worry to know that some form of modern medical facility was waiting at the other end of the plane ride. I had been feeling alone and cut off from the rest of the world for over eleven hours. The nurse continued to check Cameron's vitals, as did the doctor. Mauroof and Arjun sat off to one side, both looked tired as they stared out of the window to watch the world fly past on our way to Malé.

I suddenly realised that I felt really tired. The events of the night had started to take their toll and I also realised I was sweating profusely. The towelling dressing gown Jeff had taken from the hotel, instead of the lighter one I had requested, was only exacerbating the problem; it meant that poor little Cameron was snuggling up to a sweaty body. I clutched Cameron tight, not enough to hurt him but enough to ensure I did not drop him; all the while I worried that I might be doing something wrong or that something awful could happen right here on this plane.

Numbed by the constant drone of the engines, I absentmindedly turned my head toward the window of the plane and looked out. I was surprised at what I saw; a huge expanse of water rushing beneath us that made up the lagoons between the atolls, all broken up by the pockets of lush green vegetation and white sands of the islands. It looked serene, almost surreal really. As I squinted and looked harder, I could just about see holidaymakers dressed only in swimsuits, frolicking in the turquoise waters without a care in the world. And why shouldn't they? After all they were in paradise with every available amenity at their disposal. It just seemed so strange; all those people totally unaware that the low-flying aircraft above them was making a mercy dash to the hospital to save the life of a premature baby who was only hours old.

{Jeff}

I remember looking at the pilots, and it felt peculiar to me that they were chatting away as though nothing was different to any other day and I guess it wasn't, for them. They probably talked about their past weekend or what they would do for their own next holiday. Whatever it was, the topic kept them amused, just a normal day at the office, hundreds of feet in the air, while I was going through one of the most harrowing ordeals of my life.

'They look like they are having fun,' Clare said almost rhetorically to me, as she nodded her head toward the window indicating the holidaymakers below.

Her words abruptly returned my thoughts to the present, disrupting my inner musings. 'Not a care in the world,' Clare continued to mutter as she looked down at the beautiful island we passed over. 'As it should be on these paradise islands, I guess.'

I didn't answer Clare, instead I craned my neck around to look out of the window and see what she was referring to. I was sitting in an immensely uncomfortable position and was just beginning to comprehend why parents would dispense with their own well-being in favour of their children's. It was something I had been told and read about; but only then did I start to gain a full comprehension. Still sitting in the row ahead of mother, baby, doctor, nurse and machines, I again turned back toward them, half strangling myself in my contorted position while I tried diligently to hold Cameron's oxygen mask in place.

'It looks lovely, doesn't it?' I paused, and I wondered for a split second if Clare heard me. 'You know, we do have a seaplane. Maybe we should land and go for a swim?' Though I'd tried to lighten the mood, Clare did not respond, apparently too petrified to move.

{Clare}

I was numb. I kept wondering why on earth we had thought it would be a good idea to go somewhere so remote for a holiday when I was seven months pregnant. We had been so self-assured, rejecting Dr Amir's urging that we consider somewhere less remote. I immediately decided to suppress the thought, pushing it to the back of my mind and trying to leave it there. Good decision, I thought, feeling better the moment I did. After all no amount of guilt was going to help at this point.

The doctor looked back and forth between us. I think he was trying to read our mood and concerns. He then decided to give us some good news. 'Your baby is doing well, and his vitals are still very good. Considering all of the commotion and these deafening engines, he seems remarkably unfazed by the whole thing.'

{Jeff}

As I looked round from Clare to face the doctor, the look on the nurse's face stopped me cold. Her face was white, and she looked shocked, despite the doctor's reassurance. *What on earth has drained the colour from her face?* I thought. Just then one of the crew knelt beside the nurse and without another word smiled and ushered her to the rear of the plane, where he put her in a more comfortable crew seat and handed her water and a sick bag. It was then I realised that the poor girl was airsick. I felt a pang of guilt as I watched the colour flood back into her face. At least the crew were experienced, and in a matter of minutes she returned to tending Cameron. As the nurse regained her colour, I felt a wave of emotion. That wonderful young woman had just used mind over matter to cure her airsickness and thus better ensure Cameron's safety – the safety, that is to say, of a newborn whose parents she had never met until a few hours earlier that day.

'Jeff!' Clare called to get my attention. I instantly wondered what might have been coming next. 'I am worried about the landing,' she stated.

I was genuinely bewildered at her tone. 'Why? You have been in seaplanes before. What's up?'

'Just in case something happens to Cameron. What if I drop him if it gets bumpy?' she said, and as she said his name, I realised how natural it felt and how well it fitted him.

I looked affectionately at Cameron, who at that point didn't seem to have a care in the world. Despite all of the noise, attachments, machines and people talking, he was asleep, breathing lightly, with both eyes closed for the first time in a while.

'Nothing will happen to him; you are doing really well,' I replied, without taking my eyes off of our beautiful baby boy. I couldn't comprehend the contented look our son wore on his face. 'These pilots are the best that the Maldivian air taxi service has to offer, and I'm sure the landing will be smooth,' I said, and only hoped I was right.

Just then we started to see a built-up area, something more than just the thatched roofs of luxury villas. It seemed like civilisation had been thrust upon us as we felt the plane start to descend. Soon we approached a landing area, a strip of water designated by marker buoys for the taking-off and landing of the seaplane service. The open, rectangular strip of glassy water at that moment was reserved for the sole use of our evacuation team to land.

The pilots stopped their jovial chat as they professionally went through the landing checks and prepared the plane for arrival. As the engines cut back, I felt like I could once again hear. The plane glided effortlessly over the water just a few metres above the rushing sheen, then scrubbed off the last few MPH before beautifully and gently coming to an uneventful floating position, as we bobbed on the water. The pilots then lost no time in directing the plane into the dock, where engines were turned off and propellers stopped.

Civilisation was just outside the window. The whole experience felt like one spliced from a movie depicting travel in the 1920s on a steamship, as a horde of people suddenly arrived at the door of the seaplane pulling old-fashioned steamer-trunk baggage trolleys. Behind them followed a VIP welcoming committee with cold towels and freshly squeezed fruit drinks. It had been a normal day at work for them, as they serviced the high-end customers on their way back from paradise before setting out on their often-long trips home to normality.

As mixed purposes collided, all of the arriving entourage got in the way and started to turn the arrival into a bit of a fiasco. I disembarked the aircraft and fought my way to through a marauding crowd, who started to notice that it was no ordinary flight arrival. I quickly made the point clear that things were getting out of hand, shouting, 'Where is the ambulance?' I looked at Mauroof, who also tried to comprehend the scene that was unfolding in front of the plane.

'It should be here!' he replied. He looked concerned until suddenly his face begun to brighten. 'Oh look, there it is!' We had all missed its arrival in the midst of the hustle and bustle. He pointed toward the top of the docks where a more modern ambulance stood waiting. 'Let me get someone to organise the crowd and have them move away from the plane,' Mauroof said, there was no way to get mother and baby off the plane skin-to-skin with that number of people milling about and just gawking.

Just then a lady with a big friendly smile on her face approached me, 'Hi Jeff, we have been waiting for you. Let me help with anything you need. It's not just my job, I want to make sure you guys are taken care of.' I almost walked away, thinking that she was about to ask whom and what might have been inside the plane when I realised she had said my name.

'I'm sorry, with all of this commotion I didn't hear what you said.' I had been genuinely bemused with my surroundings and desperately hoping the hospital was not too far away.

'It's okay,' she beamed, and revealed a very reassuring smile. 'It's me, Toni, I have booked your trips to the Maldives before, though we have never met.' I realised instantly that she hadn't been some nosey bystander, but someone who knew us, even though we had never met before. Perhaps she could actually help.

'Oh, Toni, I'm so sorry, I thought you were one of this maddening crowd.' I said this with as much of a smile as I could muster while distracted by the mayhem around me. I realised I was being a little abrupt, but with my son's life on the line the pleasantries I would have normally afforded slipped a touch. 'This is mad, people everywhere, how are we going to get Clare and Cameron out and into the ambulance?' I said as I continued to stare at the crowd.

'It's okay,' Toni beamed back. 'The hotel staff have gone off to get help, and they'll have a clear path in no time.'

And with that, a couple of uniformed men looking like security guards politely and ever so calmly moved the workers away from the fuselage of the plane.

{Clare}

Meanwhile, I was still inside the plane looking out of a tiny porthole. I wondered how on earth Cameron and I would disembark the plane safely. And what was more; I wondered what the crowd were doing there and why they were gathered around the plane in the first place. I assumed, correctly as it would turn out, that there had been a rumour of a premature baby arriving from one of the remote islands and everyone wanted to come and see. This turned the dock into something of a carnival atmosphere.

'Where is the ambulance?' I asked both the doctor and nurse, although it was a moot point as they too were stuck in the plane with me and the crew, while Mauroof and Arjun had been working out a way to get us all off the safely.

'Don't worry, Mrs Curtis,' replied the doctor. 'I am sure they are just inquisitive, as you are somewhat of a first here. I don't think we have ever had a premature baby born to holidaymakers here in the islands before.'

I thought about his comment for a moment. It was quite the revelation; among all the holidaymakers that had visited the Maldives – and it had to have been in the hundreds of thousands if not millions of people over the years – we were the only ones ever to have given birth to a premature child, and on one of the furthest islands as well. *That figures*, I thought scathingly to myself.

'Mrs Curtis,' a crewmember put his head through the door, 'it's safe for you to move now.' And just at that moment the nurse carefully took Cameron from me and the doctor then painstakingly removed all of the tubes and cables, allowing Cameron to be free.

I was shocked for just the briefest moment. On seeing my face, the nurse then said with a reassuring look, 'Don't worry, we'll just get you in the ambulance and I'll pass him back to you.' Then she smiled at me, which eased my concern immensely.

As I clambered out of the seaplane I felt like a celebrity, but not in a good way, with people taking photos and lots of inquisitive looks. I wondered to myself what sort of person, what sort of tourist, would want a picture of dishevelled me as part of their holiday snaps?

Meanwhile Jeff was up at the ambulance with a woman who seemed to be helping. They looked down to the plane moored up next to the dock and as it floated on the water. The nurse was helped down from the plane with Cameron held securely and lovingly in her arms, and she was followed by one of the plane's crewmembers, who carried all of the machines and drip bags.

As I reached Jeff at the top of the jetty by the ambulance, we both instinctively looked back, to ensure we could see our newborn. And there he was, still asleep as the nurse carried him off the plane onto dry land. As the nurse pushed through the entourage with Cameron held securely in her arms to reach the ambulance.

{Jeff}

The door of the vehicle was open wide, and I took the opportunity to look in. What I saw startled me; there was hardly any medical equipment in there, there was not much more than in the ambulance we had left behind on Manadhoo Island, yet it was better than nothing. I jumped in with the notion it would do, and found myself a seat on the floor, as there was no stretcher or seats.

Before the nurse entered the ambulance, she returned Cameron to Clare, but I observed that no drip was put back, just the monitor clamp, which elevated my worry slightly. After Clare carefully entered, Mauroof and Arjun followed her, and then Dr Mehedi and Toni also embarked, together with an assistant. If you counted the ambulance paramedic, there were no less than ten people squashed into the back. I knew that we only needed to cope for a few more minutes, because Malé just didn't look that big.

With the doors securely closed, we set off, down a long straight road all the way to the end, which was very near to the sea. We turned ninety degrees right and went a short distance, before again turning ninety degrees right. I noticed we were returning on a road situated on the opposite side of the island to the one that we had just come down.

Seeing the quizzical look on my face, Toni then remarked, 'That's the runway to the international airport. We can't cross it, so we have to go around.'

I thanked her, though it struck me as unusual that the hospital would be on the other side of the airport. I said nothing however, as I was tired and just wanted to get our son to safety. In truth, the adventure had gone on far too long in my opinion. All I wanted was for it to end so we could carry on with life with our new family safe and sound.

After only a few minutes the ambulance stopped, and we all clambered out. Everyone made way for Clare and Cameron to exit. She clutched Cameron firmly but lovingly and that, despite everything else, made me smile inwardly. I saw that Clare was retaking control. Sure, she had a huge amount of help around her, but I knew she felt confident by then to handle her own child, no matter how tiny and delicate he was, and it was obvious the nurse understood that as well, as she didn't try to interfere with the sterling job Clare was doing.

I looked around at my new surroundings as the last few minutes flashed through my mind; we had literally gone from the seaplane port to a boat dock on the other side of the island. It started to occur to me that the island was so very small and consisted of nothing much other than sea and air terminals.

'Where is the hospital?' I asked, part exasperated, part inquisitive.

'It's on the other island! Malé, the capital.'

What?

I wasn't sure who said it, but as soon as I heard it my focus shifted further afield where I could barely make out another island some distance away. I then begun to realise that in comparison with where we stood, the island in the distance was a sprawling metropolis with taller buildings. Obviously, that was our destination, but nobody thought to tell us we still had miles to go.

'Aren't we already on bloody Malé?' I blurted out, despite already knowing the answer. It was the mildest profanity I could muster. After all, I was surrounded by good Samaritans and didn't want to offend them.

It wasn't the first and it would not be the last time that I was only in receipt of part of the information flow. I was just learning that to reach the destination hospital in Malé, it would require two more forms of transport. That being the case, without argument we all clambered onto another boat that sat waiting for us and set off across the water, once again.

Chapter 14

The Art of Distraction

{Jeff}

The boat ride seemed shorter than expected to me, and in no time, we were over the body of water and approaching the dock. Clare, on the other hand, had been counting the seconds for the entire journey. We could see the dock, but we were both wondering where we would make land.

'Where are we going to dock?' she asked. 'There doesn't seem to be any space along any of it.' And as we got closer it was apparent the huge dock was lined two or three boats deep before you could see the land, wherever you looked.

'We'll have to moor off the side of another boat and climb over the rest to shore,' stated the captain, who had been silent until that point.

'You do realise I have a premature baby here with no protection from the elements and nothing proper to carry him in?' Clare said defiantly. 'We could drop him in between the boats on the way over, you know!'

I clenched my teeth. It was a ridiculous notion that we would carry Cameron over all those boats. My head spun as my brain worked through all of the possible problems or accidents that may occur, and I came up with zero solutions.

'Here,' said the nurse quietly to Clare. 'I'll take your son over,' and as quietly, effortlessly and expertly as she had done earlier, the nurse then scooped up Cameron and with a hop, skip and a jump made it over three boats moored side-by-side in no time. Before I had time to consider the consequences, she stood waiting on terra firma, with Cameron safely in her arms and as far as anyone could tell, enjoying himself. It seemed that the airsick nurse was much more accustomed to being on water than we were.

I helped Clare climb over the parked watercraft, inelegantly stumbling over the rocking boats myself, after ushering Clare onto the quayside without incident.

'Where's the hospital?' I asked. I felt a sense of déjà vu as I spun around and saw nothing but low-rise offices and the fish market. 'Where are we exactly?' Inside I was boiling over, as there was no ambulance or hospital in sight.

'It's on the other side of the island,' Doctor Mehedi offered. 'But don't worry, the island is only a few kilometres square. It won't take long and then we will be in NICU.'

I took a moment to consider the information as I looked up at Clare, who looked at something that she seemed to find a little unusual. Then I saw it for myself; as we – all ten of us – stood on the quayside contemplating our next steps, two paramedics came running down the middle of the road with a stretcher. As insane as it would have looked on any other occasion, on that day it actually seemed quite normal.

'Ma'am, please lie on here and we will take you to the maternity ward,' shouted the first paramedic over the din of the traffic that had been noisily whizzing past us only inches away. The traffic was made up almost solely of mopeds and scooters – lots of little two-stroke machines ridden at full throttle – while 4 x 4s, the obvious car of choice, slowly threaded their way through a throng of two-wheelers.

'What?' Clare's eyes shot wide open. 'That's not for me?'

'But ma'am, we were told a pregnant woman was coming in,' defended the second paramedic.

'There's no time,' I shot back. 'We have a premature baby.'

'Where's the ambulance?' Clare then asked in desperation.

'We left it up the road because we couldn't get through with all of the traffic.'

{Clare}

I decided to leave asking the question of how they thought they would get me on a stretcher through all that dense traffic five-hundred yards up the road, because I already knew the answer: there was no thought at all, just panic.

'No, we'll calmly walk to the ambulance and then you can take us to the hospital,' I said, regaining my composure and as I started to take control of the situation. I also sensed that Jeff, who had been responsible all night, had begun to be worn down by the enormous responsibility without a fully operational Team Curtis.

So, the ten of us traipsed up toward the ambulance, where once again I found myself paraded half-naked, still wearing only the bloodied dressing gown from the Cheval Blanc Hotel resort. Around me a whole personal entourage continued to follow. We moved in unison with drip bags, monitors and medical equipment and before long all were loaded into yet another ambulance.

The driver then proceeded to drive all the way back to where we had just been standing on the quayside, managed an illegal U-turn in the middle of the road, and knocked over a few parked scooters for good measure as he swung around. Without remorse for his actions, or maybe he simply hadn't noticed, he drove back up the road as if he were practising for the next Formula One race. Everyone in back of the ambulance was thrown around wildly, as of course we had neither proper seats nor seatbelts. The nurse once again held Cameron and was holding him in such a way that he seemed totally comfortable; she took the full brunt of the bumps against the inside of the speeding van.

Jeff had his back to the driver's cab, separated by a metal bulkhead. He bashed his fist on it hard, and shouted, 'We have managed to keep our son alive for nine hours. I don't think a few more minutes is going to make any difference, so please slow down or someone is going to get hurt!'

Just then the driver swung round a left turn very close to another scooter, which was being ridden by a young man who was hurled off and into what looked like a food stall located on the kerbside. Nobody remarked on it, making me think no one saw it except me. As we swung around another corner at breakneck speed, I got a final glimpse of the young man being helped up and brushed off: at least he seemed all right.

When we arrived at the A&E, Doctor Mehedi jumped out and was met by a handful of other doctors who waited at the emergency entrance to the hospital. Their conversation quickly escalated into a heated exchange. After a few moments, Doctor Mehedi reappeared at the door of the ambulance.

'We are going to have to go through triage in the A&E. I have already called ahead, and we were told to come straight to the NICU, but because we have come in by ambulance it's hospital protocol that Cameron be seen by an A&E doctor first.'

As we disembarked, Cameron still in the nurse's arms, I leaned into her ear and discreetly asked her, 'What is NICU? Is that the children's ward?' Alarmingly I had no idea what the letters stood for, except perhaps the C stood for children. I hadn't been privy to the conversations earlier that night in Manadhoo Island and had heard no one explain. Feeling rather stupid, I waited for the answer.

The nurse smiled a friendly smile and replied, 'It stands for Neonatal Intensive Care Unit. Most people that work there just call it 'Ni-cue,' but it is exactly that, an intensive care ward for babies, not just premature cases, but they do make up most of the occupants.'

The words "Intensive Care" scared me.

{Jeff}

I was the first to enter A&E. Once inside I was struck by another image that may never leave me. In contrast with the rather sparsely occupied Manadhoo Island hospital with its quiet wards and lack of people, this place was jam-packed with whole families sitting in every conceivable inch of the waiting room; there were people everywhere. As we were led to the main A&E ward, reality hit me; that is what a third world hospital looked like. It was an expansive room, packed with people. The whole scene was a mess, and by just looking one could not tell if the room was still being built or was partly demolished.

As I walked, I overheard all the doctors speaking to each other while they replaced the oxygen mask on Cameron's face with one connected to the hospital's own internal oxygen supply; they were not speaking kindly. I was unable to hear them clearly, so I was unable to ascertain the point of contention. But I had noticed that the last bottle of oxygen that we had carried with us from Manadhoo had miraculously continued to supply oxygen for the whole trip without running out I wondered how much could possibly be left.

I scanned the room and saw sick people everywhere – people with colds, children with forlorn looks, people who seemed to be suffering from quite serious complaints. *The risk of contamination in this room is ridiculous*, I thought to myself, and having got this far the last thing I wanted to do was open up more risks to our premature son. As Cameron was moved to the dirty sheets of the hospital bed, I thought,

Heaven only knows who occupied that bed before and what disease or condition ailed them.

Looking around, I counted no less than nine of the entourage still with us, they still looked to help however they could. But there was nothing to do except gawp at the sea of infirm around us. It was almost mesmerising to see so many sick people in one room, on such a small island.

'They can't leave Cameron in here,' I said to Clare with urgency. 'He needs medical attention and it's already arranged upstairs. What the hell is going on now? Why are we stuck here?'

'I have to get his paperwork sorted before he can go upstairs,' stated Doctor Mehedi. A wave of anxiety immediately made me feel sick, clearly at that point my sole concern was that Cameron was definitely in the wrong place.

'As we came in by ambulance,' Doctor Mehedi continued, 'there is a procedure that might take hours. They will not allow us to move upstairs, and they are refusing to let us leave. Sorry, but we just have to wait our turn.'

I felt no sympathy for the place, and I wasn't calm any more, either. I knew that stupidity left to reign in situations like that normally spelled disaster. I was determined to do what I always did in situations like these; take control.

'I'm going to take him myself,' I barked in Clare's general direction as I racked my brains to come up with an escape plan.

Clare then looked at me with uncertainty. 'But they have told us we have to stay here,' she said, from the wheelchair she had been placed in on arrival to await being processed herself. She had slipped into her compliance persona and was typically displaying a British acceptance of being told what to do by those in authority.

I, however, would have none of it; not this time. I listened as Clare was being told she needed to be seen by the hospital gynaecologist. To me, this translated into the message that Clare wasn't going anywhere in hurry. Moreover, they had her strapped in, which prevented her from leaving without help. As I watched on, I felt a sense of overwhelming incarceration and growing hopelessness. We had escaped Manadhoo Island only to fall into the clutches of the bureaucratic process of the

Malé island's A&E department. The sight of our helpless newborn son waiting on the dirty sheets for unnecessary disagreements to be settled was too much for me, the new father.

With a building sense of defiance stirring within me, I made a mental plan of how to escape that room, hoping that one or more of the entourage would help. I figured that I could simply take the bottle of oxygen, which miraculously still contained gas, and slip it under my arm. The nurse who came with us stepped to the side as I approached. The look on my face must have indicated I was in no mood for a conversation or debate, and that anyone who ventured in front of that broad-shouldered raging bull was going to have to tangle with the horns. Like me, the Manadhoo nurse knew this was no place for a premature baby and that Cameron's chances of survival would diminish with every second wasted in that room. But two burly nurses were standing almost like sentries in front of the room's only visible exit. It was a preposterous situation and tempers, including mine, began to fray.

'You need to go,' Clare suddenly said. I saw that she too had come to realise there was no room for procedures, with our son's life on the line. 'You need to get Cameron upstairs, now,' she said quietly.

So, I scooped up Cameron and replaced his oxygen mask with the one attached to the bottle that had travelled with us. The Manadhoo nurse looked me directly in the eyes and, without a word spoken, she gently took Cameron from me and proceeded to lead me over to the wall on which hung a curtain. She partially brushed it aside with her free arm, to reveal a door. It was odd as it was not an obvious place for a door to be located; nor would you have ever expected it if you didn't already know it was there. She opened it and without fuss or commotion simply slipped through it. I followed hot on her heels without looking back. I felt it reminiscent of being let into the concealed VIP entrance at a nightclub, as I followed the nurse into a space that seemed to be behind the admissions desk. I had observed earlier that nobody got past that desk unless they had filled out numerous registration cards and stacks of forms the size of phone books. Yet it was obvious the nurse knew where she was going.

'Where are we going?' I felt compelled to ask, despite being relieved to be anywhere but that wretched A&E, while I did feel guilty for leaving a wheelchair-bound Clare behind.

'I'm taking you to the NICU,' the nurse said. 'The hospital is under renovation. It received a grant from the Indian government last year, and some of what you see is the old hospital, which is very run down.' I felt comfortable with the answer and realised that it was the first time I had heard her voice.

We continued down a labyrinth of corridors; all dimly lit due to the building works. It felt like she was leading me deeper and deeper into mining tunnels, further and further away from the main hospital wing. At some point, I started to get worried at what I might find when we finally arrived at the hospital's NICU. I was still reeling from the notion that I had just held my son for the first time only a few moments before, albeit only for that instant, but I could still smell our new baby on the hair of my beard.

Balanced against my worry, the nurse – whose name I did not know – was leading the way with our son in her arms. She seemed to have had a certain aura about her, a presence. She was well-spoken, capable, and thoughtful. She had presumably been schooled and above all else, she was plain nice.

'Is it much further?'

'Not much,' she said quietly, and we had reached a lift door. 'It's on the top floor, though unfortunately this lift stops at every floor. We need to be patient, but we'll get there.'

{Clare}

I was sitting in my new wheelchair feeling about as useful as a chocolate teapot. I wanted to help, I wanted to be mobile, but all I could do was sit and watch the commotion. It started with Doctor Mehedi wanting to break protocol and take an ambulance patient straight upstairs without triage. But at that point heated discussions started about where the patient had actually disappeared to. Unlike the rest of them, I knew that wherever Cameron had escaped to, he was with his father and most assuredly on his way to NICU. That's all that mattered to me.

After Jeff had scooped Cameron up, he had somehow slipped out of the room without even having to 'hot shoe shuffle' around the nurses that blocked the only visible exit. I was relieved that Jeff spirited Cameron out of that filthy room. Somehow, he managed to get his huge broad shoulders, a baby, a nurse and an oxygen bottle under one arm out of the room unseen, while everyone had been looking the other way at the arguing doctors. Even I hadn't seen their actual escape route from the room. I knew Jeff loved the art of distraction, but I did have a feeling that the nurse must have been involved in their amazing disappearing act.

Suddenly I was struck by the overwhelming reality; that I had given birth to my baby prematurely while on holiday in a remote location. It had actually happened. Dr Amir had warned against us going and we had only then started to understand his worry about being so remote. As I closed my eyes, I tried to re-imagine the perfect birth that had run through my head for the last seven months. When I opened them, I started to appreciate that this romantic daydream would never happen, and I needed to come to terms with reality.

Just at that moment, one of the A&E doctors brought me back to reality. 'We are going to take you to the ward,' he said.

'To see my son?' I asked him expectantly.

'No, you still need to be processed and then you need to be assessed yourself, but we can take you to the gynaecology ward now.'

I looked over and saw Toni. Apparently, she had been quietly speaking to the staff and managed to convince them to move me immediately. And with that, I got bumped to the top of the queue. Soon I would be done there and could be transported to gynaecology. Nobody in A&E seemed to worry about protocol any more. The problem just evaporated with the disappearance of their patients.

It was only then that I realised I had not seen Doctor Mehedi for some time. The doctor had managed to accomplish his own disappearing trick, also slipping out of the room without being seen.

{Jeff}

When the lift doors opened on the ground floor, there seemed to be hundreds of people waiting. Doctor Mehedi appeared, panting, at my side. It was as if he had just been running; maybe he had. *Away from those big burly nurses,* I thought to myself, finding a small respite in an internalised humour.

'I was hoping I would catch up with you,' Doctor Mehedi panted. 'Good, the lift is here, and we can go up.'

We all stepped into the lift, followed by a mass of other people who were also waiting patiently and who then crammed in behind us, filling it completely. I didn't realise it, but I unintentionally held my breath. Ten stops and then we would be there, the top floor, the penthouse. Finally, the light at the end of the proverbial tunnel was upon us.

'Are they expecting us?' I asked. Though I already knew the answer, it had been such a long and tiring journey that I just needed to hear it again for myself. 'I have so many questions, and I really want to make sure of the facilities,' I said urgently before anyone could answer my first question. 'Will he be put into an incubator?' I gabbled incessantly.

I thought back to only several hours earlier when I had gone in search of an incubator and then built one. Soon I would see with my own eyes: rows and rows of them. I was starting to get dizzy with anticipation, counting the floors on the elevator screen. We were only on seven, with three more to go. I noticed that neither the nurse nor Doctor Mehedi answered any of my questions, and I also noticed that at every floor as many people got into the lift, as got out. It was still packed as the lift binged and the doors opened at the top floor. I wrestled through the crowd, making room for the nurse and Cameron to exit unhindered. People spilled out of the lift onto a small vestibule that contained only a single door within a solid wall, a few feet away. There was a shoe rack by the door, a double metal chair you might find on a railway platform and a broken plastic chair all facing an old TV that hung on the wall showing cartoons, and that was it.

When the lift closed behind us, there were only the three of us left there with Cameron, waiting to enter. Then I saw that two doctors and numerous nurses were standing the other side of the only entrance to the NICU, eagerly waiting for the arrival of Cameron. In went the nurse, still ever so gently holding Cameron, followed closely by Doctor Mehedi who disappeared out of sight. Eager with anticipation, I hurriedly slung off my shoes and started to cross the threshold into the Neonatal Intensive Care Unit.

After less than two steps, a hand thrust gently into my chest by a stern-looking NICU nurse. She was quite short but entirely professional in her red NICU gown, finished off with a blue headscarf which was more for religious than medical purposes.

'I'm sorry Mr Curtis, but we don't allow parents in while we assess premature babies.'

A surge of utter outrage exploded inside me. I involuntarily hunched my shoulders ready for battle, the anger inside detonated a volatile chain reaction of pent-up emotions, but before I could even speak the nurse pulled her hand from my chest and begun to hold my hand. It was as if she knew how to prevent a volcano from erupting.

'Please, Mr Curtis, it's not good for your baby if he's assessed with parents present, especially for those who have had an emotional journey. It could distract the doctors from their true diagnoses. Why don't you find your wife in gynaecology and we'll come and find you when he is ready, okay?'

She smiled still kindly and I knew I was beaten. She spoke the truth, right from the heart. If that would be better for Cameron, then that's exactly what I would do. I stared at the floor like a scolded teenager, and as I looked back it was just in time to see the door click gently shut.

I realised I was left standing there alone.

Completely and utterly alone.

Chapter 15

The Waiting Game

{Clare}

I was wheeled out of the A&E department and down a long corridor of the older part of the hospital, where wallpaper peeled off the wall and the smell of damp filled the nose. We passed a kind of vestibule with no roof that was open to the outside elements; heaps of rubbish bags and cast aside building materials filled its void. I forced myself to look in the other direction, swallowing hard. I started to worry about what Cameron's new surroundings might be, and my earlier high hopes started to diminish.

'I wonder where they are?' I said, trying to calm my mind by surmising where Jeff and our newborn son may have disappeared. I just hoped that they were able to make it to the NICU. The not knowing grating on my mind immensely.

'I am sure that they have made it,' Toni the travel agent reassured me. Since meeting us at the airport and jumping in our various modes of transport, including the treacherous 'keystone cops' ambulance ride, Toni had not only proven very knowledgeable, but also provided a sympathetic and competent female confidante for me to talk to.

Mauroof and Arjun walked a few paces behind us, both on their phones as they organised as much as they could on the move, although what exactly I could not be sure.

'The NICU is on the top floor?' I asked as we reached the lift and the nurse pulled my wheelchair to a soft halt.

'Yes, it is, but you are being taken to the second floor which is gynaecology. Don't worry, I am sure Cameron is in good hands by now.' Toni explained as she pushed the call button for the lift.

'We have just left the oldest part of the hospital,' Toni continued. 'Unfortunately, or fortunately, depending how you look at it, you are in the new part of the hospital, but the ward is still quite old so don't expect too much when we get up to gynaecology. Although don't worry, the NICU is relatively new.'

I didn't want to anticipate what 'relatively new' meant in reality and only hoped that my own stay would be a very short one. I was told that I needed to see the hospital gynaecologist to ensure that the sutures had been made correctly and that there was no postpartum infection. I pointed it out myself in fact earlier that morning; I had been on my feet much quicker, out of necessity, than would have normally been recommended. I'd even mentioned that I hadn't even received my *tea and toast*; a British custom that I had been truly looking forward to, once the pain of a natural childbirth passed. In fact, until that point, I never really considered myself to be a patient either. A mother fleeing to save her son's life, maybe. But a patient myself? No.

I played out what had become the waiting game from the wheelchair, wishing I could have been more help. As a mother I felt uncomfortable about not being able to care for our newborn; as Cameron's mother shouldn't I be there? But what could I have done in reality anyway? On the other hand, I experienced relief during this brief interlude from the intense responsibility of handling my tiny premature baby, for which I also felt immensely guilty.

When the lift arrived, and the doors opened, there was an enormous number of people who waited to use it. All departments including the maternity ward were serviced by that same lift, meaning pregnant women hours from delivery, babies born in the last hours or days, and families with young children in hand – all mixed and milled around the lift in a frenetic state of worry and excitement. I looked around, trying to take everything in, when suddenly a pregnant lady standing directly next to me, who also waited for the lift, smiled kindly.

'The worst is over my dear, you are a mum now,' she said to me.

I had never met the woman before, nor did I know whether she knew my whole story; but I felt an overwhelming urge to be hugged, and for the first time since it had all begun, hot tears stung my eyes as they begun to roll down my cheeks. The kind woman held out her hand and I hung onto it as if it were a life preserver. I felt a connection that could not be explained, a consummate bond with a woman who knew I was a new mum without words being spoken.

Finally, the lift stopped at the gynaecology floor, the doors opened to reveal a hallway that led to an old wooden door that was locked from the inside and could only be opened by a nurse with a key card. Apparently, they had been expecting me, and unbeknown to me at that point, I had become a little bit of a celebrity as *the lady who had given birth to a premature baby on holiday.*

'Welcome to the gynaecology ward, Mrs Curtis. Please come in and we will show you to your bed,' said a pleasant nurse who opened the door and ushered both Toni and I in, leaving Mauroof and Arjun to find a place to sit in the corridor. Being men, and no relation, they were not allowed into the ward.

One of the other nurses took me from Toni and wheeled me deep inside the ward where there were six beds with only curtains for privacy. It was basic and quite old but at least the ward was clean, as opposed to what I had seen downstairs. Toni followed us in and helped the nurse move me delicately onto the bed. I took a deep breath and tried to calm my mind.

'The doctor will see you soon,' said the nurse, as I settled myself in the bed and Toni sat lightly on the edge. 'She is quite busy today, but we hope to be able to get you seen as soon as she is free. Until then, please do make yourself as comfortable as possible.' With that the nurse glided from the room.

'When Jeff arrives, he'll have to go down to the foyer and do all of the admission formalities,' Toni said, making conversation. 'Don't worry, I will help him. My only concern is that they can sometimes be a little wary of outsiders and don't always take foreign credit cards. But it won't be a problem; we'll work through it.'

I stared up at the ceiling in an attempt to calm my mind which was all over the place. I wished we were at home in Dubai. Being unashamedly self-indulgent for that split second, I wondered what we might have been experiencing right then, if we had left those two days early, as we so nearly did. I almost certainly would have had an emergency caesarean in a proper hospital with the best available medical care at hand, and tea and toast! I tried to erase these frustrating thoughts, I knew hindsight was a wonderful thing, and we were where we were, so I had to keep optimistic and as positive as possible.

I could only imagine the hoops that Jeff was about to jump through, although we were somewhat used to it, as in fairness Dubai could also be frustratingly bureaucratic. Indeed, in that moment, I was grateful we had Toni close at hand to help, especially in light of the fact Jeff hated filling out forms and had no tolerance or patience for bureaucratic behaviour. Coupled with his lack of sleep, I could imagine he would be in no mood to face the hospital admissions desk.

Toni on the other hand seemed very mild-mannered. I could easily have imagined her being extraordinarily patient with the most demanding of clients who were spending lots of money to get luxury and who came with high expectations. It thus gave me comfort knowing that she was nearby, perched at the end of my bed, in addition to the ever-resourceful Mauroof and Arjun, who were just outside the ward if needed.

{Jeff}

I arrived in the hallway to the gynaecology ward courtesy of the very slow lift, with its all-stops service. It binged and its doors slid open. As it was so tightly packed with bodies, I had no choice but to join everybody in getting out, even if I hadn't wanted to. However to my amazement everybody then turned around and packed themselves back into the elevator before the doors closed, leaving one lone figure standing there. Me.

I looked at the bedraggled Mauroof and Arjun, who were sitting there slouched in their chairs trying to sneak some rest. Upon noticing me, their eyes and bodies perked up and immediately started to straighten, not just in their chairs, but also in their clothes so as to present a smarter impression of the hotel's staff. I held up my hand and waved at them, my gesture meant in salutation and suggested they should remain *at ease*, as an officer might gesture to the off-duty enlisted. Like soldiers, these gentlemen had earned their rest and I did not want them to be uncomfortable on my account.

'Mrs Curtis is through those doors,' Arjun said pointing. 'Toni is in there with her and of course we're waiting for news here outside.'

'How is Cameron?' Mauroof interjected before Arjun could continue.

'I honestly don't know,' I replied, and then recounted the last hour to them. The story led to how I came to be standing outside the NICU alone, and then after waiting on the bench outside for any news of Cameron and hoping for any indication at all about his health.

'At last someone opened the door,' I continued, 'but it was to suggest that I wait with Clare in her ward.' Then after a pause, I said, 'Is there any way I can get into the ward?'

'Yes, of course.' Mauroof then leapt off his chair, as if to express his apologies. 'I'm so sorry we have consumed your valuable time'.

'No, no, it's okay,' I replied, noticing a slight apology in Mauroof's tone. I didn't need to go straight in. Talking to the two gents had been respite in itself for me. 'Actually, probably more respite for Mrs Curtis,' I joked with them.

We all smiled.

I stepped to the front door of the ward, which had glass in the top half, making it easy to attract the attention of one of the nurses on the other side. She deactivated the magnetic lock and let me in.

'Mr Curtis?' the nurse correctly presumed as I stepped through the doorway. With my big beard and determined British look, I was rather easy to distinguish among the locals.

I nodded in confirmation.

'Come this way, your wife is just through here.'

I followed her to where Clare sat on the top end of a hospital bed with Toni perched delicately on the other. On seeing me, Toni jumped up, prompting me again to assure her I appreciated her help in the situation and not to stand on ceremony on my part; our relationship was no longer client and service provider, we were fast becoming friends.

'Where's Cameron? Why are you not with him?' Clare said in a panic.

'It's okay, it's okay,' I replied softly, as I stood beside her bed. 'He's with the doctors. Apparently, the person who has been on the other end of Doctor Mehedi's phone conversation all night is the head NICU consultant here.'

I began to recount the same story that I had just told Mauroof and Arjun and about that damn lift stopping at every floor. The *lift of doom*! as we would affectionately come to know it.

'So where is Cameron exactly?' Clare enquired, though rather more calmly this time.

'He's on the top floor, above us here.' I lifted my head and eyes upward to indicate. 'And although it may take a while to get there as that damn lift services every floor and seems to hold an untold number of people–' I paused, rolling my eyes this time 'it seems for the first time in his life, Cameron is now in the hands of neonatal professionals. Although we can't be with him, he is receiving the best medical care the Maldives has to offer.'

Although of course, I had no real idea of what that really meant.

'Yes, the lift is awful, but what is the NICU like?' Clare asked. 'Is it clean at least? Do they have good facilities?' Her voice was demanding, needing to be assured of her newborn's wellbeing.

'I know you need answers, just as I do,' I sympathised with her. 'I just don't know, Clare. I was stopped in the threshold as you know. The door has a small window but it's impossible to see through it. And although the nurses were well-dressed and seemed incredibly nice–' I stopped abruptly as my eyes met Toni's.

'What's wrong, Toni?'

'I am really sorry, Mr Curtis, but we do need to get Cameron registered as a patient. Otherwise they may not be able to administer the much-needed medicines.'

Toni gave me an apologetic look as she imparted this troubling information to me.

'Okay, let's do it.' I said wearily.

I had no objection to that. I am always one for getting things done with immediate effect. I knew that if things are not actioned at the time they were first discovered, procrastination has a tendency to set in. I would make no exception that day despite my fatigue. I kissed Clare quickly and turned to Toni. 'No rest for the wicked. Come on then, let's get this bureaucratic mess over and done with,' though inside I was cringing at the very thought of jumping through more unnecessary hoops.

Quickly I found I wouldn't be disappointed. After waiting forever for *the lift of doom*, Toni and I proceeded straight to the admissions desk, with Mauroof and Arjun in tow. When we arrived, we took a numbered ticket like everyone else; it suggested our turn would be quite a long way off. We waited for half an hour before Toni finally leapt to her feet with just a hint of impatience and approached the reception desk. She demanded we see the manager, pleasantly but firmly, and to my surprise he came right away.

'Why are we waiting so long?' she asked. 'My client has a baby in NICU, and we do not know whether they can administer medicines without the registration. Can we please get it done to ensure the baby is given the very best care?'

The manager nodded and then extended a stack of papers to me, which Toni kindly intercepted. I hated filling out 'daft' forms requesting largely repetitive information.

'I need a credit card,' the manager then said. I suddenly felt like I was checking into a substandard hotel.

'A credit card? For what? I have medical insurance.' But as the words left my mouth, I knew my protests were futile. I presented my card to the manager.

'Sorry sir,' he replied without blinking. 'We don't accept those.'

'What? You don't accept Visa?' I stared fiercely at the manager; my patience being tested once again.

'No. No foreign cards.'

Intervening, Toni gently laid the completed forms on the desk and motioned for me to follow her to a cash machine. Medical care in the Maldives was relatively inexpensive and it can be paid for with a minimal cash deposit.

For the next thirty minutes we trudged round to multiple cash machines to look for one that would accept any of my cards. None, of course did. Although I had numerous internationally issued credit and debit cards, none worked. I was unsure of my next move, and I turned to Toni in exasperation. 'What now?'

She withdrew her own card and inserted it in the slot. In a few moments, money came out and she handed it to me with a smile. 'I trust you,' she simply said.

With that we rushed back to the admissions desk and paid over Toni's hard-earned cash. I was so grateful, and I noted that I would pay her back with interest once the time came.

'Now we need to admit your wife,' the manager stated as he handed me the receipt.

'What?' I sighed.

For a moment I couldn't believe my own ears. There we were in an emergency situation with our newborn son's life on the line, and we were being processed like we were renewing a driver's licence.

'That was to admit your son. Now we have to admit your wife.'

With proverbial smoke starting to billow from my ears, I tried to hide my frustration as we charged back toward the cash machine that accepted Toni's card, from which she willingly withdrew more money. We then returned to the admissions desk, only to find another stack of forms that needed to be filled out. Once again Toni snatched them up and filled them out within a matter of minutes. As she handed them over to the desk clerk, she also presented the second tranche of her hard-earned cash to the manager. At least this time it was quicker, because we knew the routine.

'Can you take the papers to the first floor, please?' The manager accepted the money, but not the forms Toni had just completed. I could feel my temper rising.

We trudged to the lift in order to go up to gynaecology registration on the first floor. By sheer dumb luck, this time the lift was already on the ground floor. So we clambered on board with a hundred other waiting people. We slowly rose up one floor and out we sprang to the gynaecology admissions desk, where we were presented with more forms and immediately told that we should go back to the general admissions for reasons I was not able to comprehend. We reluctantly returned back to the ground floor and were immediately told their information was wrong. Apparently, we needed a stamp from the first floor before we could get a seal from admissions. It was established hospital protocol that no one had mentioned to us before.

I took another deep breath, and Toni and I spent another thirty minutes going between the two admission desks in the quest to legally admit Clare to the hospital. Entire rugby games have been played in less time than it took us to admit both Clare and Cameron to the hospital under emergency conditions.

With the paperwork complete, I was now desperate to see Clare and Cameron. After all the time spent processing paper, I had no idea what had become of them. But just as I turned to go to the lift, a hand laid gently on his shoulder.

What now? I thought

'Hello, my name is Paul,' a man said formally. 'I am the honorary consul to the Maldives for the British Embassy.'

My heart stopped. Why would the consul be here to see me?

Oh God, what had happened to Cameron?

Chapter 16

The Harsh Reality

{Clare}

Having just been examined by the gynaecologist, I pulled on my soiled-and-tattered Cheval Blanc bathrobe. I longed for means to just wash myself after the birth, however at that point it was the least of my worries. As I turned, I saw Jeff walk into the room. He looked pale and dejected.

'Oh my God!' I exclaimed. 'What on earth has happened to Cameron?'

'Nothing, no, nothing. I just had a shock myself. I have been running in circles trying to get you and Cameron admitted to the hospital. Toni here has been brilliant by the way. And I met the honorary consul to the Maldives. I didn't know what to think.'

I stood there somewhat stupefied, emotions running in overdrive. For a moment I felt I might have been transported into a scene from *that* movie '*Inside Out'*. I could see that Jeff was flushed; it suddenly became clear it was due to his thinking that something horrible had happened to our son. The urge to smile had taken over and I gave him a big hug. We both held each other extra tight, and when we released, I said, 'Oh, silly you. It's just our government's representative in the country. I guess he's honorary as they don't have a full-time embassy here.'

'Well, I know that now,' Jeff sighed, with an embarrassed look emerging on his face, 'but when he introduced himself, I thought I would have a heart attack. Honestly, I thought it was the coroner and that he was there to tell me something horrible had happened to Cameron.'

I looked at him and knew why I loved him so much. He wore his genuine concern and heartfelt passion on his sleeve, even when he was in the midst of action.

'I have never needed help on my travels before,' he continued. 'But it really threw me when he said, 'honorary consul'. Anyway, apparently Toni had called him before we arrived at the hospital, but he was held up in meetings all day and wanted to come by and introduce himself. He explained he would need to wait until we know Cameron's condition, but once we do, to expect twenty-four to seventy-two hours on the safe side to get his travel documents.'

I couldn't believe what I heard. Twenty-four hours had suddenly increased to seventy-two hours. Seventy-two hours meant three days. Resisting a wave of panic, I replied, 'They want to keep me here overnight just to be safe.' I tried to put a positive spin on it, but the look of dismay that crept onto my face likely had given away my true feelings. I still didn't considered myself to be the patient. In my mind we had only meant to make a quick stop in Malé and fly home soon thereafter; but as realisation set in, my mind turned back to the situation around me. Other patients were only feet away from me, separated by a flimsy curtain. It was very hot and clammy and there was zero privacy. For a brief moment, despair gripped me. I didn't know if I could take any more. I was in desperate need of a shower and just wanted to curl up with Jeff in a private hotel room somewhere far away. The ordeal started to bleed into trauma. I desperately needed somewhere to hide away from the world with my family; just me, Cameron and Jeff, away from all of the insanity.

Just at that moment Toni walked back in and handed me some essential items, including some disposable underwear and maternity pads that she had purchased downstairs while running more errands on our behalf. Toni's mere presence gave me strength.

'So, I have managed to get Clare a private room for the night,' she exclaimed gleefully.

I tried to process the news, but my mind was blank, and I could only manage a weak smile in appreciation for Toni's hard work.

'Don't look too pleased,' Toni said, as my small relief had washed back into a feeling of blankness. 'It's private and hopefully clean, but it is in a general ward back in the older part of the hospital.'

I was happy to have been offered some privacy, but the notion of staying in the older part of the hospital did give me some cause for concern.

'Ready then?' Toni asked.

'Yes,' I replied. 'Let's do it.'

So we set off, wondering what our ordeal would behold next.

Waiting outside the gynaecological ward were Mauroof and Arjun, who had been beavering away on their phones. Leaning on the seats beside them were white take-away bags.

'Arjun took the liberty of going to buy some sandwiches,' Mauroof said, as he motioned toward the bags.

Arjun offered up the contents, though we hadn't even thought of food. We just stared at the bags, almost as if we didn't know what to do with their contents, we just didn't feel hungry given the circumstances. Toni politely refrained, having eaten lunch earlier, and it was obvious to me that both Mauroof and Arjun had been waiting for us before eating anything themselves.

'We are going over to settle Mrs Curtis into her room on the general ward,' Toni said, and it was agreed Mauroof and Arjun would stay there for the time being, while we would check me in to what I had hoped would only be a temporary abode.

'We are here for you,' Mauroof said in his pleasant tone. 'Renato, the hotel manager, has told us to stay here as long as you need us, and we are happy to. If you are here for the week, we will be with you.'

'Thank you,' I said. I wanted to say more, to express my gratitude, but in the moment I couldn't think of anything else appropriate to say.

Jeff, Toni and I stood in the corridor, silently waiting for the *lift of doom*, and listening to the antiquated contraption go through its cycle before arriving ten minutes later. When we reached the ground floor, we meandered back through a myriad dimly lit corridors toward the building works, until we eventually arrived at a small bank of lifts in the mysterious older part of the hospital. A lift arrived swiftly, as it serviced only three floors. When we exited on the third floor, the difference was profound. The old ward was dark and dreary with an eerie starkness. It totally lacked the chaos and energy of life of the part of the hospital where we had just been.

For a moment another surge of panic rose up inside me. I wondered if I would be all right over there, so far away from my baby. A certain worry began to set in as I felt the unwelcome presence of something that was withering away. As we traipsed down the hallway, my mind filled with the vision of being a prisoner walking to her cell, her life destroyed, her future bleak. We passed solemn patients suffering a multitude of different ailments. I was overwhelmed with a feeling of despair, a deep depression started to set in, and I still didn't know how my baby was.

We passed a bank of private rooms on the left and the right, maybe ten in all, each door numbered, until we reached the last door, which didn't have a number. A nurse who stood nearby pushed open the door as she explained that it was a VIP room, reserved for dignitaries, 'But we are opening it for especially for you on this one occasion.'

I then realised that, despite the gloom and darkness, Toni had really used her ingenuity to ensure I would receive as much privacy and comfort as possible in the circumstances. This was a good move, not a bad one. It was progress, not failure. And although the room was very basic, the toilet had running water despite the basin and shower being dry; apparently buckets of warmed or hot water were provided for each patient as required instead.

'That was nice of them,' I said to Toni. 'Thank you. Whatever you said or did, it's certainly nice to know I'll have some privacy tonight, being in an unfamiliar place and without Jeff at my side, after what has happened.'

I had actually begun to wonder if I would feel too alone, but I pushed the thought from my mind, like every other negative thought that had surged through my brain since my waters had broken.

{Jeff}

With Clare set, I suddenly realised that I didn't have a bed for the night. 'Can I stay in the room as well?' I asked. It was a women's ward, so I already knew the answer. However, by asking the question at least I would start the conversation of where I would be staying.

'Unfortunately not,' Toni said, stating what I had already presumed. 'In fact, you cannot sleep in a bed in this hospital. But don't worry,' she continued. 'Mauroof, Arjun and I have been working on getting you a room. There is a five-star hotel, but it is on the opposite side of the island.'

The whole island of Malé is relatively small so the opposite side couldn't have been that far, however as I would learn shortly after, the overcrowded roads presented a hazard that could delay or interfere with my travels should something arise, so it was not the most convenient location.

'However we took the liberty and have organised a hotel that's closer. It's a basic one, but it is very clean and has a restaurant.' Toni screwed up her nose, indicating she hadn't been sure if she had done the right thing.

I nodded in the affirmative as my weary mind processed the information.

'This hotel is very close to the hospital and the Cheval Blanc staff are bringing all of your belongings as we speak. But if you would like, we can move you to the five-star hotel tomorrow.'

'Thank you,' I said. Right then, everything was about Cameron and his well-being, his survival. It was not about my own comfort. 'I am sure the hotel that's closer will be fine.' I smiled politely as I lowered myself into the plastic chair next to the bed. It was by then mid-afternoon and as my backside landed in the seat, I realised I hadn't actually sat, apart from the rides in the plane, the boat and the three ambulances while en route there, for nearly forty hours.

Exhaustion quickly began to take hold, but just then the door opened, and a nurse poked her head through. 'Mr and Mrs Curtis, Cameron has been assessed so it is possible for you to see him now.'

{Clare}

Jeff's backside barely brushed the seat of the chair, but on hearing the news he leapt to his feet. A new burst of energy also surged through my body at the thought of seeing our son. It had been hours since Jeff last saw him disappear with the nurse and the doctor. Although those hours passed incredibly quickly with the number of hoops that we had been forced to jump through, we were both certainly ready to see Cameron and ascertain his condition.

Toni escorted us, newly energised and eager, out of the room, through the ward, and to the lifts; the lift was there in no time. Once on the ground floor we began to negotiate the corridors back to the newer part of the hospital, and even though there seemed to be ever more people that filled the walkways, we made it through in record time to the *lift of doom.* As expected, it took the lift an age to arrive, as we stood there in silence and anticipation.

On reaching the top floor Jeff banged hard on the NICU door. A kind-faced nurse with a headscarf opened the door and motioned for us to come in. Except she stopped Toni, explaining that only immediate family were allowed.

Toni graciously motioned that she would remain right outside the door and stood aside so Jeff and I, the worried parents, could see our son for the first time in hours.

'I need to take you through some formalities,' the nurse started. Inside we walked through a short corridor to a small washbasin where slippers and hospital gowns, all clean and sterile, waited. 'Firstly, everyone coming into the NICU must wash their hands thoroughly with the special soap and water, is that understood?'

We both nodded.

'Then they must wear the sterile flip-flops there, and they must put on the sterile green hospital gowns over their street clothes. It's purely to stop anyone from bringing in any bacteria or infection into the ward. Is that understood?' Her words were firm but kind.

Again, we both nodded. The nurse then took us through the do's and don'ts and the basic rules of the NICU. As much as I wanted to see my son, as anxious as I was, I listened intently as the last thing I wanted was to infect him or any other baby in the ward. I fought exhaustion to remember every detail. When the nurse finished, we both hurried over to the sink and washed up, ready to move on with our tour.

'Now, that's the rules,' the nurse reaffirmed to Jeff and me. 'We can now go through and see Cameron, after I explain a few further things.' My impatience tugged hard at me. I was desperate to see if Cameron was okay, how his assessment had gone, whether there was any permanent damage. The nurse was stern but wore a kind look on her face as she continued perfunctorily with the rendition of her learned verse, 'We have assessed Cameron and we are taking every precaution for him. When you last saw him, he was wrapped just in a pink blanket…'

That bloody blanket, I thought. I had never envisaged wrapping our newborn son in anything other than blue. Again, I pushed the thought to the back of my mind.

'You have to prepare yourself for what you are about to see,' the nurse said next. 'For some parents, it's particularly harrowing to see their child with all of the wires and tubes that are going into him.'

Jeff looked over to me, I looked back to him with wide eyes.

'Cameron is quite bruised on his ankles and wrists where the island hospital attempted to get a line into him at the very beginning.'

Jeff saw me as I swallowed hard. I caught him doing the exact same thing. I was mortified that my poor son was bruised and likely in pain because he had been born without proper medical facilities.

'The harsh reality,' the nurse continued, 'is that Cameron has a lot of tubes in him now, two into his belly button which are directly into his umbilical, and he has a feed tube which goes into his mouth and directly into his stomach. He has a cannula for us to provide him with nutrients and there are a lot of machines, all with warning signals and flashing lights. It can be intimidating for any parent to see for the first time.'

I had listened intently to the nurse, but absolutely nothing could have prepared any parent for what I saw next. There on the bed was my tiny, helpless, premature child who was so scrunched up he looked as though he might fit in the palm of a large hand, strapped to a mass of machines with wires and tubes that swarmed and surrounded around him like the tentacles of some sea creature. I gasped.

My maternal instinct was to rush over, pick him up, to hug him, but I couldn't see how that would have been possible. Instead I simply put my finger under his palm. Instinctively Cameron's hand curled around it slightly and clung onto it. The new wave of emotion that hit was hypnotic, the relief that he was still alive, the feeling of being a new mother combined with the guilt of us having put poor Cameron through this.

All Jeff was capable of was to put his hand at the base of my neck reassuringly, to let me know he was there, to let me know he saw what I did, and that he too was intimidated by seeing our baby wound in the machines' mass of tentacles. We could barely see Cameron. He was a tiny speck, so small lying among the monitors, needles, tubes, lights, and sounds. Even the strongest couple would be affected, and we were humbled and awed by the intertwined miracle of science and birth.

At that moment a doctor walked up beside us and for a few seconds looked on, giving us a little time to digest the spectacle and absorb the awe of what we saw before us.

'It's okay to feel intimidated,' Doctor Sayed finally said. He spoke with compassion, looking directly at Cameron. 'Nothing we can say can prepare you for this; but at least we hope to lead you in gently.' By the look of concentration on my face, and the tilt of my head, Jeff could tell I was struggling to fully understand the doctor's accented words; though as he talked his reassuring tone did wonders. 'We have put him on a ventilator, but this is only a precaution. He was breathing on his own when he came in with a 98 percent blood saturation. That's a very good sign, but he spent nearly ten hours breathing unassisted and this would have tired him out.'

I just stood watching Cameron and listened to the doctor at the same time, observing and processing, it was wondrous, and I felt completely rapt.

'At less than thirty-one weeks,' the doctor continued, 'the bronchioles in his lungs would not have formed properly, so we have given him an injection to help their development; pretty standard. We have also put him under anaesthetic to give him some time to heal. He is a true fighter, and now we must help him get some rest.'

It's true, I remember thinking to myself. *To be here at all, under these circumstances, to have breathed unaided for ten hours across stormy seas, he is a fighter, a true Curtis by birth, there is no doubt about that. This kid is going places.* Although, as we both looked at Cameron, surrounded by all the medical machinery, a realisation set in that he wasn't going anywhere just then!

'When do you expect him to come off the ventilator?' I asked the doctor. I think I was still in shock; I was frightened as I looked at my fragile son, feeling all the more guilty. If we had got him to medical help sooner, if we had left the island two days ago, or if we hadn't have come away at all, maybe I wouldn't have gone into labour and could have delayed the birth, preventing Cameron's journey through that ordeal.

'It could be as soon as later tonight,' the doctor replied. 'We have twenty-four-hour care here, so we will not leave him on the ventilator longer than is necessary.'

I understood. It was a precaution to make sure no complications developed. That gave me a little relief from my anguish.

'Our main concern with any premature baby is infection,' the consultant continued. 'It's why we take so many precautions with washing hands and covering clothes and leaving shoes outside, to keep the room as sterile as possible. Sepsis is the primary concern, so we are always on the lookout for signs. He has jaundice, you can see from his yellow colour, but full-term babies also get that to some degree as a matter of course, so we tend to treat it as a low priority.'

'What—' I started to say then stopped, because the doctor continued.

'We have screened his blood for any infections, and we can see something that is unidentified, again not unusual, but we are running a course of antibiotics as a further precaution.'

So many precautions, I thought. It was good to be cautious, but I couldn't help but feel the doctor was hiding something, not telling us the whole picture so as not to worry us. Again, I looked over to Jeff. Our eyes connected and without him saying a word, the telepathy between husband and wife permitted me to know he was thinking the same thing. But we both knew Cameron was now in more experienced hands and it was best to sit and wait, to be patient. We had made it this far and now we were at a point where even though time worked against us on the whole, in the short term at least time was on Cameron's side. Time was the best healer, an old saying we had heard growing up. Though neither of us is particularly religious, the power of positive thinking is a salvation Team Curtis faithfully embraces.

For a time we stood there watching Cameron's chest move up and down aided by the ventilator, and for that time, it was as if life itself stood still.

'Why don't you both get some rest?' the consultant said gently, sensitive to the fragility of the moment. 'From what we can see, you have been functioning on limited if any sleep for what, forty-eight hours? Things always look better from a rested mind, take my word on that from many years' experience.'

The nurse put her arm reassuringly around my shoulders. As Jeff looked across at me, he would have seen my muscles begin to relax, a faint loosening of my grip on fear itself. So many parents had been through that ward with the same worries, of course, but I knew from watching them that the doctor and nurse were in their element. And besides, as harsh as it seemed, the medical team knew logically that some babies made it and some babies didn't. And though uncertainty manifested itself, right then there was nothing more that either Jeff or I could do about it but worry the worry of all new parents.

'Come on,' Jeff said to me as he put his own arm around my shoulder. 'Let's get you back to the ward.'

'I want to kiss Cameron goodnight,' I replied, as I tensed to lean forward from his grip and then stopping tentatively. 'But I'm not sure that's even possible with all the wires and tubes and stuff. I certainly don't want to give him an infection.' Then I pushed through my hesitation, as my motherly need pushed me on, and I leaned over ever so carefully. I whispered to Cameron, as if we were the only two beings in the universe. 'Sleep now my little prince. You've had a big day today and you need your rest to make yourself big and strong for tomorrow.'

Jeff then walked over and said his nun-nights as we left Cameron's side, we then disposed of our gowns into the washing bin and removed our flip-flops at the door.

Outside, a weary-looking Toni was watching what looked like a cricket on the television screen. When she heard us, she looked over. 'Clare, I will take you to the ward. Jeff, when I am done, I will meet you at the front entrance to take you to the hotel.'

We all rode the elevator down to the ground floor where we were met by a very tired-looking Mauroof and Arjun. Toni then dispatched me to the older part of the hospital and promptly returned to direct Jeff outside.

{Jeff}

Taxis were in abundance at that time of night, so we did not have to wait long. Ten minutes later Toni and I pulled to a stop in front of a plain building located next to a huge building site.

'Here we are,' Toni said.

As I looked out into the night, I thought of home and Dubai with its incredible building boom underway. Dubai, home away from home, I thought, hoping that building site next to that hotel wouldn't be as noisy as those at home.

Toni paid the driver and we then walked through the reception door, where the manager rushed over to greet her like an old friend.

'I'll leave you here,' she said to me, as the hotel manager released her from his bear hug. 'They have a restaurant if you are hungry and they will print and photocopy anything you need.'

With that and a quick bear hug in my direction, she was gone.

'Let me show you to your room,' said the manager. 'The aircon is on and it's set low as I've heard you like it that way.' I smiled, wondering what else Toni had told the manager; she had been plain brilliant.

'Thank you,' I replied.

When we arrived at the room, it was adjacent to the elevator. I bid the manager goodnight and went inside. As I stood there, I felt alone, isolated, and wished I could have the comfort of my wife's body lying against me that night. But alas, she was elsewhere. When I finally looked around, I realised I was standing in a suite of sorts, it had two rooms and ensuite bathroom. I was astonished to see that Renato's team had already delivered our entire belongings; an amazing feat considering we never travel light.

I didn't know whether I wanted to shower or just collapse in the bed. I walked through to the bedroom where I found more presents from the hotel, another one of Renato's kind thoughts, no doubt. I stripped down to my boxer shorts and realised it had been precisely forty-two hours since I had last slept. I lay back on the bed just to contemplate whether to eat or shower. When my head hit the pillow, however, I instantly fell into a deep sleep.

{Clare}

Back at the hospital, I also slipped into bed, but lay staring out of the window, unable to relax. I let a torrent of thoughts swim through my mind, in the hope that exhaustion would take me. I felt alone in the room with only my thoughts for company. Cameron was in another part of the hospital and Jeff was in a hotel somewhere close by, ironically my family separated by the recent birth. Just then, the phone by my bed rang.

Who could that be at this hour? My heart started racing and I answered quickly, 'This is Clare Curtis…'

'Mrs Curtis, you must come, you are needed urgently in the NICU.'

Chapter 17

The Paperwork Vortex

{Clare}

Despite forty-two hours of sleep deprivation, I leapt out of bed wearing only my new hospital nightgown. As I bolted out the door, I grabbed the first robe in sight, somehow of course it happened to be that bloodstained one that had followed me everywhere. My fresh stitches tugged at the skin between my thighs, but I moved as fast as my fatigued legs could carry me. I had to know what had happened to Cameron. Was he dead?

We knew infection was a real danger and we had been forewarned that if sepsis took hold he may not survive. Had he caught something in the A&E? My head spun as the possibilities kept coming.

By the time I reached the *lift of doom,* I was slightly disorientated, but I did not let this slow me down. The nurse who had arrived shortly after the phone call to collect me from the ward could hardly keep up. Whenever we arrived at that lift it was always on the farthest possible level away, and that night was no exception. It seemed frozen in space somewhere near the top floor. *Who programmed this ridiculous thing anyway?* I wondered in exasperation. Then I took a deep breath and calmed myself, realising I couldn't possibly climb ten flights of stairs, as my stitches were already hurting. I had started to wonder if I had done any permanent damage to myself, the pain beneath was intensifying, but like every other personal issue, I simply put it to the back of my mind.

'Oh, come on!' I unintentionally shouted out loud to the lift as if it could hear me.

'Ma'am, please, slow down,' the nurse said when she finally caught up, out of breath. 'You could pull out your stitches.'

'What has happened to my son?' I asked in anguish.

'I'm just a ward nurse, ma'am. They told me to bring you here right away.'

Oh my God, I panicked. *What has happened that they need to chaperone me?*

I needed Jeff, but it was only when I reached into the robe pocket that I realised I had left my mobile next to the bed. Damn it. I looked up at the lift lights. One more floor to go.

Finally, the lift arrived and delivered me to the tenth floor. The moment the doors opened wide enough to alight, I bounded the few metres toward NICU and pounded on the door with the unbridled intensity of a mother whose baby's life depended on it. Almost immediately a nurse appeared at the glass window of the door, she looked a little confused and tried to hide her slight annoyance at all the commotion outside the quiet of the NICU.

'What on earth is wrong?' she exclaimed to me as she opened the door. 'As the mother of one of our babies, you are most welcome any time. There is no need to break the door down.' She smiled, trying to lighten the mood a little.

'I was told I needed to come here urgently,' I erupted. 'What has happened to my baby?' I started to search the nurse's face for an answer, looking for even the slightest twitch or change in demeanour in which to base my next emotion.

'He's fine for now,' the nurse said softly. 'In fact, we were just discussing that it might be time to take him off the ventilator.'

I stood wide-eyed as I tried to take it all in. *Have I totally overreacted?* I asked myself as tears stung my eyes.

'It was a good precaution to have him on a ventilator, of course, but his vitals are good. His lungs are working and overall he's a very strong boy, especially taking into account the journey he has taken.' She smiled as she finished the sentence.

'He's fine?' was all I could muster. 'May I see him then?'

'Of course, as soon as you wash up and put on a clean gown.' The nurse motioned with an outstretched hand toward the sink, all gleaming and clean.

'So, Cameron is fine?' I repeated.

'Well, he's not completely out of harm's way, but given the circumstances he's doing much better than we expected. Why would you think otherwise?'

'I was told to come to the NICU urgently.'

Over my shoulder another NICU nurse who was checking a chart looked up. 'I'm so sorry Mrs Curtis, but I think there has been a misunderstanding. All I needed was to give some new medicine to Cameron. For that you must sign a form. If you were still awake, that meant I could start giving him his new medicine tonight, without delay.'

She handed me a form that I signed and returned. Then I washed up and discarded the bloodstained robe, for good this time, in favour of a sanitised gown. Then I moved tentatively around the corner and, despite knowing he was there, I was still profoundly moved to see him only metres away, sleeping ever so calmly and looking so small and helpless, still entwined in the mass of wires and machines, which seemed to only get thicker with time. Just being near my baby gave me a sense of calm; I saw he was still alive, and I realised I just needed to be near to him.

For the longest time I just watched his chest rise and fall. The motion of my son's breathing relaxed me like nothing else could. Although the ward was still overrun with its miniature patients, each with their own machines, the darkness coupled with the rhythmic vibrations of all the equipment made the whole atmosphere feel quieter, almost serene. It felt like something out of a science fiction movie.

Suddenly feeling dizzy, I knew I needed sleep badly and was quickly becoming obsolete in my role as a mother, due to fatigue. So I kissed my fingertips and pressed them onto Cameron's cheek, then turned on my heels and made my way out. Instinctively I reached for my phone to call Jeff, but again realised it was not there. Besides, what could he have done? He needed sleep as much as I did; I would tell him the next morning.

As I passed the reception desk on the ground floor, one of the few ladies working the nightshift recognised me.

'Mrs Curtis, there are more forms for you to sign.'

I'm notorious, I thought, as another stack of papers was shoved my way. I grimaced inwardly and accepted them with a forced smile. 'Fine' was the only word I had energy to say.

The forms were for my medical care and the medicines I had been given on the ward; non-urgent details I could easily address the next morning. I suddenly realised I didn't know how to get back to my room, so I tried to retrace my steps as best I could until I eventually came back to the lift taking me a few floors to my ward. I shuffled toward my private room as I made a mental note to lock the door. Once inside, I lay my head down on the pillow. Within moments, just as the sun peeked over the horizon, I slipped into a deep sleep. Whatever nervous energy kept me awake earlier had now depleted. As daylight flooded the room, it was not going to wake me; nothing could have by that point.

{Jeff}

That same sun poked through the curtains of the hotel room, entering the corner of my eye and causing me to squint from the bright light. I instantly arose upon realising it was a new day. I had taken enough rest and could relax more when we eventually returned to Dubai.

I surveyed the room as my mind processed the images before me. Our suitcases were lying in both rooms and a bulging A4 envelope sat on the table. Not remembering the envelope from the night before, I swung my feet to the floor and went over to pick it up. The envelope contained the balance of our valuable belongings held in the previous hotel safe. I then set about making some order of it and afterwards putting the envelope and our passports into the room safe, inside the wardrobe.

Next, I turned to my suitcase. Inside it I found items neatly folded, but they presented a mishmash of both of our belongings. It was still way too early then for fathers' visiting time or to call Clare, who would hopefully be asleep, and I didn't want to wake her if she was.

To pass time, I set about reordering some of the chaos in the suitcases. I found my wash bag and with no delay I made for the shower. Even though the pressure was low, the clean water still revitalised me, giving me a desperately needed feeling of freshness.

On leaving the bathroom I felt like a new man, ready for anything. With the room in an orderly state, and me washed and dressed, I suddenly realised I was famished. As luck would have it, time had ticked on and I was sure that by then breakfast would be available in the hotel restaurant. So I headed downstairs to eat. I entered the hotel lobby and sought to gain my bearings.

Though the hotel was small and basic, it was at least furnished with equipment that enabled me to communicate to the outside world if the need arose. The Wi-Fi also appeared reasonably good, which was a bonus.

The receptionist smiled as she handed me another huge stack of papers that immediately darkened my mood. *More paperwork,* I groaned to myself, but thanked the receptionist as I headed through the door to the small restaurant opposite reception.

I sat down with the forms at a small table in the corner. It gave me a good vantage point to see people coming and going. Both Clare and I loved to 'people watch' and wonder what filled their day.

''Good morning,' I said to the waiter, with a smile, 'Double espresso if you have it, black coffee if you don't.' The server nodded and sprinted away. I then started reviewing in my mind what I needed to do to start the evacuation process from Malé:

Get a local sim card.

Make copies of our passports.

Organise paperwork for Cameron's departure.

Ten minutes later I was in the reception area, waiting for my taxi to the hospital. I had tried unsuccessfully to reach Clare on her phone and though I desperately wanted to talk to her to see if she and Cameron were okay, I also hoped she had got some sleep. She had, after all, just given birth.

On realising a taxi was not forthcoming it was suggested that I try hailing one on the corner, so I slipped the paperwork into my backpack with the intention of doing it later and exited the hotel.

Then just as I put my foot onto the street, a scooter whizzed by, narrowly missing me, and then another, and another. I looked around and saw scooters everywhere. Hundreds of them were racing down the tiny roads and thousands were parked on both sides of the streets for as far as the eye could see. It was manic: almost pandemonium. After attempting to hail a cab for fifteen minutes, one finally stopped at my feet. The vehicle was packed inside, they simply made room for me and we all rode together.

It quickly became obvious why scooters were favoured in the capital. With an abundance of people everywhere, and small, cramped roads, it was the opposite of the carefree paradise for which the more remote islands of the Maldives were known. A scooter was the only way to manoeuvre through it. Malé, the capital of the Maldives, was a mini sprawling metropolis, a business centre and market town all rolled into one. Nearly a hundred and thirty thousand people from poverty-stricken neighbouring countries had flocked there in pursuit of a better life. And by the looks of things, they had all bought their own scooters!

{Clare}

The moment I woke up I poked my head out of the room and asked for the latest news on Cameron. The nurses looked blankly at me and offered me pain medication and a couple of buckets of hot water instead. This reminded me how dirty and uncomfortable I felt, as I still hadn't been able to properly clean myself since I gave birth.

I took the buckets into the bathroom, where there was just a hole in the floor and basic essentials. As I gently cleaned myself, I was suddenly aware of just how uncomfortable I felt, no real pain but just plain, downright uncomfortable. I also realised how hungry I felt. I quickly pulled on a change of clothes that Toni had left for me and wondered where I could find food.

'When is food served on this ward?' I asked the nurse as I once again stuck my head out of the door.

'Food is not served to inpatients. The family normally brings it in,' the nurse replied. 'But you can call the cafeteria and pay for it yourself.'

I called the cafeteria and when asked what I wanted, I had absolutely no idea.

'Do you have toast?'

'Of course. So, one order of toast? Is that all?'

'Yes, thank you. Oh, maybe a tea as well,' I added. Putting down the receiver, I realised Jeff had left some money under the phone should I need it. The food came quickly and as I ravenously consumed my tea and toast my mind started racing. I had so much to do and would certainly need help, assuming Cameron had made it through the night.

Then I remembered that I was meant to be having my baby shower that week back in Dubai. Panic took hold as I realised I needed to let people know that the baby shower would be cancelled. I wanted to speak with my sister Ann most, but it was still the middle of the night in the UK. In fact, it was still early in the morning Dubai time, but I knew my friend Mhairi would be awake as she got ready for work. I called, and the phone just rang and rang. I tried again five minutes later, and just as I was about to give up Mhairi answered.

'Hello there,' came a bright Scottish voice.

All of a sudden, I had no words.

'Clare, are you okay?' said Mhairi.

All I could think of was, 'The baby's here.'

'Say that again.'

Tears stung my eyes again as I said; 'Cameron. That's his name. He was born yesterday… on a remote island.' Speaking those words released a massive wave of emotion, and the next thing I knew I was sobbing uncontrollably.

'Oh my God!' exclaimed Mhairi. 'Is he all right? Are you all right?'

I had to gather myself and wiped my tears with the back of my hand. 'The doctor said his vitals are good, but the next forty-eight hours are critical. Could you cancel the baby shower? Do you mind? And I might need some help getting some baby things, as this was on our to-do list when we came home.'

'Don't worry about any of that. I will sort it. I am sure he's a fighter with a good Scottish name like that. Just let us know whatever we can do to help.'

{Jeff}

Just arriving at the hospital, I untangled myself from my fellow passengers, paid the fare to the driver and escaped the cramped enclosure. On my breathless arrival at the gynaecological ward, however, I was told that Clare had left for the NICU some thirty minutes earlier. So, I made my way to the *lift of doom*. On arrival I was not disappointed, as the usual mass of people congregated around its doors. As always, the lift was floors away, not moving. Eventually I arrived at the top floor, the doors opened, and I entered the foyer just in front of the secured NICU door, just where I'd been standing alone the day before. Nobody else was there, just the television playing cartoons. But when a nurse finally passed the glass pane in the door, she didn't give me directions to Clare and Cameron. Instead she handed me a paper prescription and said, 'We need medical supplies.'

'What do you want me to do about that?' I asked bewildered. *Don't hospitals everywhere stock their own supplies?*

Apparently not in the NICU in the Maldives; it's the father's job to take prescriptions and purchase whatever medical supplies might be needed. I didn't delay, I scraped together what was left of the local currency Toni had loaned me and headed straight to the hospital pharmacy. Though it would be the most expensive, the cost was not an issue. The health of Clare and Cameron was all that mattered, and the hospital pharmacy was closest and presumably the best. Unfortunately, it proved a futile trip in the end; of the five items listed, only three were in stock.

'What should I do?' I asked the hospital pharmacist with genuine worry.

'There are many more pharmacies outside. You must look there,' the pharmacist suggested.

I thanked her and ran out the door, down the corridor and out into the street, I hadn't noticed before, but I counted at least twenty pharmacies. The two closest pharmacies, however, didn't seem to carry much of anything. At store four I found one of the items and then I found fortune at store five. It had in stock the last remaining item. With supplies in hand, I rethreaded my way through the buzzing scooter traffic and back to the *lift of doom*, which had just left the moment I arrived. I could not believe it. And it was then that I was struck by another epiphany; I could save an abundance of time and frustration by scaling the ten flights of stairs. So, I gritted my teeth, and strode at full pace toward the stairs, with intention of using my own legs. However, just like that, my world turned upside-down as the corridor spun uncontrollably around me.

The next thing I knew, I lay flat on my back on the floor, immobilised in pain. Had there been an earthquake? Had there been a landslide? Uncertain what had hit me, I did a mental body check and found that pain emitted from my right big toe; it throbbed like hell. I realised I had simply misjudged my first step; I had foolishly stubbed my toe on the very first step of the ten flights of stairs, which had sent me crashing to the floor so hard I was stunned senseless. From the swelling, colour and pain I was pretty sure my big toe was broken.

'I'll take the lift,' I grumbled to myself under my breath. I was in severe pain as I hauled myself off the cold stone tiles.

I arrived at the top floor some twenty minutes later with a throbbing toe, and a desperate need to see my wife and son. I carefully shed my shoes. My toe was a mess, I could barely walk; I hobbled to the door and knocked. The nurse opened the door with a big smile and thanked me for the medicines. Then she ushered me to the sink, where I got washed up and dressed in a gown. With a painful limp, I proceeded into the ward where I had last seen Cameron the previous night. Clare was already there, sitting on solitary guard at the bedside, providing part motherly vigil, and part company for her sleeping son.

Then, just as I was about to speak, I realised there was no ventilator. Instead, Cameron was wearing a woolly hat with a Velcro tab that held a minuscule oxygen mask over his face and no machine breathed for him. *What a brilliant little contraption, so simple yet so effective.*

{Clare}

As Jeff rounded the corner, I was about to ask him how he was, but my thoughts were disrupted by his limp, 'What have you done?' I could see his toe was bloodied and had started to swell.

Jeff waved his hand dismissively, 'Fell down the stairs. Well stubbed it, up the stairs to be exact, but either way it was stupid, and it hurts!'

The subject was left there for more pressing matters, Cameron's welfare. I had already held court with the nurses when I had first arrived that morning. Jeff took a plastic chair and we began discussing what might and might not happen, what were bad signs and what were good.

Just then the door behind us swung open and in strolled a smartly dressed man, who was beaming from ear-to-ear.

'Hi Jeff,' he said with outstretched hand. 'And you must be Clare,' he beamed toward me, then leaned in and gave me a peck on both cheeks. 'I'm Paul, the honorary consul. I've just talked my way into NICU, which was not an easy task. I have good news and bad news, which is why I have sneaked in. Which would you like first?'

'There's never good news in these scenarios,' Jeff remarked sceptically, 'just facts and bad news.' We both eagerly anticipated what Paul was about to say.

'Well,' continued Paul, undeterred. 'You are in a great facility, at least you are for this region. The Indian government gave this hospital a grant just last year, adding some new machines and staff with lots of training.'

That's the facts, I thought on Jeff's behalf.

'I'm afraid we're having a little bit of a paperwork vortex at the moment.' He paused. 'It looks as though it might take a week to get Cameron out of the country.'

Chapter 18

The Rollercoaster of Emotions

{Clare}

After a lengthy discussion with Paul, it transpired that while we could apply for an emergency travel document for Cameron from the UK Government, it would only be characterised as a one-year passport. However, we needed to get back to Dubai where my gynaecologist awaited with his neonatal colleagues to take Cameron into specialist care; but Dubai only accepted five-year passports. According to Paul, there was talk in the consulate that International SOS could evacuate us back to London without the need for the five-year passport, except this route presented medical challenges for Cameron. So, we were stuck.

Firstly, the insurance company would only move the patient if the medical facilities were better in the destination. Secondly, and more importantly, an air ambulance would have to make one, maybe two, fuel stops en route to the UK, and the doctors were concerned this might be detrimental to Cameron's health.

We listened to Paul, but Jeff and I had other ideas that we would pursue later that afternoon. It was not going to be straightforward, but I also knew Jeff was quite adept when it came to matters of this kind.

'I'll not come back to the hospital this afternoon,' Jeff suggested to me. 'I'll set up a makeshift office in our new digs and with two phones and my iPad I should be set to get us out of here and back home to Dubai.'

'I think you have to take control again,' I replied. 'And if there is anything I can do to help–' I stopped mid-sentence, knowing that wasn't really possible.

'No, I have it covered. Right now, you need to be with Cameron. I guess there's not much I can do here anyway.'

We had learned on our first induction that the amount of time that fathers were allowed in the NICU was rather limited. While mothers could spend twenty-four hours a day there if we wanted, fathers had to vacate any one of the three wards within the NICU any time a mother was breastfeeding, making it very difficult as a practical matter for fathers to spend any length of time with their newborns.

I looked over at Cameron and sighed, 'Talking of breastfeeding, the nurse will come in a few minutes to give us a talk on it.' I looked at Jeff. 'He will only take three ml every few hours through the feed tube.' I pointed at the tube that entered Cameron's mouth and took its contents directly into his stomach. 'But the milk may not be ready inside me yet as he is premature,' I added bleakly. I knew how important breast milk was to a baby and I was petrified that this might be another thing I would fail at, having failed to hold my baby in my womb for 40 weeks as I was supposed to.

'I'm sure it will be fine, and you'll do great,' Jeff stated enthusiastically. He knew me well enough to realise the importance of listening to me at this point, but he couldn't help himself, so I just rolled my eyes at Jeff's forced enthusiasm, and at that moment the nurse walked in.

'Hello, Mrs Curtis. There is a free room across the hall. We can go there if you are ready to try to produce some milk.' She smiled and led us to another, empty ward, with Jeff in tow.

Once there, Jeff closed the door and whispered to me, 'I presume it's okay for me, being a father, to stay during this, whatever this is?' He added not exactly sure what to expect at that point.

'Of course,' said the nurse overhearing. 'Hopefully having husband and family near will help with milk production; for today it's simply a matter of seeing if there is milk there. Once we know there is, the body will do the rest.'

I looked around the room, which looked more like a storeroom than a baby ward, with stacks of chairs and washing liquid bottles everywhere.

'Where is the breast pump?' I enquired. The only equipment in the room was a solitary incubator in the corner. 'I don't see a breast pump anywhere.'

'For today,' the nurse said confidently, 'we will just use manual manipulation.'

Both Jeff and I became wide-eyed. *We will use what?* I thought to myself. It sounded almost barbaric, especially given the other modern machinery being displayed throughout the ward.

'Don't looked so shocked,' the nurse said with a laugh. It was obvious she had been through this many, many times before with many, many parents. She then offered me a chair and asked me ever-so-nicely to open the front of my shirt. I did as I was told, and then the nurse asked permission to show me what she needed to do. I apprehensively nodded, exposed my breast, and the nurse nimbly went to work, manipulating and squeezing in a therapeutic motion.

Jeff looked on and he didn't seem too sure what to think. It was simply in an effort to feed our son, but given the experiences of the last forty-eight hours, everything just felt so bizarre.

'What should Clare expect to experience?' Jeff asked eventually. He asked because, he knew that I wouldn't, and he could tell by looking at my face that I was silently uncomfortable, internalising my worries as I always tend to do.

'Well,' nurse said with focus, 'We are trying to see if there is milk. By doing this we should see something to signify that the body knows that milk should be produced.'

We watched but saw nothing. *I knew It!* I was failing at everything.

'Nothing so far though, I'm afraid,' the nurse said, 'but it's not a concern because this is sometimes the case with premature labours.'

I looked down at my body and I tried to mentally will the milk to appear. The nurse then showed me what to do, so that I could take over the exercise. Jeff looked as though he felt like a spare part, as there was a limit to what he could do to help, except being there for support. The nurse encouraged me have a go at it without her assistance, so I applied my own hand to manipulate milk from my breast. Yet despite concentrating as hard as possible, nothing came out.

'Oh, this is no good!' I exclaimed, frustrated and annoyed at my body's resistance to doing what was so needed.

'Well,' said the nurse, 'even if the milk is there it might take a while for the body to dispense it. We must be patient.'

'Would it help if we bought a breast pump?' I asked. 'Aren't they designed for this very purpose? Maybe we could get one tonight?'

'That would certainly be a good idea, although at this stage manual expressing may still be better,' the nurse answered.

She started to help me again and then with everybody concentrating as hard as possible on my nipple, something dramatic happened; a tiny droplet of liquid no larger than a bead of sweat and not particularly white made a glossy appearance.

'There you go,' said the nurse with satisfaction, as if she knew all along that it would happen. 'Milk!' the nurse suddenly exclaimed. 'Mother's gold!'

'Where?' I asked in bewilderment. I had expected white liquid like the kind you put on your cornflakes. 'It's nothing.'

'It's something,' said the nurse. 'And something is a very good sign. It means your body is producing milk.'

'But, but – that's not enough to feed anyone!' I cried with concern.

'Mrs Curtis,' the nurse stated kindly but firmly, 'believe me when I tell you this is a very good sign.'

Jeff nodded his head up and down, still none the wiser at what was happening around him, but he just went with it.

'In fact,' the nurse continued, 'I think we should stop now and then you can try again at the hotel tonight. Try and express milk every three hours if possible, as the body is very good at replenishing its own supply. But right now, you need a good sleep and don't forget to drink enough water.'

The nurse then did the strangest thing. She took a cotton bud and dabbed it on the small droplet of liquid at the end of my nipple. She then took it to the other room and wiped it onto Cameron's lips.

An organic bond.

I was amazed, my body had produced "milk" and hopefully would continue to do so to give Cameron the best chance. This was so important, and I knew that a mother's milk was made up of incredible stuff. Not only did it give the baby essential nutrients, but the mother's glands adjusted the proteins and fats each and every time it produced milk, to ensure proper nutritional delivery at each feed, thereby boosting the baby's immune system and helping them to fight infections. When able and allowed to work, the human body was truly an amazing machine.

With just this one drop, it was decided that I would adjourn until later in the day and that we would seek out a breast pump. Although with no cash and no ability to use credit cards, it would be yet another item that Toni might have to buy on our behalf.

We exited the NICU door in search of lunch – we were both starving – and just as we walked out of the door, there was Toni sitting on the 'station bench' waiting for us.

'Hello Toni,' Jeff said, amazed that she'd been sitting there waiting for us the whole time.

'Hi guys!' Toni said enthusiastically. 'I just wanted to make sure you had enough money for lunch, and if there was anything I could help you with, I wanted to be here.'

'We have enough cash for lunch, thank you,' I replied, we were truly thankful for her help. 'Although where would you recommend nearer to the hospital for lunch, and we also need to buy a breast pump, ideally somewhere that will take our credit card.'

'Let's ride the lift down together and I will show you the street where you can eat. I know you guys like to eat healthily, so we can find you something suitable. For the breast pump I think I have found a shop that might take international cards. I'll take you there tonight, as it is closed during the day.'

Just from that simple news that there was a store selling baby essentials, and it might take international credit cards, I was elated. Though we knew by then we would have to stay on the island longer than hoped, Cameron was in a stable condition at that time and NICU was far superior to the rest of the hospital. I felt a hint of optimism.

As we walked across the main road, scooters flying by, taxis rushing in and out while dropping people off and picking more up, the world around us seemed to be stuck in a state of mayhem. Toni seemed oblivious to it all, as she patiently showed us the street to go down for lunch. We said our goodbyes with plans of seeing her next around dinnertime.

We perused the menus on restaurant windows until we found a place that looked quite funky. It said it served 'meat and veg' so we ordered exactly that and finished off with a little treat consisting of a cappuccino. The servers were good and the food very acceptable.

'I think we should make this our go-to place for lunch,' suggested Jeff. 'So wherever we are, we'll agree in advance to meet here and have some lunch together before attacking the rest of the day.'

'That's a great idea,' I replied.

That was good, we loved routine, and we were finding ours; we knew we were trapped there for a few more days than expected, but we could handle that if we had things to occupy us. We felt comfortable and welcome in what seemed to be our new sanctuary. After finishing every last morsel, plus a second cappuccino, we left the restaurant in higher spirits. Even *the lift of doom* couldn't wipe away our positive vibe – although Jeff did look twice at his nemesis, the staircase, as he limped past it.

Back in the NICU, we meticulously went through the motions of removing our shoes, scrubbing our hands, and donning the gowns to ensure we didn't bring any contamination into the ward to infect Cameron, or for that matter, any other baby.

As I rounded the corner into the ward ahead of Jeff, I saw a menagerie of medical staff around Cameron's incubator, including the top consultant, which was unusual in itself, especially since it wasn't time for rounds.

'Oh my God, what's happened?' I gasped, leaping the last few feet. The thought flashed through my mind that the top consultant's presence with people huddled around must mean something was seriously wrong.

By that time Cameron's hat and oxygen mask had been removed; the cute little woolly one with Velcro that held the mask to his face replaced by two tubes blowing oxygen just below his nose. Even with a little less equipment, he was still surrounded by a tangle of machinery, doctors, and nurses, who all seemed dour and concerned. It didn't look good.

'We are just consulting, madam,' said Doctor Sayed in response to my outburst. 'We have found some abnormalities in his blood work.'

'What sort of abnormalities?' I only just held my resolve, as I moved from such a nice, happy place during lunch, to one of fear and dread once again.

'Right now, we are just not sure,' Dr Sayed replied. 'We have already given him a course of antibiotics, but another infection has shown up. It might be something relatively benign, but there is no way of knowing. We must make a decision on whether to increase the strength of the antibiotic. The worst case is sepsis, which can be fatal for premature babies.'

One thing can be said for Dr Sayed. He never held anything back or sugar-coated it. He had revealed the full story instantly, all the potential worries and concerns, which was a simultaneous source of great relief and great anxiety.

'What should we do?' I asked.

'Inshalla. We have to wait and pray to God,' replied the consultant matter-of-factly. Then he returned to his group consultation, after which they made the decision to up the antibiotic strength slightly, as well as add another round.

By now I was beside myself. I knew that it was a different culture there, and that people used words differently. In the UK, if a doctor said *pray to God*, it normally meant the patient was on the brink of death. Living in the Middle East for so long, I knew the direct Arabic translation might be used with less gravity, but in this instance I wasn't sure what the doctor meant. Jeff knew there was nothing he could say that would better the situation and that whatever he might have said could have only served to make things worse. He knew the bond was the strongest between mother and baby, so I was sure he also knew that I felt the anguish in every cell of my body.

'Sorry, Mr Curtis,' said a nurse ever so quietly. 'One of the mothers wants to breastfeed, so we will have to ask you to leave the ward until she is done, just for now.'

'Of course,' Jeff replied. His head was hung low, he squeezed my hand as he turned and left the ward as requested and went back to the hotel, leaving me on my own with Cameron. Once again, we found ourselves separated and alone as we both contemplated what might happen next.

As our son's health started to deteriorate at an alarming rate, all we could do was wait.

Chapter 19

Daisy and Ermintrude

{Jeff}

Hours passed. Eventually, I decided to return to the hospital, only to be told to sit and wait outside while a mother breastfed. Before long Toni appeared once more at the lift door with a huge smile.

'Why are you out here?' she asked me. 'Shouldn't you be in there with Clare and Cameron?' She tipped her head sideways, bemused.

'I was thrown out. Someone wanted to breastfeed, so they asked me to leave.' I was dejected, having been outside for quite some time and felt something of a spare part. Again.

'I have come to help you buy your breast pump. Maybe we can get Clare, then go to the store before you guys go back to the hotel for some rest. You have been up for hours again.'

With the prospect of getting a breast pump, I managed to get a nurse's attention and pry Clare from Cameron's side. We took the *lift of doom* that provided its normal slow service, but once outside in fresh air we took a quick taxi to the shop.

On entering the shop, Toni asked the shopkeeper the critical question, 'Excuse me, do you take international credit cards?'

And when the reply came, 'Why, of course, madam,' all three of us stood there frozen to the spot, not sure that we could believe our ears.

Then, simultaneously, Clare and I picked up shopping baskets and started to pile baby appliances and accessories into them. It was the first time in days that our cards had worked, and a spot of retail therapy seemed just the salvation we needed. When we were done, we once again thanked Toni profusely for being a lifesaver; she had gone above and beyond the call of duty. By now we were exhausted, all of it had taken its toll on us in every way, unlike anything we had ever experienced before.

'Shall we get something to eat, then shower and sleep?' I asked Clare as we returned through the entrance of the hotel.

'No, I want to go back to the hospital,' Clare replied. 'I want to ensure Cameron is okay.'

'You are dog-tired and need rest, for Cameron's sake,' I replied firmly. 'You'll be no good to him right now anyway, so let's eat. The restaurant is right here, and then we'll go to the room.'

I had forgotten that Clare had not been to the hotel before. It was only our second day in Malé, but it felt like a month already. I was eager to show her our new home for the next few days.

'Okay, a quick bite and then I would like to see the room, sort my clothes and try the pump,' Clare said.

We took what was to become my usual seat in the restaurant and ordered a quick meal. As with breakfast, the meals were simple, quick, and tasty; just the right combination, for right then food was fuel with which we gained energy to help Cameron, and nothing else. When we were done, Clare followed me upstairs, where she was pleased to see we had two connecting rooms with an ensuite that gave us some space to spread out a little.

'What's this?' she said, pointing at the small dining table for two.

I had been busy in the early hours and unable to sleep, so I had moved the furniture around and set up station right next to the plug sockets, with everything charging, including both of my phones and my iPad.

'It's my Passport Acquisition Desk,' I replied and with a smile I puffed my chest out in jest. I then took the sterilising unit from its box and then the breast pump and placed them together on the desk next to the iPad. 'Actually, now it's my Breast-Pump-Sterilisation-and-Passport-Acquisition Desk!'' I chortled.

Clare joined me but was only able to offer a thin smile, and then she looked over at the piles of clothes I had meticulously created, when I had sorted the mix from the suitcases.

'You know,' said Clare who spoke louder as I had moved to the other room. 'I have just realised that I only have maternity clothes for the beach with me. It will take a week or two for my bump to go down; I don't have anything that fits!'

'Don't worry, I'm sure we can buy something or ask Toni,' I replied from the adjoining bedroom.

Suddenly I heard a very strange noise from the living room and wondered what an earth it might be. As I rounded the corner, I saw Clare standing there half-naked with her back to me.

'Good God what is that?' I feigned shock, while finishing in a laugh.

'It finished sterilising, so I thought I would try it,' Clare said. She turned around to reveal one exposed breast and the other covered with what looked like a plastic ice-cream cone plopped on the tip. Even more odd was the sound of a half-demented cow coming from the machine beside her, to which Clare was connected. The whole thing looked preposterous.

'This one is Ermintrude and this one is Daisy,' said Clare, pointing at each of her breasts in turn, and on that note, we had a light moment which we enjoyed as much as our guilty consciences would allow. In the back of our minds we knew poor Cameron was weathering a barrage of needles and new antibiotics back at the hospital, which sobered us quickly.

When our laughter subsided, I suggested we go to bed, so we could get up early to see Cameron. Clare replied, 'I'll be in once I have finished trying this breast pump. There is something coming out, but it's very limited.'

'More than earlier today, when the nurse manhandled you?' I asked in a failed effort to reignite the moment. Clare frowned; she hadn't found it at all funny. 'I'll come through in a minute,' she said, forcing that particular conversation to an abrupt end.

{Clare}

The next morning after a good sleep, things seemed slightly rosier. Jeff exited the shower to find me wearing purple pregnancy trousers and drowning in his large white shirt, complete with beach shoes and a hat that befitted a festive clown.

'What do you think?' I asked, as I took a modelling pose.

'Positively preposterous,' he beamed, and I was happy that he was able to find humour to start the day. It was a really positive step.

'Are you really going to wear that?' he asked me, bewildered when I didn't start to remove it. For a moment he thought I might be serious, as the days just kept getting more and more surreal, and then he realised that I was.

'I just need to be comfortable right now,' I answered. 'I know I look daft, but nobody knows us.'

'Fair enough,' he said, taking his oddly dressed wife by the hand and leading me down to breakfast.

We took up position in Jeff's normal spot and before we knew it my herbal tea and Jeff's double espresso had arrived. We ordered and ate as quickly as we could, then ran out to catch a taxi to the NICU.

After exiting our favourite lift, we quickly went through the NICU routine and, all gowned, rounded the corner into the ward, where we found another child placed in Cameron's old space.

We looked at each other with wide eyes; where on earth was Cameron?

'It's okay,' said a nurse from behind us. 'We moved him into his own ward. Since your husband spends more time in here than most of the other fathers, we thought it would give you some more privacy.' *Oh my God.* I thought to myself. As welcome as the gesture was, my heart was still beating out of my chest from the shock of not finding Cameron where we'd expected.

Jeff smiled his appreciation for the additional privacy, which also meant spending less time outside the ward. 'How are his bloods this morning? Does he still have an infection?'

I knew blood was drawn from each child every morning to scan for anything nasty, and I was also acutely aware Cameron had been suffering from some sort of infection the previous night, so I was hoping to start my day with some good news.

'It's good news, madam,' said the nurse, smiling. 'He still has a slight infection, but we've ruled out sepsis for the time being. Of course, it can return any time, so we have to be on the watch.'

Why do these people always have to end on a sour note? I thought. *Is there truly something to worry about? Are they just trying to keep a little perspective? Or are they just like that culturally?* I looked at Jeff for some answers and support. He smiled back as if to say, don't worry, it's good news for now, and that's all we can ask for.

The nurse suddenly thrust a piece of paper toward Jeff, causing him to look down upon it as if it were on fire. It was a prescription for all of the medicines that Cameron needed, and it was twice as long as the one he'd received the previous day. Jeff grimaced. He had only just arrived and was desperate to spend some time with Cameron. But he was being sent back out again.
{Jeff}

Fine, I thought. *Get the medicines, call International SOS, sit with Clare and Cameron, and then after lunch sit down at my Breast-Pump-Sterilisation-and-Passport-Acquisition Desk to sort out some UK paperwork.*

'My shopping list,' I said with a smile, and off I trundled on what I hoped wouldn't be another never-ending journey trawling the local pharmacies for everything on the list.

My hopes were to be dashed. After two stops, it felt as if somebody had called ahead to make sure that a maximum of only two medicines were available per pharmacy. Not only did none of the pharmacies have everything on the list, each only had a few items, which was distressing. Though I had to travel farther afield to do so, I eventually managed to collect everything on the list. Rather pleased with myself, I brought back my treasure trove and presented it to the nurse, who took the bundle of bags with a smile. And then as I tried to enter, she held up an authoritarian hand.

'Sorry, Mr Curtis, but another child was just admitted to your son's ward, and his mother is breastfeeding. It is not possible for you to come in right now.'

I wanted to complain – I wanted to say, *just move her to another room, I want to be with my family!* – but I thought better of it.

'Could you call my wife, please?' I asked politely, and the nurse fetched Clare as quickly as she could. Clare poked her head out of the NICU door, where I stood patiently in the vestibule.

'Hi, sorry,' she said, 'another mother…'

I gave her a look that she need go no further with her explanation.

I might as well start the hunt for Cameron's passport,' I said. 'Shall we meet for lunch at our place?'

Clare smiled. 'Yes, that's fab. I'll meet you there at 2pm.' She pecked me on the lips, then added, 'I have the lactation consultant coming in five minutes to give me some more help.'

'I presume that's something to do with breast milk production?' I asked, and Clare nodded.

'Cool, I'll see you at 1pm,' I said, just as the doors of the *lift of doom* binged closed, and it descended without me.

{Clare}

At a quarter to one, my stomach groaned. The lactation consultant had emphasised to me the importance of eating to produce breast milk, so I left off early to go to the restaurant, eager to fuel my body in order to feed our son. The simple circle of life. I was also looking forward to a few moments alone with Jeff. A thirty-minute respite over a grilled chicken wing would be pure heaven. When I entered, I was greeted by a man that I hadn't seen the previous day.

'A table for one for the beautiful lady?' he asked with a wry smile.

I looked at him and laughed inside. This guy obviously thought he was some form of charmer or maybe a joker, but I thought nothing more of it.

'A table for two please, my husband will be joining me soon,' I said.

The waiter smiled coyly, suggesting he thought that my words might be a ruse to scupper his flirtation.

'Of course, come this way. I can show you to a very private table, and the aircon is better over here.'

I followed him to the back of the restaurant, where it was indeed quite private, and I reflected that it might prove to be a hideaway for us in the coming days.

'May I help the lady with her shoes to be more comfortable?' And without waiting for an answer, he scooped up both of my feet and positioned them on the bench of the semi-circular booth. Then he took my shoes off and began to massage my feet.

'Thanks, but I don't think you want to massage those right now. They have seen better days, I'm afraid.' I was feeling a tad uncomfortable with him and found the whole situation rather odd.

'It's okay, madam, I know what women need.' Undaunted, he started to rub my shins in such a way that he seemed to be getting off. 'You look tense, why don't I give you a shoulder rub?' he said, lecherously.

And just like that, he jumped up and suddenly moved behind me, trying to rub my shoulders. He then started to get rough, making me feel like I was being pinned to the seat, I tried to get up; but he only intensified his pressure.

'Wait! Stop!' I finally demanded.

Only then did I realise, far too late, that this guy wanted to be more than flirtatious. His hands were all over my shoulders and he pushed down toward my breasts. I looked around for someone to help, but then I realised that he had put me so far in the back corner of the restaurant, so close to the noise and clatter of the kitchen, that nobody could have heard or seen what was going on.

Suddenly I felt very scared. I felt sick, like it would never end. I was being violated. *Where is Jeff?* I thought. He was always five minutes early. 'Please, stop!' I begged, angrily. 'I just gave birth to a premature baby only forty-eight hours ago!'

When he still didn't stop, I screamed, 'Please! Leave me alone!' Being the eldest of two girls born to a father who always ensured his daughters were streetwise, I suddenly remembered what he had taught me and how to get situations like that under control. I smacked his hands as hard as I could, and then tried to push him away. Only he caught my wrist and tried, in vain due to my resistance, to force my hand into his trousers.

'My husband will be here any minute,' I growled. 'You fucking touch me one more time and I'm calling the police. My husband's on his way and he won't be happy!'

That lecher just did not understand the word *no*. He came closer and this time launched himself at my breasts. Nobody was going to help me, and I had to stop it myself. Somehow, I managed to turn sideways and use his own weight as a counterbalance, which sent him crashing headfirst with a crunch into the side of the bench seat. I turned to him and he was looking less aggressive.

'This is your last warning. I have had a shit couple of days, I don't need this, and I don't need to fight off scumbags like you.'

He looked beaten, he begun to apologise but I would have none of it. I quickly gathered my things, unsure of what to do next, unsure of what on earth had just happened. Had I led him on? But how could I have? For God's sake, I looked like Coco the clown.

When I reached the main part of the restaurant my legs felt weak, and I didn't have full command of myself. I made a beeline for the booth we had sat in the previous day, out in the middle of the restaurant. I just hoped the waiter hadn't followed me, but I dared not look back. I plonked down just as Jeff came through the door, smiling, totally unaware of what I had just been through.

He seemed happy to see me waiting for him in our new hideaway, where we had hoped we could pretend, for a few brief moments a day, that we weren't trapped on a desert island with a sick premature son, unable to move him due to the world's bureaucracy.

'Hey, how's ma boy?' He mimicked his own father's words.

'Yeah, he's fine,' I said flatly, looking back into the restaurant and watching my attacker dusting himself off after his fall. I felt sick inside, violated, but in a weird part of my brain my British sense of humour was thinking, *Well, if you can attract a man's attention looking like this...* Or was that just my defence mechanism? Was I actually in a state of shock? I felt I needed a bath, to wash the filthy memory of his hands away. He hadn't got that far but I was very scared and very angry. I suddenly felt very alone on a small island in the middle of a huge ocean, despite Jeff being right there at the table.

‘What’s wrong?’ Jeff asked, concerned at my obvious discomfort.

‘Oh, nothing. Nothing.’

He could tell something was wrong. And it didn’t have to do with Cameron, as he knew I would have said so straight away. He knew I was trying to conceal something. So he pressed on.

‘Clare. It’s me, Jeff! What’s wrong? There is obviously something I am missing here.’ I looked up at him, guilt and fear in my eyes.

‘I think I’ve just been molested.’

Chapter 20

The Green Stuff

{Clare}

'What the fuck?' Jeff leapt up from the table, his eyes searched the restaurant for the unknown culprit.

'Jeff, you need to calm down,' I stated firmly.

'Calm down? What the–? What on earth?'

'Please.' I begged.

Jeff couldn't find the words or the attacker, so he sat back down. He needed to control his anger; right then if he had found that guy, it would have been likely that he would have ripped his head clean off.

'Okay, tell me what happened and what you want to do about it,' he said as calmly as his fury would allow.

I explained most of what happened as Jeff listened. When I got to the end, he was beside himself. His agitation was obvious, so I tried to placate him, 'The last thing I want is to have a huge issue with locals and the police. The only thing that matters right now is Cameron and getting off this God-forsaken island.'

He looked at me with proverbial smoke coming out of his ears.

'Let's just get up and walk out,' I said, 'then forget this place ever existed.' I looked directly at him. 'I'm made of strong stuff. Let's just erase this from our minds and move on with life!'

And so, that's exactly what we did. We simply got up and walked toward the exit to leave. Adrenaline surged inside Jeff's body. As I held his arm, I felt every muscle expand from its normal size as he tensed them. We both knew for Cameron's sake that there was nothing Jeff could do to better the situation. We were guests in a foreign land, and any aggressive move he might make would no doubt have serious repercussions for all of us, not least Cameron. I laid my hand knowingly on his elbow, as he opened the front door we slipped out onto the street.

Not only had we not eaten lunch, something both of us so desperately needed, we had lost our sanctuary, a place in which we could momentarily escape the harsh world outside and pretend that our predicament didn't exist. As we walked up the street, it reminded me that we didn't belong here on Malé Island, where at any moment something untoward could befall any of us.

'Let's just get a sandwich and head back to the ward,' I said, as I felt like I just wanted to hide away in the hospital and be with Cameron.

We bought two sandwiches from the vendor at the entrance to the hospital. By that time we didn't really care what kind, scoffing them down at the elbow-high tables nearby. Then we headed back for our ride in the *lift of doom* up to the NICU. Rather surprisingly, after a shorter wait than usual, we found ourselves back in NICU, washed up, sanitised and ready to see Cameron.

As I looked around, I was astounded at how many other premature babies there were in the hospital. It had filled up again, presumably more patients coming from the outer Maldivian islands. Maybe it was something in the sea air, or to do with the storm, that had brought on an outbreak of early births?

Once again, a crowd had gathered around Cameron's incubator, where our pale-skinned, blond-haired, blued-eyed premature baby continued to be a curiosity to inquisitive admirers.

'Hello, everything okay?' I asked as I pulled up a plastic chair next to Cameron's crib.

'No,' came the level reply from the head consultant. 'We have found some green liquid in the bag of his feed tube. We think it may be sepsis.'

These were words every parent in NICU dreaded.

'Oh, my God!' I exclaimed. 'Are you sure?'

'Well, it could be the start of bile production in his stomach,' said the consultant.

'So, it could be a really good thing, or it could be a really bad thing; but we just don't know at this point? Is that what you are saying?' Jeff asked from behind me.

{Jeff}

From my point-of-view, it was way too soon to speculate, especially since the medical staff seemed to thrive on delivering negative information.

'I suppose you could put it like that,' the consultant replied. 'Although it's a little early for bile production in the stomach. That's why we believe that it is highly likely that it's sepsis.'

Clare put her head in her hands. 'What do we do now?'

'We pray to God,' the consultant replied.

I had already decided to stay at the hospital to give Clare and Cameron moral support, rather than return to the makeshift office where I would only be worried and distracted. Assessing the situation, I knew Cameron was on zero oxygen assistance by then and breathing normal air, which was a great development, despite the latest news. However, I had detected that our son was a little yellow again, which prompted me to ask, 'Is that normal?'

The consultant replied, 'He does still have jaundice, but that is pretty normal even for full-term babies, so it's the least of our concerns. If he can get through the next round of antibiotics infection free, we will start the light therapy.'

At that I pulled up my own plastic chair, and sat beside Clare, and together we both looked at Cameron. He seemed to be managing everything quite brilliantly, notwithstanding the total rollercoaster ride of the last few days. He had jaundice but now he was producing the green stuff to boot.

What a good kid, I thought. Cameron just got on with it, barely stopping to cry along the way. In fact, Cameron was such a chilled baby that the staff put babies who would not stop crying on either side of him, in the hope of calming them. Indeed, the staff even started to call him, 'Calm Cam'.

'Excuse me, Mr Curtis.'

The pleasant request came from the nurse behind me, the one responsible for looking after Cameron during the dayshift. I spun round.

'I am so sorry to ask, but a mother would like to breastfeed. As you know, you'll need to leave the NICU.'

In the circumstances, of course, it was certainly a reasonable request, but what was not understandable was why the mothers were not moved into another room and the door closed, leaving everyone satisfied. Yet, as always, I smiled and promptly complied with the request. I got up from my plastic chair, replaced it in the corner, having only gained a small respite in the seated position over the last few days.

'I'll go back to the hotel and make some calls, see if I can speed up the passport process,' I said. And with that, I left.

Back at the hotel, I sat in a chair staring at the wall. A fully charged breast pump sat on one side, next to a fully sterile steriliser. Plugged into the wall and charging were my phones and iPad. I stared at magnolia wall paint that wasn't actually such a bad view, compared to the view out of the window, which was a building site heaped with rubbish. I already had plenty of those waiting for us at home in the ever-expanding metropolis of Dubai.

Considering my options, I made the decision to fly back to Dubai overnight. I desperately needed to run some errands and once there I planned to knock on a few doors to see if I could arrange any emergency travel document for Cameron. I'd just finished booking the flights when the phone rang. It was International SOS. They would call once or twice daily to check in, support relatives when things were tense, chat about the patient's condition, and ensure the medical care being received was acceptable.

I spoke to the representative for about thirty minutes. On the one hand, I filled them in on the developments with Cameron and Clare, letting them know what was being done without conveying a sense of panic; on the other hand, as when I had first spoken with them from Manadhoo Island, I emphasised the continual challenges and desperate need to leave the island as soon as possible.

It seemed that International SOS were also talking to the nurses in the hospital, so they had got a broad overview of the situation, although I felt to a degree that the nurses were overselling the quality of medical care delivered. The nursing care was certainly without reproach, but I had to admit, due to the facilities and lack of substantial funding, the hospital could well be described as sub-par to most anywhere else in the rest of the Western world. Truth be told, we needed to get Cameron out.

When I hung up, I felt better. Someone was out there who could help us, eventually. I requested International SOS also start speaking with Clare, both to get a fuller picture and because she had started to feel very isolated, especially after what had happened earlier in the day.

Eventually I turned to the task of calling the UK passport office. But when I searched on the Internet, there didn't seem to be a department that dealt with precisely what I needed. Not just because our case was so extreme, but also because it was unclear which number was appropriate for people calling from outside the UK. I sighed and dialled one anyway.

'Hello,' I said politely. 'I am stuck in the Maldives with my wife, who has just given birth to our two-month-premature son.' I elaborated as necessary and ultimately reached the point, 'We need help getting back into Dubai. We need to get a five-year passport for him.'

The woman was of no help whatsoever, wishing us well and transferring me to another section. There I sat on hold for what seemed like forever. It gave me a strange feeling like the frustration of sitting in a black cab stuck in London traffic with the meter ever ticking but without actually going anywhere. My phone credit depleted with every second I spent on hold.

'Hello,' a bored voice eventually said.

'Hi,' I said, but after relating my story, she replied, 'I am sorry. I am sure that you would prefer to be at home, but in these situations, we cannot deal with the passport.'

She then transferred me to another department that proved to be equally unhelpful and indifferent to our plight. I was coming to realise that Cameron had slipped into a bureaucratic void in which no department was qualified or brave enough to act. Whatever image presented itself in the minds of those people, it certainly hadn't been of a sick premature baby with tubes sticking out of his stomach, mouth, legs, arms, hands, and head, who was turning yellow and who showed positive for green liquid coming out of his mouth.

Dejected, I stared out of the window at the rubbish that lay unattended in the construction site opposite and watched the street, where thousands of scooters were driving chaotically in every direction. Just when I thought it couldn't get any worse, I noticed that a hard, tropical rain had started to fall outside.

My thoughts continued to darken until they were jerked back to the present by the telephone I held. It erupted in a loud buzzing. 'Hello?' I said in a monotone as I answered it.

'Hey man, it's Luis,' said a friendly voice.

Luis was Portuguese but had met his Scottish wife Mhairi in Bahrain twelve years previously, before moving to Dubai. His English was so impeccable that you would be forgiven for assuming he was British, and he even exhibited an occasional Scottish twang. We counted Luis and Mhairi amongst our closest friends.

Luis had heard from his wife what had happened and was sure that I would make a mad dash back to Dubai to sort everything and refuse to accept any help. He was right. But during the call Luis made a fine argument and I agreed to let him help.

After thanking Luis profusely, I dived into the long list of documents and their locations. When I put the phone down, I felt humbled and reassured. With unbelievable pressure on my shoulders, I was glad to have good friends back home.

A short while later I arrived at NICU where Toni was waiting for me with a beaming smile.

'Hi,' she said, 'I'm not stopping long, but I thought Clare might want to borrow some more clothes. She held out a large, stuffed bag. 'Clare is a little taller than me, but some of this might fit.'

'What a nice thought,' I said. 'Thank you.'

'Have you sorted your passport issue?' she asked.

'No, it seems to be escalating. In fact, we may be here longer than expected at this rate, but I daren't tell Clare that.'

'I'll see you tomorrow anyway,' she said. We had seen her intermittently numerous times since our impromptu island incarceration. She had been unbelievably helpful, and just a good friend. She continued, 'If there is no resolution, I'll take you to see a friend of mine who can help, if anyone can. He's the Minister of Tourism.'

'Thank you, Toni. I appreciate it,' and with that she went on her way; but when I rounded the corner at NICU, the look on Clare's face immediately told me something was seriously wrong.

Oh God, I thought, *what now? Could anything more go wrong?* 'What is it?' I asked.

'They think Cameron may have a hole in his stomach,' she replied, as tears flowed down her cheeks.

Chapter 21

The Mosquito

{Clare}

Jeff held up his hands in a calming manner. 'Okay,' he said evenly to me. 'What are they doing about it?'

'They are waiting for a portable X-ray machine so that they can have a look inside his tiny stomach. If they find something, then it is possible to deal with it, but not here in Malé. He would have to be moved to somewhere else. But with his paperwork issues, they are just not sure where.'

'Okay,' Jeff said again, already deep in thought as what to do next. 'Let's take one step at a time. When the portable machine arrives, we'll learn if they find anything. Let's hope they don't. If they do, we'll deal with it then.'

So we sat and waited for hours, as the portable machine was in high demand. By then it was also very late at night and well beyond visiting hours for fathers; but the nurses took pity and allowed Jeff to stay with me, given Cameron's potentially serious condition.

Finally, the machine arrived, and the X-ray was taken. The radiologists then consulted with the nurses, and hushed whispers were spoken out of earshot of anxious parents.

'I can see a black hole, or mass on the X-ray!' I shot at Jeff. 'Oh my God it's bad news,' I cried in anguish. Jeff could see what I meant but we were too far away to really see the X-ray properly. Yet there was definitely a black portion in the middle of the body. We were ragged with worry, trying in vain to read someone's lips and decipher what was happening. Then the radiologists departed with concerned looks, taking the huge machine with them, but they never divulged a word to us.

Jeff couldn't hold back any longer. 'What did they find?' he demanded of anyone who would listen. The nurses all looked at him sheepishly and walked away without answering, leaving us highly upset and confused.

'Excuse me,' Jeff said to a junior female doctor we had seen in the corridor. 'Can you help? We really need some answers.'

The doctor came in and examined the X-ray. As she did, not for the first time in the last 72 hours I studied the expressions on her face for any reaction, anything that might give us a clue to the result. She moved to the end of the table and made a phone call, and then turned to Jeff and said, 'The consultant will be up to see you shortly.' That was it.

Shortly meant a few more hours, so as time inched into the wee hours of the night, Jeff and I lived on frayed nerves. We had been approaching twenty-four hours without rest again. When the consultant finally arrived, we both stood to attention.

'I am sorry to have kept you, but we had an emergency on the children's ward,' he said. 'I have looked at your son's X-ray and I can't see anything on there to be concerned about. Bear in mind he likely has sepsis, but he is on the best antibiotics and his last bloods indicated a lowering of the infection. So, Mr and Mrs Curtis, I ask you to please go home and get some rest.'

We weren't sure whether to be happy that the green regurgitation wasn't caused by a blockage, or to be concerned that he still had a serious infection; but we really had no choice, so we did as the doctor suggested. We once again turned to our little baby boy and kissed him goodnight. It just didn't feel right that we had to leave him every night. As we exited the hospital, taxis were in abundance and the streets were eerily quiet, except for an occasional scooter or two whizzing past. This enabled us to arrive back at the hotel in record time.

I took the sterilised cones for the breast pump out of the steriliser and turned on the infernal machine to milk Daisy and Ermitrude. Jeff made a beeline for the bed and crashed into a deep sleep with his clothes on, again.

{Jeff}

The next morning, I awoke to what sounded like a cow dying in the next room. I promptly pulled open the door to see Clare sitting on the sofa staring into space with a cone over Daisy.

'Have you been pumping all night, or did you just get up?' I asked, as that was the exact position I remembered last seeing her in, the night before.

'No, I just got up. I am pumping every three hours presently, like clockwork, and I am getting more milk now. See?' she showed me.

'But still, it's not coming out in the hundreds of millilitres, just tens and twenties, so I have a long way to go and it's getting rather painful.'

'That's more than enough milk for now,' I said. 'As long as you keep ahead of Cameron's feeding plan, it will be fine.'

Cameron was actually not yet taking breast milk until the infection or whatever it was cleared. This gave Clare some time. But as soon as Cameron was able, he would need three ml of breast milk every three hours, which would quickly elevate to five ml then seven ml and eventually ten ml. The idea was to get his stomach working with low doses. Being so premature he hadn't yet developed his sucking ability, so couldn't yet take milk from his mother's nipple or for that matter a teat from a bottle, so we were a little unsure of the exact procedure to feed him.

'I know we don't need it yet,' Clare said, 'but still I'm not producing as much as some mothers and I feel like I am being left behind.'

'You always do,' I countered. It had come out a little harsher than intended. 'It will be fine, you watch. Your milk will come as soon as Cameron needs it. Your body will do it completely subconsciously.'

'I may need medicine to increase the milk flow though.'

'Okay,' I replied. 'And so what if you do? After all you've been through, and I do mean *all*, that really is the least of our worries. What day is it today, anyway?'

'It's Wednesday, why?'

'I have completely lost track of time. I thought it was Thursday already.' Days had passed like the scenery on a bullet train and the rollercoaster had got faster and bumpier.

'Let's go down for some breakfast,' Clare suggested. I realised I was famished again, and wholeheartedly agreed.

{Clare}

'Eggs this morning, sir?' asked the server of Jeff.

'Yes, please,' said Jeff, 'and maybe a chocolate croissant, too.'

I raised my eyebrows, as it was completely off routine for Jeff to consume both gluten and sugars together.

'What the hell?' Jeff said as he flapped his arms to show he didn't care. 'Worse things happen at sea. Can you make the double-espresso into a flat white as well, please?' he continued dangerously. Clearly, caution had gone to the wind.

'What the hell? I'll have exactly the same thing,' I said with a smile, cognizant that Jeff was having a 'timeout' and feeling I needed to join him.

Although wearing Toni's clothes, and feeling better for that than wearing the preposterous outfit of yesterday, I was still very aware of my protruding, post-natal bump. *What the hell is an extra bit of sugar going to do now?* I thought. *Caution to the wind!*

When we finished, we were full to bursting. Jeff walked me to the corner where I caught an overcrowded taxi and off I went to keep vigil over Cameron.

I arrived at the hospital alone. Over the last twelve hours I had accumulated more milk than before and was quite pleased with myself. This put a smile on my face, which I still wore as I approached to the nurse's station.

'I've brought my milk in,' I said to matron, with whom I had built a good relationship with over the short time. She had helped me learn how to produce milk and what I needed to do as a new mother. For the first time in ages it felt to me like I had done something right. I proudly unzipped the cooler bag to show the matron, only to find to my absolute horror and devastation that the milk had leaked out of the bottle, into the bag and onto the floor. In my haste I had not put the lid on correctly!

I looked at the milk on the floor and then slowly up to the matron. Tears stung my eyes. Of all the things that had happened in the last few days, it suddenly felt like I had hit a new low. I let out a little sob, and said, 'Can I do anything right?'

The matron was having none of it. 'Your baby needs feeding, and you need to express some more.'

'Express some more!?' I gasped. 'It took me twelve hours to get that lot, and my boobs and my nipples are so sore!' Although sympathetic to my feelings, the matron took my arm firmly and led me into an empty room and sat me down. I felt completely numb as the matron got to work on Ermitrude.

{Jeff}

I returned to the hotel room to start firing off emails after I mentally sorted out all the different time zones – the Maldives, Dubai and London. I finished my task relatively quickly and then headed to the hospital, which I decided to do on foot with a large umbrella swinging over my head to repel the torrential rain that seemed never ending.

As I entered the hospital, shaking off the excess water, I looked at my watch and realised it hadn't taken as long as I expected, despite having limped most of way due to my toe injury. My big toe was still very black and blue, and sore as hell.

'That looks painful,' a voice said from behind me, and when I turned round, I was pleased to find the honorary consul who bounded gleefully toward me. 'Is that broken?' he asked, pointing to my swollen toe.

'I'm not sure,' I replied. 'But it hurts like hell.'

'Well, you certainly don't want it X-rayed here,' Paul snorted.

'Oh, why?' I said, suddenly very concerned. 'Are the X-rays no good here?'

'No, it's not that. I just don't want to open a third file for your family.'

We burst out laughing. It was a truly funny comment that had caught me completely off guard, but it felt so good to really laugh from the bottom of my belly. The stress of those last few days needed any relief it could get, even if only temporary, and I only wished Clare was there to enjoy it too.

'Are you going up to see Cameron?' Paul enquired seriously.

'Yes, I'm joining Clare until London opens. She arrived a few hours ago. Then I'll continue my quest for the right documents to allow us all to travel back to Dubai.'

'Okay, well, I just came down to check on you and make sure you were alright. Please give her my best. I'll drop by the hotel later.'

'Sure,' I replied, but Paul hesitated. 'Unfortunately, Mr Curtis, and I think I should tell you this now, so you don't get your hopes up, I think this is going to take more than a week to sort out.'

I felt my stomach sink, as it confirmed what I had been dreading.

'I'm afraid Cameron has fallen into a category that has never been thought of before. Getting a five-year passport isn't that easy, even in emergency conditions.'

Paul paused, then continued uneasily. 'Even though I have borne witness to seeing Cameron and have indeed taken a photo of his blue eyes and blond hair, there are no five-year passports on the horizon, no chance of being admitted to Dubai, and no way to get to the UK on medical grounds.'

'How about Singapore?' I asked immediately.

'It's possible, I guess, but why?'

'Well, I have a lot of friends there, and it's closer and has an excellent medical centre.'

I was quite happy with myself for having just thought of a new option. If we were going to have to stay someplace away from home for a month or more, this could work well as I had travelled there on business numerous times and knew the city well.

'Let me check what documents they would need,' Paul said. 'I will let you know tonight.'

We parted and I carried on toward the lift, but now in deep trepidation of just how long this whole ordeal was going to last. Just as I finished my sanitation routine at NICU. I entered the ward and found Clare sitting with Cameron inside her shirt. At that point Cameron didn't need oxygen assistance, so he could be handled much more easily, despite the interlacing tubes that went in and out of him.

'What's this?' I asked. I was both surprised and pleased at the same time, a smile formed on my face.

'It's KMC,' said Clare with a satisfied smile, as she held her own baby again. 'Kangaroo Mother Care. It's what Doctor Mehedi must have read about, the idea of skin-to-skin contact that started in South America not so long ago. Apparently, they have used it extensively and it's claimed to improve survival rate substantially. So here I am!'

'Well, you are positively glowing,' I said, as I continued to smile. 'And Cameron looks very comfortable all wrapped up in Mummy's shirt.'

'You know,' Clare then said to me, 'it's not stopped raining all day, and it seems to be getting worse.' She shot a worried look outside the window.

'Welcome to the islands,' I replied. I was uncertain of what she was getting at, so I was unsure how to reply as I detected a hint of worry in her voice.

'With the rains come mosquitos, and with mosquitos come disease, and although it's not a huge issue here, there are known cases of dengue fever.'

As absurd as it had initially sounded, Clare had not been kidding; she was quite serious.

'I am sure that there aren't any in Malé,' I countered. 'I've not heard that it's prevalent in this area.' I hoped this would conclude the issue and stop Clare from worrying.

'Okay, but there are other nasties like malaria,' she continued undeterred. 'I mean, look! The window is open over there, you can hear and see the rain, yet there is no mosquito net.'

Realising she was right, I turned to a nurse. 'Excuse me, do you know the window is open?'

'Yes, thank you,' the nurse replied. 'We like to have fresh air for the babies.'

'But what about mosquitos?' I replied.

'A small bite won't hurt. Besides, the fresh air is good for them.'

'But what about dengue fever and malaria?' I pressed.

The nurse just laughed quietly as she walked away, it had been as if I were joking. But I wasn't at all convinced, and though I felt the care was generally very good, it struck me there was a relaxed attitude to diseases from insects, maybe something historic that made them complacent toward such risks, which were commonplace in the islands.

By the time I turned around, Cameron had been returned to his open incubator. Although KMC was amazing, apparently there can also be the potential for over-stimulation. But more importantly, Cameron was off antibiotics as infections seemed, for a while, to have subsided and without the protruding tubes that he originally had inserted in his bellybutton, it was time for him to receive his first breast milk fed through the feed tube.

{Clare}

'I have some of your breast milk here,' the nurse said looking directly at me. 'We will try him on three ml, and if he holds it down and nothing comes back up his feed tube, then we should be able to increase him to four or five ml on the next feed.'

'Okay, let's try,' I said. Jeff and I held hands; we had both been willing with all our heart, with all the positive will in the world, that it would be successful. *Please, no more green stuff!* I thought.

To feed Cameron, the nurse put three ml into the syringe connected to the end of the tube in Cameron's mouth that went directly to his stomach and lightly depressed the plunger just a smidge and then removed it to start the gravity flow.

'It's quite slow, isn't it?' Jeff said. The flow was very slow; but in the grand scheme of things, the slower the better: the smoother the better. Just three ml of liquid goodness slowly but surely drained into Cameron's stomach before our very eyes.

We waited, and stared wide-eyed at Cameron and his feed tube, and waited to see if any green mucus or milk would flow back up the tube. Then, a little milk splashed back out.

'Oh no!' I exclaimed. 'There is a problem, it's come back up.'

'No, no, it's okay,' the nurse said reassuringly. 'That's just a very small drop that was still in the syringe. It looks fine, it looks like he has taken it well.' The nurse smiled genuinely and looked positively relieved.

'Okay then,' the nurse said. 'I'll be back in a minute and we'll see how he's doing, but for now, it looks good.' And then she walked over to the next incubator to feed the next baby in turn.

Feeling energised, I allowed a positive feeling to wash over me. I had been pushing any positive feelings away, not allowing myself to feel too good in case something went wrong. And then I saw it – two of them, actually.

'Jeff,' I said sternly but quietly, whispering so as not to wake the sleeping Cameron. 'Do you see it?'

Jeff rubbed his eyes. 'See what?' he replied. 'What am I looking at?'

I pointed, dancing my finger up and down.

Jeff followed my finger and then looked at me as if I might have finally gone mad.

'It's a bloody mosquito! Two of them, look. You have to kill them before they bite Cameron.'

Jeff's chin dropped.

For the next few minutes, Jeff followed one of the mosquitos around the incubator. But there was no way to swat it without wreaking havoc on all the wires.

After about fifteen minutes, the mosquito settled on the electric socket, which is when Jeff desperately swatted at it with his hand; but he was too late. It danced in mid-air, where he tried clapping and squashing it between his palms. The first time he missed, so he tried again, and again and again and again. I noticed the nurses began to watch him intently, no doubt they wondered what on earth he was doing.

{Jeff}

Then I saw the second mosquito, and with my peripheral vision watched them both as they landed simultaneously on the same solid surface away from any important equipment. I swatted hard with my left hand and then my right, then again with my left and then with both hands.

I looked out of the window to help refocus my eyes and became conscious that the rain fell harder. It had been going non-stop for nearly thirty-six hours. 'Just don't sit there, can you help me?' I said to Clare. Actually, it was less a question and more a statement of exasperation. I needed help with these evasive monsters.

Clare begrudgingly rose from her chair and began to do the same thing – chase, swat, clap, stomp, equally to no avail.

Thus, as Wednesday drew to a close, the nurses of Malé's IGMH hospital's NICU stood motionless and completely bewildered by this strange European couple performing what could only be described as some form of primitive rain dance, that consisted of an elaborate hand-slapping and foot stomping ritual around the incubator that held their sick premature son.

Chapter 22

The Flood

{Jeff}

Thursday morning; we woke to the clapping of thunder and flashing of lightning. Cameron had been stable for twelve hours, which was comforting, but we could only wonder what would happen next.

It was still dark outside, with weather reminiscent of the night Cameron was born, a storm that felt so violent it could make the gods shudder. I got up and looked out of the window. It reminded me of my mother's words when I was a young boy, not to look out of the window in a lightning storm. Fear gripped me.

I looked down at the construction site and the huge hole that yesterday had been ready to receive a foundation of cement. It had started to look like a swimming pool filled to the brim with brown, murky water. The rain had swallowed it, leaving only a brown, glassy surface. As I looked out to the distance, it dawned on me that where roads ran the day before, only canals ran that day, it was like the waters of a rural Venice. Where scooters once drove, only boats could pass.

'You know,' I started, looking over to Clare who was lying in bed with her head buried in her pillow. 'It doesn't look good out there. I think we may be sinking.'

'Don't be so dramatic,' she said, pulling the pillow off her head. She wrestled out of bed, shuffled across the room, and proceeded to hook up Daisy. Or was it Ermintrude?

'Seriously, I cannot see any firm ground,' I said pensively. 'Literally just water. Malé is so flat the water has nowhere to go.' I looked over and realised that Clare was only half listening. She had adjourned to the front room and had started up the infernal machine that sounded like a half-demented cow, which was providing a vacuum to suck the milk out of her.

I showered, then dressed and thought I would go down and speak to reception, since no one else in our world would be awake yet. 'It seems very bleak out there,' I said to the receptionist, as I exited the lift on the ground floor.

'Good morning, Mr Curtis. You are earlier today than usual. I'm afraid the restaurant isn't even open yet. But yes, it seems we have caught the end of a tropical storm. The rains have come very heavily, which means that the island we are on may suffer from flooding for a while. It's not that usual, but it does happen.'

So I returned to the room where Clare was just dressing. 'How bad is it out there?' she asked me.

'Bad enough. I think the taxis will get through, but it's over a foot deep in spots. A mosquito's perfect habitat,' I finished with the thought of last night's mosquito debacle too readily in my mind.

By the time we got ready the restaurant had opened. We ate and then walked out to get a taxi. With my big toe so swollen it couldn't fit into a shoe, I was only wearing flip-flops, one of which I immediately lost in the torrent of water running along the kerb outside the hotel.

{Clare}

I sat in the small reception, as Jeff left me to go and change his footwear. I then realised I hadn't contacted my work to let them know I may be delayed. I decided it was best to SMS message my managing director with an update. He had been a great support so far, and had told me I did not need to worry about things on the ground. Ever the professional, I wrote him another message which read, 'Hi Nigel, we had a nerve-racking day yesterday as Cameron was sick during the previous night and we feared infection. He is stable again and we have resumed his tube feeding so we are moving forward again. (As you can imagine, we are pretty knackered.) Still no final date on moving but we hope Monday. Can you let me know who is taking over which of my clients and I will start to draft the relevant emails to them, DFSA and copy in the right people internally? As always, if you need me, just text and will get back ASAP.'

I still have this on my phone today and look at it from time to time. It reminds me of the peculiar situation that we found ourselves in back then.

{Jeff}

Up in the room I searched for some suitable attire. Until that point, I had been wearing beach clothes every day and had only packed one pair of beach shoes. To mix it up, I decided to put on some Chelsea boots I had brought in case of any hotel policy on dining. Shorts, a T and a pair of brown Chelsea boots was my attire for that day. If my wife could get away with dressing unconventionally, then so could I.

When I exited the lift to reception, I caught Clare by surprise with my new outfit. 'What do you look like?' she gasped.

We both rolled our eyes simultaneously.

I grabbed her hand and led her out of the hotel. The rainfall had become lighter, but the gutter was still a torrent. We managed to get a taxi straight away, a record, a miracle or both, especially given the floodwater was up to the bonnet. I felt like we were on a boat again, and how the carburettors did not flood was beyond me.

We arrived at the hospital to find a huge crowd waiting for a taxi. Though the driver helped us out, I grimaced when I still managed to dunk my right boot into the water and get soaked. I was fast running out of footwear.

When we arrived at NICU, the predictable happened. I was handed another long list of medicines that meant I'd be turning around and going back out into the flood. Familiar with the routine, I headed out the hospital door and promptly bumped into several other NICU fathers with the same mission in mind.

'The water is too high!' one yelled, as he looked at the flooded road before us.

'There is no way to get across,' said another as he backed up a step.

I surveyed the water level and said, 'Well, I guess we'll have to brave it.' With that I waded out into the knee-deep current, struggling not to further injure my foot as I pushed through the water that was carrying all sorts of muck.

'Let us know how you get on,' someone yelled to my back, as I felt the cold wetness saturating my socks. I cursed myself for the stupidity as I wore my expensive boots outside today in the first place. What had I been thinking?

When I reached the first pharmacy, I was greeted as the first customer of the day, but as usual could only secure a couple of the medicines needed. After a few hours of wading through freezing water, approaching every pharmacy within several blocks of the hospital, I had almost collected what I needed and started to venture back. But I still lacked one item on list. I could only hope they still had a supply left in the ward.

I handed the nurse the white paper bag full of goodies.

'Thank you,' she said, then glanced down at my boots. I followed her eyes to the pieces of twisted leather that looked like they had been stolen from a homeless person; all sodden and wrecked, they were no longer good to anybody.

'You know, you are the only father to have brought medicine so far today,' she said, almost in consolation for the state of my shoes.

'I couldn't get one particular item,' I said, pointing at an indescribable word on the list. 'Do you have it in stock? Is it important?' I wanted to understand the size of my dilemma.

'Unfortunately, we do need this one and we are almost out in the whole ward. In fact, there is a low stock everywhere. We aren't even sure how we can get any more at this point,' the nurse said with remorse. To top it all off, there was a mother breast-feeding, and although I only intended to stay a few minutes and see my son, that seemed out of the question.

With no other options, I decided to attempt to return to the Breast-Pump- Sterilisation-and-Passport-Acquisition Desk at the hotel. Outside the hospital it was a zoo, everyone tried every which way for a taxi, so I trudged several blocks in the murky flood water until I managed to flag a car not yet swamped by needy passengers.

{Clare}

At the hospital, the nurses were trying to organise a routine brain scan for Cameron. They would normally have called up one of the two portable machines, but as fate would have it, one was temporarily out of order and as a result the other was in unusually high demand.

I was told that all premature babies have bleeds on the brain, and not to worry too much if something showed on the scan planned for Cameron. Most bleeds occurred in an insignificant part of the brain's right cortex and were benign. Of course, some bleeds did require an operation, which would have been tricky in the circumstances, as that was not something the Malé hospital could handle. And given the weather conditions, there was zero chance to secure a medevac anytime soon.

'For now, we have no choice but to transport him to another part of the hospital for the scan,' the nurse told me. We transferred Cameron from his open incubator into a huge, old-fashioned, covered incubator. I watched with a general sense of worry, as all the wires and tubes were disconnected and reconnected to my tiny baby before the enormous contraption and its myriad working parts was wheeled to the *lift of doom.*

In my growing unease, I couldn't help but notice that the hole cut out of the side of the incubator for the wires and tubes had not been sealed. It was just a gaping hole. *Didn't that defeat the object of transferring Cameron in a covered incubator?* I thought to myself. I was unsure whether to point this out to the nurse – *surely they knew what they were doing?* – but it was my son after all, and I didn't want to unnecessarily expose him to the elements while outside the sterile ward. After a few minutes of internal negotiation, I finally blurted it out and confronted the nurse about the hole.

'Don't worry,' the nurse replied compassionately as she took some linen and draped it over the hole. 'How's that?'

Though I was not completely satisfied, that did seem a fair compromise under the circumstances. The main goal was to conduct the brain scan as quickly as possible to ascertain if there were any further problems in terms of Cameron's health.

Eventually we made our way down to the ground floor, where we manoeuvred the incubator to the older part of the hospital, which reminded me of how very basic some of the facilities there actually were. Moving through the hospital corridors made me feel like a freak at the circus, with everyone stopping and staring at us.

As we rambled along, all of those stares made me begin to worry about what Cameron and I would encounter next. In fact, the oddity of it all led to some people pushing me aside to get a better look at whatever was inside the chamber. I resisted them as much as I could, wanting to protect my son from encroachment; I tried hard to resist the urge to physically push people back and out of the way.

On arrival at the X-ray room we found a queue of people occupying the chairs outside a faded and peeling green-blue door. We were told we had to wait like everybody else. And as we waited, once again curious onlookers started to pull the linen back to see what was inside the incubator. This caused me to panic until the nurse kindly but sternly moved people away, at the same time she assured me we were next in line.

Finally, the huge doors opened, and we were ushered inside, to a small reception desk with a curtain surrounding an old X-ray machine. The doctor came out and introduced himself, and the process of removing Cameron safely from the incubator began.

Cameron, unlike his mother, seemed to take the whole situation in his stride, looking wide-eyed at all the bodies around him. I held his hand as the doctor placed him on the bed and started the brain scan. After a few minutes the doctor looked at me with a smile. 'All good.'

With that he moved around to check Cameron's pelvis, which presented its own nuances. Cameron had been born breech, and in the early weeks he would lie in a frog-like position, known as hip dysplasia, with his legs spread astride and his knees bent high. 'It's a normal secondary effect,' the doctor noted, 'that in a breech birth the frog legs may need correcting in the future. Nothing to worry about now though, from what I can see.'

I nodded my head, and because the doctor was generally pleased with the X-rays and everything else, I felt a huge sense of relief, but despite that tears pricked in my eyes.

{Jeff}

I sat back and rubbed my eyes. After a few phone calls, I had worked out that I could fly to Colombo, the capital of Sri Lanka, to pick up the medicines needed for Cameron that afternoon, then turn it around in less than half a day and be back by midnight. The flight would only be forty minutes, and I had arranged to meet an old contact of mine from the oil days who would bring the medicines to the airport.

The next issue I needed to address was slightly more interesting. Earlier in the day someone had posted *congratulations* on my social media wall, rather than through a private message. Now I needed to manage dozens of congratulations on the birth of our new son. I tried to answer everyone's questions individually but that was impossible, so I started to cut and paste updates about our situation. This was to become a daily occurrence. Despite that, so many individual messages kept coming, in the end I just had to stop replying.

I needed coffee, but before I left, I decided to open one last email from one of my closest and oldest buddies in the UK, Richard. Instantly I was glad that I did. It provided just the right tonic.

'Dearest Jeff,' it started, 'I know you are having one of the hardest moments of your life right now and are almost certainly inundated with people asking how you are. Just so you know and for something different to read, this is how my life is going.'

Richard went on to recount his ordinary week, in a way that only he could, no amazing drama, just a normal week of one of my best friends and his family. It was truly what I needed. For a fleeting moment, seeing life through the eyes of my friend made me feel just a little less stressed and less guilty and less tired. Just normal. It was one of the best things to have happened in those past few days, yet the simplest. I made a mental note to buy my friend dinner when I next saw him.

Just then the phone rang. The caller ID showed Paul, the honorary consul. 'Hi Paul.'

'Hi, Jeff. I just thought I'd check in and see how things were going.'

I summarised the developments since we'd last spoken and mentioned I'd be popping over to Colombo for essential medicines.

'Have you tried the private hospital on the other side of the island?' Paul asked. 'It might have supplies that nobody is aware of and would save you a big trip.'

'I thought we were in the private hospital!' I said surprised.

'No, you are at IGMH: Indira Gandhi Memorial Hospital,' Paul said, equally surprised at my surprise.

It was only then that I realised what had happened. All the planning and calls that we had made before the trip, should an emergency occur while we were in the Maldives, concerned a completely different facility; one that was on the other side of the island. In a way, we had been at the wrong hospital all along and until right then I had been totally unaware.

'But I wouldn't worry,' continued Paul as if reading my mind. 'The NICU at IGMH is by far the best facility at the moment, because of the grant they received last year.'

We said our good-byes, and as I hung up my head was spinning. I found a new pair of shoes, equally as inappropriate as the ones I'd worn earlier, and rushed out the door.

As luck would have it, the hotel had a car, which was right outside. I jumped in and it whisked me to the private hospital, the one I had spoken to many times but never visited. It was almost exactly the other side of the island, but interestingly there was less flooding over there. I asked the driver to wait and I ran inside, where I quickly found the way to the hospital pharmacy. I took a number and was soon called to the counter. I showed the assistant the name of the medicine on the prescription.

'Yes, we have that in stock,' she said.

'Great!' I immediately replied, grabbing my wallet to buy whatever stock they had left before someone else bought the last few units. 'How many do you have?'

The assistant stepped back and motioned her hand toward the shelving behind her, which contained numerous crates, each holding 25 units. 'How many do you want?' she asked, unaware of the shortage on the other side of their tiny island. I stared at the hundreds of units that just sat there all pristine in unopened boxes.

'How much are they?' I enquired, as I looked at the last $100 in my wallet, curious how many that would buy.

'It's fifteen Maldivian Rufiyaa per box,' she replied.

I glanced at the currency exchange in the hospital lobby to see the current exchange rate, then I calculated in my brain. 'That's a buck a pop, right? I'll take two crates.' She looked confused as to why I might want so many, so I elaborated. 'There is none in the IGMH NICU.'

'Oh,' she said, then put the two crates on the counter as I handed over the money. There would be an ample supply for all the patients in the IMGH NICU today!

Chapter 23

Passports, Ministries & the Foreign Office

{Jeff}

Having eaten our usual breakfast at our usual table, there was no need for me to go to the hospital that morning, as I had stocked up on all of the needed medicines late the night before. I was back at my Breast-Pump-Sterilisation-and-Passport-Acquisition Desk, contemplating life and waiting for the workday to begin in Europe.

'Think!' I suddenly said to the wall opposite me. 'What next?'

The words were a product of my exasperation with reaching one dead end after another. I didn't think I could face another barrage of, 'Try this number, and good luck.' Then I realised I needed to stop calling the help lines. It was time to speak to someone higher up Her Majesty's governmental food chain. I took a deep breath and dialled.

'Hello,' a voice said at the other end. 'How can I help you?'

I summarised the whole passport rigmarole and felt I may finally have been getting somewhere until the voice said, 'But how do we know you haven't just bought a baby from the Maldives and are trying to smuggle it back?'

At first the words stunned me. Bought a baby? Smuggle a baby out of the Maldives? That people might do such things had never even entered my mind. Apart from the fact the honorary consul had seen Cameron and could testify, Clare still had her bump, the medical reports would have shown the baby's name and age, and to top it all off, Cameron was blond with blue eyes! What part of that was even remotely similar to a Maldivian baby?

'You know, I just thought of something,' the voice said.

'Please, what?!' I asked, hoping at last for some words of wisdom. However, in a stroke of bizarre comedy, he not only remained nonsensical about our whole ordeal but he remarked, 'Well, things could be worse. You are in the Maldives with azure seas and white sands, at least you can have some extra vacation time on the insurance company, can't be too bad, huh? Enjoy your time!'

What an idiot!

I was taken aback, and not for the first time I felt I wanted to strangle someone. Not only had salvation not come flowing through the telephone receiver, I was now in receipt of possibly the most impertinent comment I had ever heard. We were stuck on a flooded, overcrowded, scooter-infested small island metropolis. Our son was in need of immediate medical attention outside of what the facilities could provide there. I then realised the line had gone dead some time ago. I was so angry, if I hadn't needed the phone, I would have likely thrown it against the wall, or out of the window into the building site next door.

What now? I needed help from someone inside the UK, and ideally in London. I needed someone with contacts in high places who could move them up the queue and get us out now. This wasn't going to happen via a phone assistant.

So, I dialled my parents' number.

'Hello?'

When I heard my father's voice, I immediately felt a pang of emotion. I also thought it was strange that my father had answered, rather than my mother. We made some small talk before my father explained that my mother was out. After finishing the call, I immediately called her mobile. I had an agenda and wanted to see if she could help out.

'Hello, is everything okay?' my mother asked.

'Yes, as much as can be expected,' I replied. However, it quickly became apparent that she was hours away from home and riding in someone else's car. My plan was dashed for the day, but there was nothing she could do.

We hung up and I re-dialled my father. 'Of course I will, son,' he said, 'but I don't think it will do much good without you there in person.'

'I have to try, Dad!' I said with anguish, and with that we again hung up, so that he could quickly gather his things and rush for the next train to London.

{Clare}

While I took a break from the NICU, I called my sister Ann to give her an update. Before I could get three words out, Ann said, ‘Clare, please do let me know if there is anything, anything at all, I can do to help. Honestly, I can get on a plane, fly to Dubai, fly to the Maldives, absolutely anything. I can drop everything and be with you in hours.’

‘Ann, that is so nice of you to offer, but honestly at the moment there is nothing anyone can do to help here on the island. What we need more than anything else is a passport for Cameron, so we can leave the island. Maybe that’s where you might be able to help, as we may need somebody, a relative, to deliver the passport to us.’

‘If you need me, just let me know.’

‘I’ll obviously keep you informed,’ I said. I knew that when Ann hung up, she would immediately pack her bags and wait for any call to help.

{Jeff}

Meanwhile, I continued to send more emails and update social media to keep family and friends updated on our predicament and Cameron’s prognosis. As I posted, I found that while I was very worried, it was also somehow therapeutic at the same time. To write about the health of my premature son was a little surreal, as were a lot of other things I had experienced of late.

Just then the phone rang. There was no caller ID, so I swiped my mobile and answered. ‘Hello?’

‘Jeff, it’s Malcolm. Mate, I’ve been following from here in Dubai and we have been trying not to disturb you. I am sure that you will have too many people contacting you already, but needless to say, we’re here if you need anything.’

We said our good-byes and hung up. I hoped I would see my friends very soon, in either the UK or Dubai. All were good people, and all were sorely missed, not to mention, Team Curtis had a new son we desperately wanted to introduce to everyone.

My phone rang again. ‘Hello?’

'Jeff, it's your dad. They didn't take me very seriously. They were annoying to say the least, and they had no interest in helping. Sorry.'

'Oh, crap,' I gasped, not meaning to offend my easy-going father but knowing that my very persistent, very convincing mother may have been better tasked with the mission.

'You know, son?' my father said after a long pause, 'you need your mother. She's better at these kinds of things than I am.'

We both knew he was right, for my father is one of the most relaxed men on the face of the planet: the kind who rarely got involved with any type of confrontation. It simply wasn't in his DNA to argue with ignorant, stubborn or lethargic administrative types.

My mother on the other hand was the natural warrior, who was always ready to ensure that a sense of fairness existed and who always fought to uphold the side of the underdog. Once again, we said our goodbyes; as I hung up, I knew I would have to wait until the morning to speak with my mother and see if she had any further ideas.

Just as I hung up with my father, the phone rang again. *Grand central station!* I thought to myself. It was as if suddenly the whole outside world had noticed that Clare and I had gone missing from everyday life and were coming alive to help us try and return home from the marooned island.

'Hello?' I said, wondering who it was this time.

'Helllooo, how's the Maldives?' a friendly voice said. 'Sunning yourself no doubt!'

I enjoyed my brief conversation with Paul, a tall, jovial Dutchman who speaks impeccable English with barely an accent. His words were authoritative yet jovial, conjured up in the way only he could. Just as we were about to end the call, Paul suddenly interjected, 'Oh, and by the way, as I'm such a good friend, when you make this into a film, I want to choose my own actor to play me!'

I chortled. *A film, indeed! Who would ever watch that?*

Suddenly the room phone rang. It was Toni in the lobby of the hotel. She had come to collect me – for what, I wasn't sure – but I was hungry, so I promptly agreed to meet her downstairs in the restaurant.

'Hi Toni,' I said as I exited the hotel lift, finding her waiting for me. My spirits were renewed after talking to my family and friends.

'I have come to take you to the ministries,' she said. 'I know the Deputy Minister of Tourism, and I have met several others. I was thinking we could go and see if they can help.'

'Okay, I'm game for anything. But I do need something to eat before we leave. Would you like to have lunch or join me for coffee?'

'Coffee would be nice,' she replied.

After gaining much-needed sustenance, Toni took me in a taxi, stopping outside a building that contained most of the ministries for the island. It was far grander than I had expected, which both intimidated and encouraged me. Toni entered, with me in tow, and as there were no working lifts, we walked up a grand staircase. She was obviously familiar with where to go and sped on up. As for me, my toe cooperated but it did hurt.

Eventually we reached the personal assistant's desk outside the office of the Deputy Minister of Tourism. There was an exchange of pleasantries and we were invited through to the next office. As we entered, the deputy minister was sitting behind his desk.

The deputy minister smiled, and we began to talk about the night Cameron was born and the series of events that had followed. The deputy minister was both shocked and relieved that his countrymen had helped to save Cameron's life.

'If there is anything I can do to help,' he said, putting his hands together in a sort of triangle at the base of his chin, 'please don't hesitate to ask.' It was a sincere remark, but you could tell it took him off guard when I immediately took him up on the offer.

'That's very kind,' I said. 'Is there any way that you could help me expedite a passport, or even issue one for five years from the Maldives just to allow Cameron into Dubai?' I didn't beat around the bush with my directness, being gentle but firm in my request, but it didn't seem to matter.

'I am afraid we wouldn't be able to help get a UK passport, but maybe the minister can help gain a Maldivian passport.'

He added the latter more in the manner of a question, as he thought out loud, and with that we all got up and walked down the hallway to a door marked, 'Minster of Tourism'. The deputy minister knocked, and we entered when beckoned.

The minister and deputy exchanged pleasantries, followed by introductions to Toni and me. The minister then indicated he had been kept reliably informed of the situation and Cameron's progress. Again, I wasted no time in asking if he could help gain a passport for Cameron.

The minister wrinkled his nose in thought and tilted his head, as if loosening up an idea. 'Well, I am afraid there is not much I can do, but maybe one of the other ministers could help.'

My stomach sank but there was a hint of hope in the minister's tone. This enabled me to embrace a certain optimism as we walked down the hallway to the next minister's office. After knocking we entered and exchanged pleasantries, but he sent us on our way as well.

That continued for at least an hour until we ran out of minsters. Each and every minister had been a gentleman, as kind and obsequious as could be, but none could help. Cameron had fallen far into his bureaucratic void, a paradox of monumental proportions, as the governments that wrote and enforced the laws had no solution to the very absurdity they had created.

When my phone rang again, I rolled my eyes. I didn't know who was on the other end, but I felt like I was back at work all over again. One grinding call after another. I answered in the hope it might be good news.

'Hi Jeff, it's Paul,' the honorary consul said, enthusiastically. 'I have some paperwork for you to fill in and if we make the last DHL it should go out tonight. Where are you? Shall we meet?' I relayed my current position to Paul who said he would pick me up, and with that he was gone.

I relayed the conversation to Toni and though we were both disappointed with our morning's work, we agreed the situation was complex and unique, so it had been worth the effort of making the enquiries and establishing contact with the ministers. If nothing else, when we did find a potential solution, any one of them might be able to expedite a result, should we fall foul of any further bureaucratic entanglement from the Maldivian officials, as the ministers had now been apprised of our circumstances.

Just then a bright blue scooter pulled up beside me. It was quite small, with a black wire mesh basket on the front, presumably for shopping. There, sitting astride this tiny machine, was a tall, dapper Englishman: Paul, the honorary consul. At any other time and place, he would have looked out of place but right now he was a sight that gave me cause to hope.

'Hi Jeff,' he said with a smile through his immaculate white helmet. 'Are you ready?' He motioned for me to climb onto the bike behind him.

'When you said that you were coming to pick me up, I thought you meant in a car!' I laughed as I looked at my next mode of transport. Paul was very tall, and I am very broad, and for the life of me I wasn't at all sure how the logistics of it would work. But, like jumping out of an aeroplane, I had faith. So, I hopped on the back and hoped that the bike wouldn't topple over and crash.

Fortunately, we only had a few hundred metres and two corners to reach our destination. It felt a little treacherous, but Paul seemed quite competent even with the overloaded back tyre, caused by the additional weight of his pillion passenger. As we screeched to a halt outside the DHL office, the guy was just locking the door. Paul had mentioned that once the office closed for the day it wouldn't be open for another few days due to a national holiday, which was the reason for the rush.

'We spoke on the phone,' Paul said with authority to the man closing and locking the door for the holiday. 'We have one document to send and we will be out of your hair.'

Fortunately, the man proved understanding. He allowed us in and locked the door behind us, presumably in case anyone else had seen us and tried to follow suit. I then filled out the forms and paid for the documents to be sent.

In a matter of minutes, we were ushered out of the office and back on Paul's scooter. It was late by then, so Paul dropped me off at the hotel. I stopped at the restaurant to have a coffee before I found myself back in the all-too-familiar Breast-Pump-Sterilisation-and-Passport-

Acquisition Desk. Staring at the same blank wall, I had gone completely full circle. While we had made some small progress with passports, ministries & the Foreign Office, we were nowhere closer to solving the problem.

My phone rang once more. I picked it up not knowing who it would be because I was too tired and dejected to look at the name of the incoming caller.

'Jeff, it's your mother. What do you need me to do?'

Chapter 24

A Few Days Later

{Jeff}

A few days later, my mother had made some inroads into the British Parliament. A purposeful woman, she hadn't needed to wield her umbrella in anger, nor even raise her voice; she simply visited Westminster and asked to speak with her MP. The MP in turn engaged his PA, Maggie, who provided invaluable assistance to us in our plight and was herself making good headway on our behalf.

By that time, we had come to realise that the passport would be processed in the north of England and from there it would first be shipped to London and then delivered via courier to the Maldives. Clare's sister Ann, having already enthusiastically offered her services, proceeded to arrange transport for herself from London to Manchester and then on to the Maldives, thereby cutting out considerable valuable time.

But as Clare and I had learned long ago, life was never that simple.

Ann then called me; I was sitting outside the NICU reading Gina Ford's book on babies. My last-ditch attempt at some form of instruction, in the hope that we would eventually arrive home with a healthy Cameron.

'I really don't know if they will give you the passport though. I have not been able to confirm either way.' I told her.

'At least I am doing something,' she replied, obviously happy to be doing anything to help.

'Okay,' I continued, 'but before you go anywhere, let me speak with the minister's assistant in London again.'

We hung up and I called Maggie. She answered quickly and, after dispensing with the formalities, I got straight to the point of call. 'My sister-in-law is on a train to the north of England. She needs confirmation that she can pick up the passport.'

'Mr Curtis, I have just got off the phone with them and they will not give her the passport. They will only follow normal procedure, as they must always take steps to prevent someone from trying to obtain a passport under false pretences. In addition, they have asked more questions about the validity of the Cameron's citizenship.'

She crushed my hopes, but in the back of my mind I knew that might have been coming. Of all the news stories in the late nineties that I remembered, the ones that were at the forefront pointed a critical finger at the government for handing out British passports like children's candy. After which of course passports were much harder to come by, even for valid cases, and Cameron once again fell into the paradoxical void.

It's so strange, I thought. Miraculously my son was just over a week old and not yet a citizen or legal alien in any country. Nobody would recognise him or issue him with a passport, which meant he had entered life as a stateless person. The world had changed, and people no longer gained citizenship as a birth right, passed down from their parents. They had to prove they existed before legal documents could be raised and citizenship issued, which of course was impossible to do in our case. A true enigma if there ever was one.

I immediately called Ann back with the bad news. She was outraged. 'This is simply ridiculous; a baby's life is at stake here, and people will do nothing other than follow stupid procedures that do not fit the circumstances? What's wrong with the world?!'

'Well, I couldn't agree with you more, but welcome to my life for the last eight days!'

We hung up and I took a deep breath, as I stared into space from my chair. I sat outside NICU more and more now. Toni and I had exhausted all the avenues we could think of to obtain a passport or paperwork to travel to Dubai, and the UK was still off the cards. Ann's anger mirrored my own more than she could have known.

Singapore had been mentioned and I had called a few friends there. I'd been hoping to rent a flat near the hospital for eight weeks, where we could stay until Cameron was well enough to travel to Dubai. Once medevac'd from Malé, he could not be moved in a commercial aircraft until he was able to travel without medical assistance. But even then, nothing had materialised from that, either.

My phone rang, breaking my thoughts, and it was International SOS who checked in on the document situation. They had already gained clearance to move Cameron to the most suitable location as soon as the documents were available to travel, but of course no such documents were forthcoming. I had also requested that they speak with Clare more in order to reassure her that things were in fact positive, especially with her spending so much of her time indoors by Cameron's bedside.

'Well,' I started, 'we have made no progress on gaining documents to get back home to Dubai. I have been looking into alternative accommodation in Singapore, just in case we end up there, but right now everything is up in the air.'

'Yes, your case seems to have considerable complications,' he replied.

'Indeed,' I affirmed, and then added, 'although we hear that we may be able to gain special dispensation for Cameron to enter the UAE on a legal loophole, which holds some remote promise. Still, we have not been able to obtain an opinion from anyone in authority.'

'Well, at least that's movement in the right direction,' replied the International SOS doctor.

Because the Maldives' doctors had advised against travelling all the way to the UK, and Dubai did not accept temporary travel documents, Singapore now remained as potentially the only viable option. Despite that, neither the insurance company, nor local medical team, or Team Curtis for that matter, felt that Singapore was the best option logistically; so we had decided it would be better to wait.

The whole situation just got more and more complicated; the best interests of the baby and his health only played an occasional determinative role. However, because Cameron had suffered fewer complications for a few days, it was his stable condition that led to a consensus to wait for the possibility of documents for Dubai.

Two days previous to that, Clare had made a desperate post on a social media mothers' chat group for anyone that might have been able to help with the documentation into Dubai, and to our surprise, a friend living in Dubai had recognised Clare and got the ball rolling. She was good friends with a man who was quite knowledgeable about the UAE's laws and quite well connected to the higher echelons of public life as well.

As miraculous as that revelation was, however, his progress thus far had only been to get verbal dispensation for the entry documents to be processed, which was not enough as International SOS had made it abundantly clear that no air ambulance would be dispatched to Dubai without the official paperwork in place. The last thing they wanted to do was fly us there at great expense and then be diverted somewhere else.

The details of the rule that might allow Cameron's entry into Dubai had not been explained to me. Under normal circumstances I would have insisted that I be informed of everything and would have ensured I understood it completely, but at that point in the never-ending ordeal, all that mattered to me was that it worked and was legal.

After I hung up, I checked my email and found a message from my contact in Dubai. It was good news, as someone had been located who could sign the initial paperwork. Then the only thing remaining was to obtain a signature from a senior official to legalise the entry document, but the necessary person was in a conference outside of Dubai. This didn't dash my optimism, this was still good news, although no one could find the senior official, we would at least have a chance when they did, and maybe the passport would turn up in the meantime.

So there were several potential options on the table at that point, which was much better than it had been only days earlier. Also, one thing I understood about Middle Eastern senior officials and ministers is that they all worked incredibly hard and incredibly long hours. Therefore, trying to get an audience with the right person could sometimes be an impossible mission as they were often engaged on other business. But with guarded optimism in my mind, I went to the hospital on the off chance that I might get to see Cameron.

{Clare}

As luck would have it, although visiting hours were over, the nurses took pity on Jeff when he arrived and even asked him if he would like to do some KMC, Kangaroo Mother Care, and he jumped at the chance.

Although the mother was the first and natural choice for KMC, when the mother was unavailable fathers were allowed to get in on the act, as that could also be beneficial. The nurse picked up Cameron and carefully unplugged all of the non-essential cables as Jeff unbuttoned his shirt. She then laid him on the centre of Jeff's chest: our tiny baby, still asleep with no care in the world. Suddenly Cameron stretched out his arms and hugged the bare chest he was lying on.

Jeff almost melted as he realised that it was the very first time in his life that he had properly held our son. It was an amazing and utterly unforgettable experience for both of us. Jeff tried not to make any sudden movements, as he allowed himself to feel the bond between father and son for the very first time. All the nurses and I watched as Jeff tended to his son. Emotions filled the room, with hardly a dry eye in the house.

As Jeff sat there, I realised he'd been racing around trying to solve problems and get Cameron and I out of the Maldives for over a week, and he had totally missed out on the miracle of parenting. Now, for just a few minutes, he sat there, said nothing, and contemplated all the things that they would do together as Cameron grew up.

What felt like minutes had been over an hour and we knew it was better not to over-stimulate him, so all too soon it was time to put Cameron back in the incubator. Cameron continued to be stable, but he still had ailments that were a potential cause for concern.

After his cuddles with Daddy, he was subjected to his third session of jaundice therapy, which consisted of him lying under a blue light with a makeshift blindfold over his eyes to block the direct light. Sounds simple, but Cameron would have none of it and was constantly throwing off the blindfold.

I was sitting quietly behind Jeff the whole time and allowing them to bond. He turned to me, 'Shall we get some dinner?' he asked. 'Maybe we should go back to the hotel for an early night, have dinner and try and get some good rest? You could even forego your three-hourly breast-pumping exercise tonight and get a good night's sleep?'

So that's exactly what we did. First, we stopped at the hotel restaurant for some much-needed fuel. There we had a visit from Paul, the honorary consul, who had dropped by on his way back from the main consulate in Sri Lanka, bringing with him the paperwork that would allow Cameron back into the UK or even Singapore. Unfortunately, however, that paperwork would still not have been enough to get Cameron into Dubai. We retired early as planned, although I did not forego my pumping duties, as Jeff had suggested.

The next morning started as a repeat of what we'd been doing for the last four days. But even as much as we loved routine, our sense of uncertainty and the frustrating repetition made it impossible to relax properly. Jeff had actually started to make mental notes of cartoons he had viewed on the television while stuck outside the NICU, deciding which Cameron would and would not be allowed to watch; I pumped milk regularly all day long; Jeff ran to the pharmacy for meds, and so on. It was time to leave this island and go home. We just didn't know quite how.

I began to talk to Cameron about all sorts of things. In many of my one-sided conversations I told him about his family and the friends waiting for him back in Dubai and the UK. I even made up silly little songs and told him all about Patch our cat. I would do KMC at every opportunity.

{Jeff}

Meanwhile, I had taken up residence in my usual uncomfortable seat alone outside NICU. There was nothing else I could do to obtain a passport but wait. My phone rang, and I absentmindedly removed it from my pocket while reading my book and half listening to the cricket game on the television. 'Hello?'

'Hi Jeff!' said the voice of my new friend in Dubai. I had never met him, but he was introduced to me through one of my close friends back there. He sounded jubilant as he continued. 'Believe it or not, I have that signature. You can finally go home to Dubai!'

Chapter 25

Sayonara, Malé!

{Jeff}

Dropping my book on the floor, I could hardly contain my excitement. After ten tortuous days of debacle, a burst of energy exploded inside me. I always knew we would get home at some point. The only question had been whether Cameron would be well enough to travel. But now…

You can go home! The words echoed in my ears. Had I heard correctly?

'Hi Jeff, are you there?' the voice at the other end enquired. I almost forgot I was having a conversation on the phone.

'Yes, yes, I'm here, sorry,' was all I could muster. 'Oh, my God, that's amazing, thank you, thank you so much for all of your help!' I wasn't sure how I could ever thank the man for his help, but I would worry about that later. 'What do I do now?' I asked, genuinely perplexed at what my next move should be.

'Now you call International SOS and let them know I will be sending them all the relevant documentation. I cannot send it to anyone else, due to the sensitive nature of the documents. However, once they receive it from me, they can scramble your medical evacuation in an ambulance. Call the consul now and tell him you are leaving his shores, let the nurses and doctors know, and then go and pack.'

We said our good-byes and I reiterated how much I appreciated his help, help from a man whom I had never met, and who out of the goodness of his heart and for no personal gain to himself had helped us find a legal way to escape our hellish predicament. It was a completely selfless act that I will always remember.

I knocked hard on the door of the NICU, causing a nurse to come running to see what the emergency was. I explained the call I had just received and that I needed to tell Clare. She immediately let me through with a big, beaming smile, stopping me before I ran in without scrubbing up. Quickly going through the process, I came sliding round the corner like an adolescent at Christmas time heading to the tree, joy plastered across my face for all to see.

Clare looked up from where she was holding Cameron on her chest doing KMC. My smile was so big and so infectious that words were not necessary to communicate to her that something huge had happened.

{Clare}

'We've done it! We're going home!' Jeff yelled at me. 'We're going home!' Looking for the right words, Jeff laughed out loud and then shouted, 'We have the paperwork needed, don't ask me how, but we can scramble a jet.' He was so high with joy that he danced from foot to foot. He had done it. Almost.

'That's great news!' I replied, looking around hesitantly to ensure Jeff's outburst hadn't caused pandemonium in the ward. I didn't have the heart to shush him, as I wanted us to savour the moment, for I had also done my part by making sure Cameron was fed, held, visited, nurtured. 'What now?' I anxiously continued.

'Now I will call International SOS, tell them the good news, and find out what they can supply to get us out of here,' Jeff said with great enthusiasm. I had to smile as I looked at Cameron and lowered my voice to a soft whisper, 'We can go home soon, son – you just hang in there.'

But as I said that, and even though my spirits were lifted, I was acutely aware that we still faced the frustrating formality of government bureaucracies, no matter from whether the Maldives, UK or UAE. I knew more obstacles would have to be scaled before we were finally set free.

I was also a mother, and as such I was starting to get in tune with my motherly instincts. Feeling a mounting sense of foreboding, I instantly started to work out the logistics in my head and they led directly to one question, *Was this the right thing to do; to move Cameron?*

All this time we had been caught up in getting back to Dubai, but now that it was a real possibility, I wanted to make sure that Cameron would remain stable and safe. Moving him and putting him on a plane could change all of that. Just at that point, one of the regular night nurses came in and congratulated me.

'Eventually, it looks like you can go home!' she said with genuine delight.

I looked at the nurse and asked if this was really the best thing for Cameron, to move him now, and the nurse put her hand kindly on my shoulder and reassured me, 'Cameron is stable presently. Getting him home to Dubai as soon as possible is best for him.'

I looked down at my tiny little bundle of joy, who at that moment had both eyes open and was looking at me almost in bewilderment. I looked back at him and softly said, 'I don't know why you are looking so confused; you were the one that decided to come early!'

And with that I gave him a kiss on the head and started working out what I would need to do when we finally arrived back home – the first task, of course, being finishing the nursery.

{Jeff}

I called International SOS to alert them we had the signature. I went over the details of the last phone call and the fact that we should be able to gain Cameron entry into Dubai, the paperwork hadn't reached them yet, but I was hoping it would just be a matter of time.

I called Paul the honorary consul. 'Paul,' I almost shouted through the phone. 'I just got news from Dubai, we have the paperwork, well almost, and we're just awaiting a fax. We're going home!'

'That's great, Jeff,' but I could sense by his pause that his brain was already working on the next possible hitch. 'Let me check and see whether we need any other documents or to fulfil any legal requirements on my side. We need to make sure they will let Cameron leave.'

'What do you mean, let Cameron leave?' I felt an immediate pang of panic.

'Well, Cameron arrived inside Clare, and he is leaving of his own accord. He doesn't have an entry stamp, so it might be a complication. I need to check.'

I felt a little bemused, wondering why Paul hadn't mentioned that before. If I had to guess, Paul had decided to avoid the subject until it became relevant in order not to open another can of worms until it became necessary. I knew that it would just be a document required, a stamp and a signature. I also knew that nobody would know what was needed or who could sign better than Paul, and by that time, I had total trust in him.

Still, when I stood up, I was hit by a wave of self-doubt. Suddenly I wondered if I was actually back at square one again and if we might face more problems with paperwork from the Maldives side. From a massive high only moments before, I started to worry whether Cameron could exit, due to a lack of an entry stamp on arrival because he had been a mere foetus.

I thought for a second, my mind spun in circles, doubts had begun to rush in. Could I really start to get excited? Maybe I had jumped the gun. I had just burst into the hospital ward dancing, claiming victory, yet did I actually know that we would be leaving and when? No, I didn't.

But I had to believe it was true; we both needed to hold on to something. And then there was the logistics of landing in Dubai before Clare and Cameron, if I didn't fit on the air ambulance.

Did I need to sign a power-of-guardianship to one of my most trusted friends, just in case I was delayed, and Clare was incapacitated? Someone who could be trusted with our son's life upon arrival at City Hospital in Dubai?

I shook my head to clear my mind of doubts. It was simple. I would act on the assumption we would leave in the next few days. If it didn't go as planned, the worse that would happen was that we would have to unpack our suitcases.

With everything out of my control, at least for that moment, I decided to clear my head further by walking around the island. The floodwaters had receded, and I had come to realise that I had no idea what anything looked like outside my confined routine. There wasn't much else to see, but there was an emotional satisfaction and sense of closure from doing a final walk before our journey home.

Back at the hotel several hours later, I was busy finishing up the packing. Everything was loaded except the wash bags and of course the breast pump and sterilisation unit, as Clare would still need these. My phone rang, and I saw it was Paul the honorary consul. *Fifty-fifty it's bad news*, I thought, looking at the screen.

'Hi Paul,' I answered, trying to sound upbeat and positive.

'Bad news I'm afraid.' Is all he said.

My heart immediately sank. *What now?* I thought.

'So, the Maldivian government won't let Cameron leave without an entry permit or some other confirmation of arrival. And before you ask, the hospital register won't be enough.'

I had been about to ask about the register, but instead asked, 'What's the good news?'

'I didn't say there was any.'

'There is always good news,' I replied, 'even if it's just the facts.' I wasn't willing to give up hope, and I didn't believe the Maldivian government would detain Cameron indefinitely.

'I'm coming to pick you up. Are you at the hospital or hotel?'

'See! There is good news, you are going to try something. Hotel,' I replied as quickly as I could, and with that the phone went dead.

Quickly, I looked for something suitable to wear for another treacherous ride on that electric blue scooter, some long trousers and solid shoes. Within minutes, Paul arrived outside the hotel where I was already waiting. I swung my leg over the back seat but before Paul could pull away, I shouted, 'Stop!'

Paul looked around concerned. 'Everything all right?'

'Yes, I just need to get a picture of us two on this scooter, because nobody will ever believe me.'

With that, I commandeered a bemused passer-by to take a number of photos of Paul and I sitting astride the electric blue scooter. The pictures would form a priceless memento later in life when it was all over, I was sure.

Once we were finished, Paul twisted the throttle and off we went, hair to the wind. With no idea where we were going, but nothing to lose, I just accepted fate and waited for what the future might hold. I couldn't help but chuckle when the scooter stopped in front of the Ministry of Employment. I wasn't entirely sure why we stopped there, but I did venture an educated guess.

'So, Cameron is to be employed?' my question was part rhetorical, part joke, but the last thing I had expected was a serious reply.

'Not quite, but close.' Paul looked me square in the eye and raised his eyebrows at the same time. He wasn't kidding.

We alighted from the scooter and I followed Paul into the building. Right away Paul by-passed the queue and strode directly to the first counter. There he asked for a person by name and within seconds two people arrived with a bundle of paperwork in their hands. Paul took it, filled in some blanks, signed it and then suddenly stopped.

'How do you spell Balthazar?' Paul asked, as he looked up from the documents. He was writing Cameron's full name. The realisation sank in that I had managed to get Balthazar in there, although when Clare recovered from this whole ordeal, I did question whether she would still be as compliant. But I loved it, it made perfect sense., it was him from bump to baby.

The two clerks left with Cameron's UK travel docs, as I stood there at the counter listening to the beat of my heart. After all the waiting and delays, everything started happening so fast I could hardly believe it; but I had the strangest feeling that it was the beginning of the end in Malé. Paul the honorary consul may have pulled off the last miracle in order for us to depart.

When the two clerks returned, they put a work visa onto the documents and pressed a red-ink stamp across the visa, smiled politely and pushed the documents into Paul's hands, then walked away satisfied. Paul in turn handed the documents to me, and I practically fainted.

'Keep these safe,' Paul said with a serious look on his face. 'These will get you out of Malé.'

I beamed a smile as I accepted the documents.

Paul dropped me back at the hotel and promised to keep in close contact as things were moving quickly now all the signed documents were in place. I waved as Paul disappeared around the corner and out onto the main thoroughfare on his electric blue scooter.

Once again glad to be off the back of the bike, I took the documents out of the plastic wallet and had a closer look at what had actually been stamped. There I found a work visa for a chalet boy, valid for one day, and across the middle a red-ink stamp that read, 'Not eligible for work.'

Well, I thought. *If it works, it works*! And then my phone rang.

'Mr Curtis, it's International SOS,' the voice said.

My heart sank, and my breathing almost stopped. By the tone in the voice on the other end, I immediately felt something was amiss.

'Please tell me you have the signed documents,' I asked as I tried not to black out with every forgotten breath.

'We have the required documentation, and we have made a request for an air ambulance to pick you up. We will let you know as soon as possible what size plane it is and its arrival time but usually it will take two to three days.'

And so it began: the final act of what could only be described as one of most trying episodes in the history of Team Curtis. Signatures were in place, documents written, and papers stamped. All we needed then was the plane and then it was, 'Sayonara, Malé!'

I returned to the hospital to meet Clare for lunch. Ecstatic and nervous, we decided to grab a quick bite at the stand-up café bar. It didn't sell healthy food, but it would have to suffice for our celebration. Nor did the capital city of the strictly Muslim island serve alcohol, anywhere. Orange juice had to do.

'When will we know more about the plane, how big and when it's due to arrive?' Clare asked me, while taking a huge bite of her oversized celebratory tuna sandwich.

'I'm not sure. The guy at International SOS was a little protective of the information,' I replied with a full mouth of food, etiquette having gone out of the window, brought on by our mutual severe hunger and stress.

{Clare}

Neither Jeff nor I slept that night, our minds rife with thoughts about the prospect of going home and everything that it would entail. As we lay in bed it felt as if the sun would never rise, but when it did, we leapt from the bed to finish packing.

As Jeff waited for me to finish dressing, I found my eyes somehow drawn to the building site next door. The hole that had filled up like a muddy brown pool in the storm, now contained its foundation cement. Oddly, I'd miss that place, I thought. Perhaps in the same way captives fall in love with their captors, or patients with their nurses: a sort of Stockholm syndrome effect, maybe.

The NICU staff had already been informed by International SOS that our departure was imminent, though they were also in the dark about the plane's ETA. I felt that was a little strange and speculated to myself that it might be called off at the last minute.

'When do you think you will leave?' the doctor asked Jeff. He had just started his rounds and even though Cameron was not officially supposed to have been his first patient, he had grown fond of the blond-haired, blue-eyed boy, so in light of his imminent departure the doctor started with him.

'The plane is scheduled to arrive this afternoon, but that's all we know,' Jeff replied.

'That's great news,' the doctor said. 'I have his file ready and will give it to the doctor on the air ambulance.' As we talked, he was going about checking Cameron, talking to the nurses and examining the morning's blood work and such. 'I hope I am here to see him leave.'

I stood there in silence, taking in the place that had become Cameron's first home, and I remembered once again that the nursery was not finished back in Dubai. The paint had been decided – Martini motor racing colours, Jeff's choice of course – and the furniture bought, but nothing was actually in the room yet. It was empty.

'You know, the nursery is not yet sorted,' I mentioned to Jeff.

'Yes, I was thinking the same thing earlier,' he replied.

'Don't worry,' I continued. 'He will have to spend a few more weeks in City Hospital's NICU before he comes home. You'll have plenty of time to finish it.' I smiled at Jeff, but only hoped that Cameron did eventually come home, and there were no more eventualities that might prevent that.

'You mean we'll have time?' Jeff said as he smiled back at me. It made a refreshing change to have a light-hearted conversation, with a cheerful optimism that we may eventually end this debacle and have a full family contingent at the end, after all that had happened.

'Yes, we'll have time,' I said with a grin.

Within thirty minutes the ward had become a hive of activity. Nurses hurried to get Cameron ready. Hospital paperwork was signed, shuffled, stacked and filed. Apparatus gathered, piled, and organised. Medical supplies were packed and sorted.

In the middle of the chaos, someone from the nursing staff requested an impromptu group photo, as the staff were about to change shift. Everyone, including the most senior consultant, crowded in, not wanting to be left out. The atmosphere in the air had literally turned carnival-like. Jeff and I sat by Cameron's incubator as we watched the folly unfold around us. For the first time in eleven days, Jeff did not have to run to the pharmacy for supplies. He could just sit and watch.

'You should go back to the hotel and pack,' the doctor suggested to us.

But Team Curtis was already one step ahead. We had completely packed, checked out of our room, and were ready to move at a moment's notice. I looked at Jeff and with genuine concern said, 'With all that's happened, I am really worried that the plane may not turn up.'

'I know,' he replied. 'I wish I could assure you that everything will be okay, but until we take off nothing is 100 percent.'

Inside, I was anticipating the last-minute problems that were so common in situations like these. By sheer weight of experience, I was sure this would be no different.

'Is anyone tracking the plane or its whereabouts?' Jeff asked the hospital staff.

'Yes,' someone promptly replied. 'It's running thirty minutes late from its refuelling stop but should be here at 13:30. The plan is to turn around and have you airborne as quickly as possible, in about sixty minutes.'

It was reassuring to hear that the hospital was tracking the plane, though both Jeff and I were doubtful about their estimated turn-around time. In the circumstances it only added to the tension, which was already through the roof.

'Has anyone told the aircraft crew that there is a body of water to cross to get to the hospital?' Jeff asked. To which the answer was, 'No'.

At one o'clock Toni arrived at the NICU, followed shortly after by Paul the honorary consul, who were both allowed entry for the special occasion.

'Not long now!' exclaimed Paul. 'Hopefully all of the documents you have will allow everyone to leave Malé and enter Dubai.'

I smiled vaguely. I was in deep thought about what might happen if any of the documents were refused; the amount of paperwork that we carried with us was staggering – the collection of signatures and stamps from people and offices we had never heard of – and the notion of travelling on the promise of strangers we had never even met was worrying. But as with every other negative thought I had survived in the last eleven days, I pushed it to the back of my mind. If something arose, we'd deal with it. And if it all worked out, we would never be able to thank them all.

At 13:33, I looked up at the hospital clock, wondering to myself whether the plane had landed. Just then a nurse rushed in. 'The plane is a little more delayed, but it should be on the ground in ten minutes.'

Those next ten minutes went by painfully slowly, just like the very first night of our ordeal, when no one knew whether Cameron and I would live or die. Indeed, the intensity and pressure on everybody in the NICU, including Toni and Paul, let alone those most involved, was almost intolerable. Everyone from that point forward had to work in complete harmony or everything could still fall apart.

At 13:54 I began to crack under the pressure, my poker face beginning to dissolve. Then I heard a voice penetrate my protective bubble,

'Sir, you have a phone call.'

A nurse was standing in front of Jeff, and she handed him the hospital phone. Who on earth would be calling now, and why call Jeff on the hospital phone?

{Jeff}

'Hello.' I said into the receiver, a little bemused.

'Mr Curtis, this is the doctor from the air ambulance service. We have landed and will be with you shortly.' The kind, accented voice of the woman immediately calmed my worries. I suddenly felt everything would be okay. 'Can you confirm if the hospital has a portable incubator?' she asked.

Oh no, not again?!

'No,' I replied in a panic. 'They won't let us have one of their new ones; they can't risk the crossing from the hospital to the airport, because they have to go by boat.'

'By boat?!' the doctor exclaimed. I heard her stop what she was doing on the other end of the phone, as if in shock.

'Yes, hasn't anyone told you?' Suddenly my stomach sank as I realised the air ambulance staff had fallen foul of the same misconception that we ourselves had experienced eleven days earlier. 'You are on the airport island,' I explained. ''There is a ferry ride to Malé Island and then an ambulance ride to the hospital. Both are relatively short distances, however it will take you more time than you would think to get here '

'How do we get Cameron to the plane without an incubator?' the doctor asked, as if she could not believe the situation she had just encountered.

'Isn't that what I should be asking you?' I gasped. 'Don't you have an incubator on board?'

'Yes, but it's bolted to the aircraft. Oh, this is a real problem.'

I reiterated the sequence of events that had to be followed in the transport and I finished to a stunned silence on the other end of the phone. 'We did skin-to-skin before,' I continued valiantly, refusing to let our momentum dissolve into oblivion. 'We can do it again!'

'It's too dangerous,' said the doctor, obviously quite astounded. 'It was dangerous before when you brought your baby in, but now that we have options it would be unwise to attempt the same again. We'll take the incubator off the plane.' And with that she hung up.

So how were they going to turn around in sixty minutes? I thought to myself. Well, they weren't!

{Clare}

At 14:32 in the afternoon, thirty-two minutes after the original planned departure of Cameron's mercy flight, the doors to the *lift of doom* opened and belched out an enormous number of people and equipment, almost too many to stand in the vestibule in front of the door. The horde consisted of a NICU-specialist flying doctor, an NICU-specialist nurse, and the four burly men commandeered from the airport to help with the incubator. Once unbolted from the plane, the incubator was strapped lopsidedly onto a wheeled ambulance stretcher, which was being pushed by the four men. The doors to the NICU were opened wide to allow them access. The doctor and nurse washed up, but not the burly men. What seemed before to be a carnival for middle school had fast become a full-blown three-ring circus.

For all of the fastidious cleanliness routines that all the parents underwent on entering the NICU, the departure of Cameron, which was completely out of our hands, brought chaos to the ward, which made both of us feel guilty.

I talked to the air ambulance doctor, a young-looking Hungarian woman who took notes as I reeled off the story of the last eleven days. After she finished with me, the doctor turned to the hospital staff and began to get a brief of Cameron's present medical status. She looked very professional, like she had done it quite a few times before.

The NICU nurses had been assisting the air ambulance nurse, who checked Cameron for herself and then made ready for the transition from the hospital incubator to the unbolted and precariously balanced aircraft incubator. The four uncleansed burly men stood by idly, as they tried not to touch anything. But as cautious as they had tried to be, one of them inadvertently walked into one of the tubes attached to Cameron.

I screamed as the tube and attached needle tore off of Cameron's skin and dangled in mid-air; everyone watched in horror. The air ambulance nurse calmly picked it up and put it back without a fuss. After that, I felt my son was in safe hands. Suddenly the time had arrived.

We were ready to leave.

Chapter 26

The Final Chapter

{Clare}

As we prepared to leave NICU, I had a feeling of anxiety. Once again, we were taking Cameron out of relative safety and thrusting him into the chaotic streets, across the rough and merciless sea, and then up in another aeroplane. As a mother I was immensely concerned about the well-being of my son.

I just hoped time would move fast – fast enough for me not to suffer a heart attack. With pressure building within me, I turned to the Hungarian doctor, 'If at any time you think this is too dangerous, or you just don't think we will make it in time, please just say so. You are in charge, but I don't like this scenario. There are too many unknowns and too many things that could go wrong.'

I was adamant that she be aware of how I felt, and that she be prepared to abort at any time had she felt something could go wrong. Nothing about the medical evacuation had proceeded in a normal fashion, so it was critical to address and thwart any potentially harmful issue before things escalated.

'We've got him this far; I don't want anything to go wrong now!' I finished.

The doctor nodded in acknowledgement that she shared my concern, gave it a thought, then said, 'I have worked in an NICU for very many years; your son is very strong. Don't worry, he'll make it, he'll be fine now!'

Thankful and shocked all at the same time, I digested these powerfully reassuring words. Then Jeff and I looked at each other. He had heard them too, and it was then we both realised that this was the first time anyone had actually said that he would be fine. Those were the perfect words to hear at that point, before we took Cameron on another trip into the unknown.

Someone had the forethought to call the *lift of doom* in advance, so we thought our parting memory of that infernal contraption was to be a good one. It was completely empty and waiting just for us. Then in concert the doctor, nurse, Jeff, myself, Toni, Paul and the four burly men all made our way out of the NICU and entered the lift, with Cameron in his new incubator strapped, somewhat lopsided, onto a stretcher.

There were too many of us for the lift to close, and I felt a momentary flare in Jeff's temper beside me; but he managed to squeeze out and asked Toni and Paul to do the same so that we could get Cameron down and into the ambulance safely. The *lift of doom*, it appeared, was going to have the last word.

By the time we all made it to the ambulance, darkness had fallen, which added to the logistical challenges. We then realised we had the same driver that had picked us up eleven days before in the chaos of the harbour and main street. However, this time when the doors closed and he headed out, he drove at a snail's pace. *He's driving too slowly*, I thought to myself, as it seemed like we would never get there; but I thought better of telling him to hurry, as that could compromise Cameron's safety.

Looking out of the back window, we saw Paul, who rode behind us on his electric blue scooter with its black shopping basket, and poor Toni holding on for dear life on the pillion seat. The ambulance was going so slowly that Paul found it difficult to stay balanced.

For some reason, perhaps to avoid the chaotic jam of scooters and central traffic, the driver went round the outskirts of the island. It was almost as if someone had told him not to drive as erratically as last time or he would lose his job. He was going so slowly that people were walking past us; it bordered on the absurd. Already hours behind schedule, I worried that it would only take one major hitch to raise the question of whether to abort then or carry on in the hope of getting airborne before the pilots were legally mandated to take a rest period. That would have meant returning poor Cameron back to the hospital again, and even potentially having to go through the A&E admissions debacle once more as he was in an ambulance. Something I didn't want to contemplate.

The Hungarian doctor could see the devastated look on my face, eventually offering, 'It's okay, Mrs Curtis, we are so late anyway that it doesn't matter. We have three pilots with us and a considerable margin of time before we'd have to stay in Malé for the night.'

At least when we arrived at the quayside the boat was docked and waiting for us. However, it was so huge it didn't quite fit, leaving a gap almost one foot wide between the boat and the quay. The Hungarian doctor scratched her head, as did Paul the honorary consul, who stood towering behind her.

'I'll ask to see if we can berth at the royal jetty on the other side,' Paul said, looking out over the flat body of water that separated us from the airport island. Although it didn't look far, we knew it was a boat-ride away. It didn't solve our immediate problem, but it would solve the same issue on the other side. 'If we can go through the VIP terminal, it will avoid delays and rubbernecking from other passengers.'

While Paul called for permission to use the berth at the royal jetty, Toni addressed the problem of how to get the oversized vessel's bow closer to the quayside in order that the heavy, lopsided incubator could at last be lifted on.

'Okay, we can use the royal jetty and the VIP terminal,' Paul said as he hung up from his call with a smile.

'Ok, let's go!' said the doctor. She looked me straight in the eye and nodded once to indicate it would be close, but she conveyed the belief that it was worth the risk.

'How do we get the incubator on the boat?' asked the nurse. It was strapped to the stretcher, with all sorts of wires connected to Cameron from the portable generators and medical equipment. 'It must weigh a tonne,' she added pessimistically.

Already painfully aware of our need for manpower, Toni was commandeering passers-by off the street. They were funnelled in toward the boat by her. Nobody disobeyed, they simply complied, not knowing what they were letting themselves in for. After a while, in addition to the already large entourage that had set out from the NICU, there must have been a total of 20-25 other people, all of whom gripped the boat and waited for their next instruction. Toni then ordered them to pull the boat as hard and as tight as possible to the dock, to eliminate the gap.

The Hungarian doctor noticed me pitching in, heaving the huge boat along with everyone else. 'Oh my God, your stitches!' she screamed at me. 'You need to let go and from now on be very careful.' But I would have none of it. I was not letting go until the incubator was safely on board the boat.

The burly men lifted the stretcher, incubator and Cameron, and hopped onto the boat. The boat swayed momentarily, then steadied. They placed the stretcher in the middle of the boat where it would be covered by a roof section. Then every one of the army of helpers that had pulled the boat into the dock jumped on board too, in case the same gap presented itself when being lifted off on the other side.

By that point more than 35 people were on a rickety old boat, surrounding tiny Cameron in his incubator. Looking on, I thought of all the people who had been involved in saving Cameron's life just to that point. It had to be more than 100. The very thought of it was staggering.

The doctor approached Jeff with her phone and to his surprise asked, 'This might be inappropriate, given the circumstances, but would it be possible to take a picture of the nurse and I with the incubator on the boat? Nobody will ever believe this story!'

It was small request and, given her help and exemplary management of the situation, Jeff instantly agreed and snapped a picture of them both. The moment the picture was taken, they resumed their professional duties, not missing a beat.

It was quite a surreal moment, causing us to have a flash of guilt that maybe we had been remiss, as we maybe hadn't taken enough pictures of our amazing journey to record the incredible story of how Cameron came to be. We hadn't taken them in case we lost him, but ironically if we had lost him, we would not have any pictures of him at all. Jeff promptly removed his phone from his pocket again and started snapping away.

As we approached the royal jetty, we realised the boat was once again too big to dock properly. The captain looked round and motioned he would try to position the bow of the boat to hold it against the dock at an angle. To do so, he powered the engines forward on full thrust. The heavers – all 25 of them – jumped off and heaved, as the burly men in unison lifted the stretcher off the boat in perfect synchronisation. Minus the help of me: I was doing as I was told, for once, following the instructions of the doctor.

There was no stopping us. We were all safely off the boat and heading quickly toward the VIP terminal. The permanent entourage accompanied us as we waved goodbye to the boat, which set out to return the enormous number of people who had volunteered their time that evening, for over an hour, to pull the boat bearing a total stranger in an incubator into the dock. Twice.

Arriving at the airport we walked through the VIP terminal, which was eerily silent; exuding a smell of damp as if it had been overly air-conditioned. Then when we rounded the corner and there it was; the passport gate. All we needed to do was pass this one single checkpoint and we were home free.

As we approached the gate, we all felt differing degrees of trepidation. The passport officer raised his hand and told us to stop. He then directed us to pass through the metal detector, saying, 'The stretcher too, please.'

'It's clearly too big, and it's obviously made of metal!' Jeff exclaimed. His patience was wearing thin as we were so close to freedom. A kind hand lay on his shoulder; it belonged to Paul.

As Jeff turned his head, Paul smiled and Toni passed through the detector in her good-natured way and explained to the nice immigration officer that the incubator was not going through the metal detector, with which he graciously complied.

All of the passports were inked with their necessary exit stamps and when the time came for the same gentleman to approve Cameron's passport, he said, 'I think we have a problem.'

Before anyone could react, Paul calmly unfolded an additional piece of paper from his pocket and gave it to the man, who then simply stamped Cameron's passport without further question. By that point nobody cared what was written on the paper; Team Curtis could literally taste freedom and just wanted so desperately to get Cameron on the plane. We wheeled him in the incubator along one side of the metal detector and outside, where an airport passenger bus stood waiting with another twenty men, all with high-visibility jackets. They were a product of honorary consul Paul's advanced planning. He had arranged the whole thing.

'The bus is to take you to the plane,' Paul explained. 'The additional men are to hold the stretcher steady, as there is no way to keep it still.'

It was there that we said our final goodbyes to Toni and Paul, who had been such an unbelievable help over our time in captivity. Words do not express the gratitude that we have for these two people, although '*life savers*' would certainly come to mind! Though it seemed impossible to process it, when we finished our hugs, somehow the situation all made sense. We boarded the bus, which pulled away with so many people holding the incubator and hanging on for dear life. The bus took us on an erratic route toward the waiting plane that was still some distance away. When we arrived, I looked up at the white side of the mid-size jet, which simply read, 'www.airambulance.com'. No doubt this was the right plane.

Three pilots exited the aircraft and greeted us. After a quick word with the nurse and the doctor about the logistics of how to get the incubator up the plane's small steps, the three pilots then simply picked the incubator off the stretcher and hoisted it in themselves. At one point, the captain was standing at full stretch under the immense weight of the incubator. I could hardly watch, frightened he would snap in half at any moment.

Once we were all on the plane, I noted that one side of the cabin looked like the stripped-out belly of a plane: completely bare, apart from a couple of blue economy-sized seats that were heavily worn; the other side looked reminiscent of a hospital emergency room, jammed with a vast array of medical equipment.

Jeff and I sat there freezing in the cold plane, keeping out of the way as the first officer bolted the incubator back into its place. The nurse hunched over Cameron, as she prepped her patient for the flight, and the doctor busied herself with paperwork.

A short time later, the doors were closed, the engines started, and the plane began its taxi on the empty airport tarmac. It was late at night now, long past our original departure time, but it did not seem to matter anymore.

The plane arrived at the threshold of runway three six and the engines were set to full throttle. As the aircraft gained speed, the nose lifted, and we were up, up, and away. I simply turned to Jeff and kissed him on the lips, snuggling up to him, falling straight to sleep for the duration of our short flight to Dubai.

I awoke to a bright rising sun, whose rays danced brilliantly off the emerald buildings of the magnificent metropolis of Dubai, before the plane touched down on the tarmac of Al Maktoum airport, runway three zero.

We were home and instantly knew our lives would never been the same again, for Team Curtis had an additional member and his name was Cameron.

A Mothers Aft Word

From Small To Mighty

{Mummy Clare}

Of course the story doesn't end there. When we got back to Dubai, we were taken to the NICU at City Hospital. As expected, the hospital had all of the state-of-the-art equipment, and the nurses and doctors were fantastic. We stayed in the NICU for almost another three weeks and in that time we once again had to face the uncertainty of infection.

There were also discussions regarding a bleed on the brain, and a new concern connected with his heart rate, which seemed to spike for no apparent reason, even though on the surface Cameron looked relaxed. In fact, one day we had just had the doctor's rounds and I had called Jeff to let him know everything seemed to be going well, but as I came back into the ward I found nurses and doctors rushing around Cameron's incubator, attaching wires to his chest and back. I just stood there. I could hear someone saying, "It's okay, Mummy; it's just a precaution," but I wasn't yet associating myself with the term "Mummy", so I didn't realise for a minute that they were talking to me.

In the end, as with so many of these scares, it was confirmed there was nothing to worry about and that this sometimes happened in premature babies, but with every scare I felt like I was being thrown back on that rollercoaster ride again and by this time I just wanted the ride to stop.

These three weeks in the Dubai NICU were different from those in Malé, although the pressure of ensuring that I produced enough milk for Cameron's daily requirements remained. Ermintrude and Daisy continued to have the life almost literally sucked out of them, but now we started to meet other NICU parents; something that didn't really happen in Malé. We learned their stories, and we saw them as they stood looking helplessly into their babies' incubators.

We would bump into each other in the Costa café every now and again; nod at each other in acknowledgement and notice how tired we all looked. In the NICU, we saw the joy on their faces when they held their babies, just the same as on ours whenever we could do KMC, and the look of concern as we sometimes stared helplessly in at our little ones. None of us had envisioned that this would be the way our babies would come into this world and we all felt immense guilt for putting them through so much at such an early stage in life.

We also learned that not every premature baby survives. It's a sad fact but every year around one in every ten babies are born too soon in this world, and not all of them make it. We would hear when a new baby was being admitted, and we would see the Mum and Dad looking shell shocked as they came into the NICU for the first time. You wanted to go over and say, "Hi", or offer some support, but part of you knew that in those moments each family needs its own little team to be rallying together. You also knew that you had your own worries and fears to deal with.

Just before we got back to Dubai, a lady called Joanne had contacted me. She had set up an organisation called Small and Mighty, to help families of premature babies. We were invited into a world of support and of information; of other parents, who had been through, or were going through, the same things and were reaching out to each other with questions and offering information. Having joined this group and witnessed the comings and goings of the NICU, I realised just how lucky we were. Some incubators were occupied and then all too suddenly empty. There were other parents who had been going backwards and forwards to the NICU for months, with no clear end in sight. Then there were those who were leaving with their babies to go home and start to enjoy being parents rather than bystanders.

It was also a new dynamic for Team Curtis. Now that we were back in Dubai with our friends as our support network, and our family just a flight away if we needed them, the strain of the last few weeks started to show. We were still a great team, but we found that small things would quickly blow up into big things. We had literally been each other's crutch for such a long time that it was only now, when we were feeling safer, that some of the stress started to creep through. I guess this was bound to happen. Our friends rallied round and I simply couldn't be more grateful for everything they did for us. I thought at some point the stress of the last few weeks would get to me and that all the emotion of what we had been through would come rushing to the surface and I would have a good old weep. But it didn't happen.

Life in the NICU is full of routine and the general chat between the mums over how their little ones were doing, how much longer they would be there and how much milk each of us pumped daily all seemed to become a normal conversation. It was also at this time we started to plan for Cameron to actually come home. In Malé, it had all been about his survival and getting back to Dubai. Now we were working out what we needed to organise before our new addition came home; buying baby clothes for premature babies, tiny nappies, selecting the nursery furniture, and picking out the most expensive and complex baby monitor available on the market.

It was also a time of firsts. Cameron had his first bottle; poor little thing! He was so exhausted by the end of it you would have thought he had run a marathon. We changed the first nappy and I started the journey of breastfeeding Cameron directly, rather than by pumping, and began to experience the concern that inevitably comes with this. I drank fenugreek tea, took seasickness tablets, because they are supposed to increase milk supply, and of course kept pumping every three hours to ensure my supply didn't dwindle. In the end, I managed to breastfeed Cameron for nine months, but it wasn't easy.

After just over two weeks, we were moved out of the critical section of the NICU. This meant that we were one step closer to going home. The doctor explained that once Cameron was at least 2kg, breastfeeding or taking milk from a bottle and achieving several other milestones, he would be able to go home. The day of the assessment, Cameron wouldn't take his milk. My heart sank as I looked helplessly at the doctor and explained that he had been taking all his bottles, up until this point, and we had successfully started breastfeeding. I felt sure he was going to say that Cameron still couldn't go home, but he didn't.

He just smiled at me and said, "Don't worry, I have been following Cameron's progress all this time and he's doing really well. When would you like to take him home: Friday or Saturday?" Excitement soon turned into panic; we were suddenly unsure about taking Cameron out of this sterile and controlled environment. You would have thought I would have jumped at the chance to get him home as soon as possible but instead I blurted out that Saturday would be best and as the doctor left, Jeff and I stood there looking at each other in shock. This was amazing news and yet we were scared.

How would we make sure our house was germ free, what if something happened, how would we stop the visitors from flooding through the door bringing all sorts of possible infections and how would we know if he stopped breathing, he wasn't going to come home with the hospital equipment still attached! As we left the hospital with fear and excitement flowing through our veins, we headed home to finalise our list of outstanding items including at least 10 different hand sanitisers!

Saturday came and I insisted on getting two balloons that said, 'Congratulations on your baby boy'. I wanted desperately to leave the hospital just as any other normal new parent but it seemed that no-one had known whether we should be congratulated, given the circumstances. So, we bought the balloons ourselves.

Cameron's birth hadn't happened the way that I had dreamed of or that you see on TV. I had to get used to that and accept the feelings of disappointment and guilt and appreciate that nothing could change what had happened. We had been through so much but still we couldn't relax. Now that he was home, I would constantly fear something would happen to Cameron and that if he got sick, he may die. I don't know whether this is normal. Of course, every new parent worries about their newborn but did I worry more than others? I was concerned about over protecting him, and yet the fear of not protecting him enough was hard to control.

I still haven't had the emotional outpouring that I was expecting and perhaps some of you were expecting to read about. Yes, there were moments, including on his first birthday, when I did have a cry. The trigger was mundane; my sister simply asked how I was doing. It was such a happy day, and it was a natural question, but the day was one we hadn't been sure we would ever see, and it was only when I was asked how I was doing that I realised how emotional I was feeling. Having spoken to other NICU mums, this lack of emotion is actually quite usual. It's partly shock, and it's partly holding it together to get through it. Once you are on the other side, the day-to-day routine of having a newborn takes over and you simply get on with it.

As I write this, it is the eve of Cameron's third birthday. I look at the clock and remember what was going on at that time, in the northern atoll of the Maldives, three years ago. It's simply unbelievable. Jeff and I still live in Dubai but we are currently in the UK, visiting family to celebrate Cameron's birthday together. He is a happy, healthy, energetic three-year-old, who starts almost every sentence with, 'Why?'

Having been exposed to the stories of others who are at various stages on the NICU journey, I am aware of how scary it is and how unprepared we all are for such an eventuality. I am also aware of the different possible outcomes and am grateful to have an amazing toddler running around us now.

I don't know who or what was watching over us that night, but someone was rooting for Team Curtis. There were so many times when a wrong decision might have changed the ending of this story, but it didn't, and I am therefore happy to say that the new member of Team Curtis is fitting in just perfectly to our crazy life.

Cameron, we can't wait to see who you grow up to be.

Some of the proceeds received from the sale of this book will be donated to 'Small and Mighty' in the hope that others may benefit from its amazing community and support.

Printed in Poland
by Amazon Fulfillment
Poland Sp. z o.o., Wrocław

60858834R00150